SAFARI PRESS

HUNTING TRIPS IN THE LAND OF THE DRAGON

HUNTING TRIPS IN THE LAND OF THE DRAGON

ANGLO AND AMERICAN SPORTSMEN AFIELD IN OLD CHINA, 1870–1940

DR. KENNETH P. CZECH

SAFARI PRESS INC.

Czech, Dr. Kenneth P.

First edition

Safari Press Inc.

2005, Long Beach, California

ISBN 1-57157-303-8

Library of Congress Catalog Card Number: 2003099234

10 9 8 7 6 5 4 3 2 1

Readers wishing to receive the Safari Press catalog, featuring many fine books on big-game hunting, wingshooting, and sporting firearms, should write to Safari Press Inc., P.O. Box 3095, Long Beach, CA 90803, USA. Tel: (714) 894-9080 or visit our Web site at www.safaripress.com.

TABLE OF CONTENTS

DEDICATION

To my mother and father, who always made sure I had plenty of books to read and a place in our home to enjoy them, though oftentimes their budget was stretched thin. Those youthful years have long since disappeared, but the fond memories of reading Edgar Rice Burroughs, Jules Verne, Frederick Selous, and Jack O'Connor remain.

ACKNOWLEDGMENTS

The literature of hunting large and small game spans centuries and continents, but few books focus on the adventures of sportsmen in China. Through my conversations with Jake Johnson, an enthusiastic and extremely knowledgeable collector of rare sporting books, I became interested in investigating these experiences more closely. Many thanks to Jake for his suggestions and for pointing me in the right direction in my search for scarce China titles.

I would also like to thank Joan O'Driscoll, head of the interlibrary loan department at St. Cloud State University, who secured scarce titles that rarely show up on the used-book market.

Matthew "Duke" Biscotti also deserves thanks. Duke read portions of my manuscript, offered advice, and suggested I contact Safari Press. I also offer thanks to Ludo Wurfbain of Safari Press, who encouraged me to complete the manuscript, made valuable suggestions as to content, and guided me through the publication process.

And last, my wife Mary deserves a veritable bag limit of praise for tolerating my seemingly insatiable habit of collecting hunting books and then disappearing, hermitlike, into my office to read and write.

INTRODUCTION

THE HUNTING GROUNDS OF OLD CHINA

Stretching nearly four million square miles across eastern Asia, China offers a kaleidoscopic landscape, varying from tropical jungles in the southeast to the windswept plains of Manchuria and Mongolia and the rugged mountain ranges of Tian Shan and Kunlun Shan to the far west. This rich and varied land has been home to a wide selection of wild game. Though Chinese emperors and nobles of bygone dynasties enjoyed sport-hunting tiger, deer, and feathered game, China was rarely recognized for its sporting opportunities. It wasn't until the steady mercantile encroachment of Europeans in the eighteenth and nineteenth centuries that the country finally achieved some notoriety as a hunter's paradise. Among foreign sportsmen, China enjoyed only moderate popularity compared to the game fields of Africa or British India, though its spectacular scenery and variety of game were second to none.

European travelers had written about China's natural history throughout the nineteenth century. Abbé Armand David recorded his observations in *Les Oiseaux de la Chine*, and Robert Swinhoe's descriptions of animals and birds in northern China appeared in various zoological journals. In his monumental work *The Middle Kingdom* (1882), S. Wells Williams provided elaborate descriptions of Chinese topography, life, and customs. He also included a lengthy chapter on the region's natural history with descriptions of various species of deer, wild sheep, bear, and wolf. As for birds, the pheasant caught his immediate attention: "No tribe of birds in China, however, equals the gallinaceous for its beauty, size, and novelty, furnishing some of the most elegant and graceful birds in the world, and yet none of them have become domesticated for food."[1]

China was also the breeding place for millions of ducks, geese, and other species of waterfowl. In late summer and fall, migratory flights brought virtual clouds of birds across the Yangtze River to the

1. S. Wells Williams, The Middle Kingdom *(New York: Charles Scribner's Sons, 1882), vol. 1, p. 336.*

early-spring nesting areas of Mongolia and Siberia. Russian explorer Col. N. Prejevalsky observed the enormous number of birds arriving in the marshes and salt lakes of Mongolia:

> For days together they sped onward, always from the W.S.W., going further east in search of open water, and at last settling down among the open pools; their favorite haunts were the flat mud banks overgrown with low saline bushes. Here every day vast flocks would congregate toward evening, crowding among the ice; the noise they made on rising was like a hurricane, and at a distance they resembled a thick cloud. Flocks of one, two, three, and even five thousand, followed one another in quick succession, hardly a minute apart. Tens and hundreds of thousands, even millions of birds appeared at Lob-nor during the fortnight ending 21 February, when the flight was at its height. What prodigious quantities of food must be necessary for such numbers![2]

Sport in Chinese history served a twofold purpose for China's population. Hunting expeditions arranged by nobles and princes displayed their prowess with weapons and their courage, signs of superiority within the culture. In addition, wild animals were destructive to croplands, and hunting parties were one way to protect important food sources from the depredations of birds, deer, wild boars, wolves, and other animals. When nobles neglected to hunt, the local population considered them indolent.[3]

The thirteenth-century Venetian explorer Marco Polo provided perhaps the most famous description of a Chinese imperial hunting expedition. During his travels, he noted the size of the wild sheep in China's mountainous west and wrote that wolves preyed upon them. In accompanying the immense party of Kublai Khan in China proper, he observed ten thousand falconers serving the emperor, who rode in a specially constructed chamber mounted on the backs

2. *N. M. Prejevalsky,* From Kulja Across the Tian Shan to Lob-Nor *(London: Sampson Low, Marston, Searle and Rivington, 1879), p. 116.*

3. *T. R. Jernigan,* Shooting in China *(Shanghai: Methodist Publishing House, 1908), p. 206.*

of four elephants. The khan's sleeping tent was lined with tiger skins, and his robes were made of sable furs. Hunting hares, stags, bucks, and roe deer was strictly forbidden to all save the emperor from March to October.

Kublai Khan's sporting adventures were a combination of ceremony and ostentation; hunting expeditions by local nobles were on a much smaller scale. They usually conducted their hunting seasons after peasants had harvested their crops and were free to beat forests and valleys to drive game toward the waiting nobility. Over the centuries that practice changed very little. The last of China's ruling dynasties, the Manchu (Qing) Dynasty, came to power in 1645. The love of sport was so great for these rulers that they created imperial hunting grounds and preserves throughout the country. They particularly enjoyed tiger and bear hunting, and at least one emperor lost his life to an enraged bruin. Trophies such as skins, feathers, certain glands, and horns enjoyed a prominent place in Chinese markets.

With the invention of gunpowder and the advent of firearms, hunting methods began to change. Chinese hunters used primitive matchlock shoulder arms called gingals into the early twentieth century. Briton Henling Thomas Wade observed a Chinese waterfowler enter the water up to his neck, with a wooden frame supporting his five-foot-barreled gingal floating in front of him. Concealed by bunches of grass and weeds stuck into his hat, the hunter waded toward rafts of ducks and "fires into "the brown" a heavy charge of iron shot. He never fires at two or three fowl, as his shot costs money. He bides his time and then fires into "the brown."[4] Wade also noted that Chinese sportsmen were able to get closer to pheasants because their lightweight grass sandals made little noise compared to the European's heavy boots.

By the mid-nineteenth century, China had been ravaged by numerous civil wars. Entire towns and villages were razed during

4. *Henling Thomas Wade,* With Boat and Gun in the Yangtze Valley, *2d ed. (Shanghai: Shanghai Mercury, Limited, 1910), pp. 140-41.*

the Taiping Rebellion of the 1860s. With a weak central government, and beset by predatory western powers, China struggled to maintain its imperial identity. Foreigners seemed to flood the land. During the latter half of the nineteenth century, British and American merchants, civil servants, and military men spent their leaves and leisure time hunting in the Middle Kingdom, while naturalists interested in bagging specimens for scientific study or museum exhibitions prowled the hinterlands.

Many Anglo sportsmen traveled by houseboat up the Yangtze River to shoot ducks, pheasants, woodcocks, and other winged game. Perhaps the earliest account of these hunting experiences written in English was Francis Groom's book *Sportsman's Diary for Shooting Trips in Northern China* (1872).[5] Henling Thomas Wade noted that shortly after the publication of this book interest among foreign sportsmen in procuring large bags increased. In December 1872, along Pasejow Creek in the Yangtze Valley, six hunters collected 1,629 head of game in a few weeks, including nearly fifteen hundred pheasant and seventy-four deer.[6] In 1901 British sportsman J. Bell-Irving recorded a three-week trip up the Yangtze that netted "29 deer, 883 pheasants, 261 ducks and teals, 5 wild geese, 24 woodcocks, 32 hares, 18 ground hog, 1 wild cat, and 4 sundries."[7] Certainly the Victorian penchant for shooting and noting large bags of game was not limited to the British Isles.

Nor did British and American sportsmen hunt only small game. High-mountain stalking of wild sheep and goats achieved considerable popularity in Asia, particularly in the Himalayas, the Pamirs, and the Hindu Kush Range. Books and articles by the likes of Colonel Fred Markham, Major General Alexander Kinloch, and St. George Littledale extolled the excitement of bagging game among

5. *This book is quite scarce; neither the OCLC (Online Computer Library Center) nor the British Library references a copy. It is referred to in Wade's* With Boat and Gun in the Yangtze Valley *(1910) and in George Lanning's* Wild Life in China, or Chats on Chinese Birds and Beasts *(Shanghai:* The National Review *Office, 1911).*

6. *Wade,* ibid., *p. 4.*

7. *J. Bell-Irving, "Sport in China," in* The Field *(February 1, 1902), p. 164.*

lofty peaks and precipices. A simple extension was to hunt sheep, bear, and wapiti in Chinese Turkistan and the Tibetan borderlands. Other sportsmen sought adventure in the remote reaches of Manchuria and Mongolia. By the 1920s, they had collected rare species such as takin and panda bear as well.

There is, unfortunately, a dearth of sporting literature concerning hunting in old China. A few articles appeared in popular English periodicals such as *The Field.* Others were printed in obscure and long-extinct journals such as *China Weekly Illustrated* and *Peking and Tientsin Times.* The handful of books published in China, England, and the United States provide insight into a style of life and sport that all but disappeared from China after the collapse of the Manchu Dynasty in 1911. Some of the authors in this anthology are virtually unknown. Others, including Kermit Roosevelt, Roy Chapman Andrews, and Arthur de Carle Sowerby, formed a formidable cadre of highly respected and experienced hunters.

Decades of civil war, world war, and communist revolution further eroded chances for European and American hunters to enter the Middle Kingdom. Books about hunting in China, never plentiful, all but disappeared after World War II. Indeed, during the decades of the Cold War, the United States did not even recognize mainland China as a national entity, reserving such recognition for the Nationalist Party government of Taiwan. By the early 1970s, only a few dozen foreigners were allowed into the People's Republic of China in toto. After President Richard Nixon's 1972 trip to China, relations between the United States and the People's Republic slowly thawed. By the late 1970s, a few foreign sportsmen had managed to hunt game on the Tibetan frontiers. In 1980 an American sportsman was granted permission to hunt sheep in the Chinese Pamirs.[8] Since that time, China's government, perhaps sensing the income generated by international sportsmen, has slowly opened its borders to sporting opportunities.

8. *See Elgin Gates,* Trophy Hunter in Asia *(New York: Winchester Press, 1971.), and Robert M. Lee,* China Safari *(New York: Sporting World Library, 1988).*

For those who enjoy hunting stories set in exotic locales, this collection offers sport painted against the broad canvas of China's geography and natural history. Each selection not only reflects the adventure of the hunt, and the variations of game and its habitat, but accurately portrays the people and customs of the region.* The interplay between sportsmen and natives provides rich insights into everyday life and travel in old China. Most important, these vignettes capture the texture and color of an era long gone.

**In order to maintain the flavor of the times when these stories were written, I have chosen to keep the Latin genus and species for the animals described just as they were written in the original text. Please note that the Latin in modern taxonomy has changed significantly since these stories were written.*

EUROPE
RUSSIA
S.PETERSBURG
MOSCOW
Kazan
Sinbirsk
Samara
Tobolsk
Astracan
Sea of Azov
BLACK SEA
Trebizonde
Tiflis
Derbent
Bagdad
BASSORA
ISPAHAN
Tehran
Shiraz
PERSIA
Arabia Deserta
Herat
Candahar
CAUBUL
Cashmere
Bokharia
Samarcand
TARTARY
Kashgar
Yarkand
CHINESE
Tomsk
Omsk
Lakes
Copper Mines
Agra
Allhabad
Benares
Calcutta
HINDOOSTAN
Madras
Pondicherry
Hyderabad
BAY OF BENGAL
CEYLON
Equator
Addon
SIBERIA
Irkutsk
Chita
ASIA
L. Balkash
Tashkend
Kashgar
Yarkand
Khotan
KUENLUN MTS.
MONGOLIA
CHINESE REPUBLIC
EASTERN TURKESTAN
TIBET
Lhasa
PEKING
Tientsin
Urga
Port Lazareff
Dairen
Weihaiwei
SEOUL
JAPAN
YELLOW SEA
Kiaochow
Nanking
Shanghai
Hankow
Kaifeng
Sianfu
Lanchow
Foochow
Changsha
Canton
Hongkong
Macao
FORMOSA
EAST CHINA SEA
Lahore
Simla
DELHI
Lucknow
Cawnpur
Benares
Calcutta
Nagpur
INDIA
Hyderabad
Madras
Pondicherry
Bangalore
C. Comorin
CEYLON
Kandy
BAY OF BENGAL
Mandalay
Rangoon
BURMA
SIAM
BANGKOK
TONKIN
HANOI
Gulf of Tonkin
HAINAN
Luang Prabang
Hue
FRENCH INDO-CHINA
Pnompenh
Saigon
Gulf of Siam
C. Cambodia
SOUTH CHINA SEA
LUZON
MANILA
PHILIPPINES
PALAWAN
MINDORO
NEGROS

SEA OF OKOTSK
Okotsk
Yakoutsk
Olekminsk
Lena
Mountains
Oudskoi
Lake of Baikal
Kiachta
Selinginsk
Nertchinsk
Saghalien
Kurile Islands
Jesso
Matsmai
Sado
Jedo
Nipon
Xicoco
Sea of Japan
Corea
Yellow Sea
Pekin
Nankin
Canton
Macao
China
Hoang Ho
Quelpert I.
Eastern Sea
Tchusan I.
Loo Choo
Bonin Islands
North I.
South I.
Volcano Is.
Tropic of Cancer
Formosa
North C.
South C.
Bashee Is.
Babuyan Is.
PACIFIC
PACIFI
NORT
OCEAN
Hainan I.
Paracels
Pulo Canton
Gulf of Tonquin
Siam
Cambodia
Saigon
Camboda R.
Gulf of Siam
Cochin China
Luzon
PHILIPPINE ISLANDS
Manila
Mindoro
Mindoro Sea
Samar
Leyte
Mindanao
Sea of Sooloo
Borneo
Natuna
Malacca
Pulo Lingen
Banca
Gilolo
Morty
Celebes
Egoi Is.
Yap Eap
Johannes Is.
Peeloo Is.
St. Andrews Is.
Saltibabo Is.
Lord Norths I.
Frewill Is.
Asia Is.
Harbour I.
Madjicosemah Is.
Todos los Santos
S. Thomas
Fatsisio
Tyger I.
C. Bolinao
Sooloo
Tropic of Cancer

CHAPTER ONE

WILLIAM SPENCER PERCIVAL

A member of the British civil service in Shanghai, William Spencer Percival spent more than two decades in eastern Asia during the last quarter of the nineteenth century. In his first book, The Land of the Dragon, My Boating and Shooting Excursions to the Gorges of the Upper Yangtze *(1889), he described his journey by boat to the tumbling rapids and high gorges near Ichang (formerly I-ch'ang), a walled city first opened to Westerners in 1877.*

"The water had a dark, uncanny, creepy look," he noted, "in consequence of light being shut out by the high overhanging rocks, the base being thrown into a deep and gloomy shadow."

Noted for its valuable descriptions of the terrain and Yangtze rapids, the book was hailed by numerous literary critics. During his journey, Percival ran afoul of local Chinese villagers when he attempted to photograph them, realizing almost too late that many of the natives had never seen a camera. He also recorded his observations of country and riverine life, noting evidence of ruined villages and landscapes left from the destructive era of the Taiping Rebellion. His second work, Twenty Years in the Far East *(1905), published posthumously by his wife, recounted various rambles in the region, including a stint with the Shanghai Fire Brigade.*

While on his trip to the gorges of the Upper Yangtze in 1887, Percival took time to enjoy a hunting excursion for wildfowl and upland game. He and his companion shot over eight hundred pheasant in three weeks, and the results of their bag ended up in the food markets of Shanghai. Percival ably described his experiences aboard a small customs cruiser threading its way to the shooting grounds, making special note of the river's pitfalls. They once were surrounded and threatened by pirates. On another occasion, he and his shooting partner rode into the hill country near Chen-chiang, hoping to bag deer, leopard, and wild boar, the latter particularly destructive to peasant croplands.

In this passage from Percival's The Land of the Dragon, *the author suddenly encountered wild boars driven into the open by Chinese beaters. Wicked-tempered and armed with slashing tusks, boar could be a formidable foe, especially at close quarters.*

WILD BOARS OF CHEKIANG PROVINCE

About the middle of April, in the year of grace one thousand eight hundred and eighty-seven, I was asked by Sir Roderick Runnimede to be one in a party of two on a proposed journey to the rapids, gorges, and glens of the upper waters of the Yangtze. It was not a scientific excursion, and there were no new countries to discover, no new people to trot out before the world, no new trade routes to open up. It was simply an excursion for health and pleasure combined, to wander anywhere and everywhere our fancy led us, to explore some small portion of this wild, romantic country, and, in short, to have a good and pleasant time.

It is seldom that any ordinary mortal who has drifted onto the eastern coast of China has an opportunity, more than once in a lifetime, to visit the recesses of the vast Chinese empire, so I accepted the offer without the slightest hesitation. In three minutes the whole matter was settled, and in less than a week we were off.

Late one Saturday evening I followed my baggage up the Bund, bound for the steamer that was to take us on the first part of our trip. The steamer was lying securely moored off the Taku jetty. She was a fine boat, and coolies were busily carrying bales and packages to stow away in her capacious hold. She was not to start until the small hours of the morning, so I amused myself with rambling about the decks and watching from on high the squabbles and comical altercations constantly occurring among the men below. Sir Roderick put in an appearance around midnight, and a little before 2 A.M. the screw commenced to revolve, and we were off.

The steamers that ply the lower Yangtze are a large and commodious fleet. The *Nganking,* the boat that was to carry us to Hankow—a vessel registering nearly two thousand tons, and larger than some of the oceangoing steamers—was most comfortably and luxuriously fitted up. The saloon, about fifty feet by thirty, was a compound of white enamel, bird's eye maple, and gilding, and it was well lighted, well ventilated, and well looked after. A good, thick carpet was pleasant underfoot; the most comfortable of all lounging chairs invited you to come and take things easy, the sofas and chairs being covered with green leather. The most scrupulous cleanliness, evident everywhere, gave an outward sign that our lives were pitched in pleasant places. At one end of the saloon stood a handsome and fine-toned piano, a violin, and some reams of music. The captain, who was a musical genius, and his chief engineer, equally good on the flute, made the time pass gaily. We carried two or three passengers who were proficient pianists, so there was no difficulty in finding performers, and the three instruments harmoniously played Mendelssohn, Beethoven, and Mozart.

The first night out we narrowly escaped running down a lorcha; we just missed her hull, but carried away a huge boom that was standing out over her stern. The boom tore away with such cracking and splintering wood that it sounded as though the whole side of the ship had been crushed in.

The following morning was bright and warm, and the fresh breeze off the broad expanse of the river was thoroughly enjoyable. During the afternoon we passed Silver Island, one of the sacred islands of the Chinese. It is an extremely pretty rock, well covered with timber, and stands out boldly from the center of the Yangtze. On its shores a few fishermen's huts are scattered about, and far up on its well-wooded sides is a fine old temple, frequently visited by strangers and residents of Chen-chiang.

In a short time we arrived at the city of Chen-chiang itself. This is the first of the ports up the river to be opened to foreign trade, and it is the great entrepôt of the trade of the grand canal. The northern section enters the Yangtze here; the southern entrance is a short distance down the river. The city was overrun and destroyed by rebels and imperialists by turns during the wars of 1840 and 1860. The country and villages for many miles around are now desolate and in ruins, since the place never recovered its prosperity after it was burned by the rebels around 1860.

Some eight or nine miles to the south is a range of mountains, the Wuchow Shan range, extending beyond Poyang Lake and far into Kiangsi province.

Not more than four or five years ago, the shooting around Chen-chiang was all that could be desired; game (principally birds) of every description was most abundant. Sportsmen made Chen-chiang their headquarters. Feathers and fur—everything, in fact, from snipe to leopard—could be found within easy distance. Each year, as cultivation advances, population increases, and people are gradually rebuilding villages destroyed by the rebels, driving the game farther and farther into wilder and more remote regions. At the time of my visit we found pheasants and other birds by the hundreds; I now hear very poor accounts from those whom I have lately recommended to try the same district.

At the time of which I write, W. de St. Croix, an old and much esteemed friend, was engaged in the service of the Chinese Imperial Maritime Customs. He was for a few years stationed at Chen-chiang and several times had pressed me to join him for a month's shooting up the Yangtze. Hitherto I had not been able to make my time fit in with his own. At last, fortune favored us, and on a bright winter afternoon I joined him at Chen-chiang. He had obtained the loan of the customs' cruiser, a boat of about twenty-five tons, manned by ten men. This boat was to be our home for a month.

Early the following day we commenced shooting near a small island on the right bank of the river, just outside the site of the Imperial lines around Nanking, where we found duck, geese, and a variety of wildfowl. The next day we crossed to the opposite bank and came into swampy ground with small, reedy ponds or lakes, about three or four hundred yards inland from the river and extending for a couple of miles into the country. On these ponds were flocks of wild swans, some otters, the usual variety of ducks, and the like. Beyond this the ground became drier and more undulating, with large patches of cane—strong, thick, and ten or eleven feet high. Farther on were low, rolling hills, covered with scrub and small timber. Here was the home of the wild pig; large and very savage wild cats (so we called them, but I think a naturalist would have given them another name, for I never heard of any cat showing the ferocity these animals did); deer, eagles, civet cats, and the like. Pheasants abounded.

The country people held the cats in great fear and were quite afraid to approach them, for the cats did not show the slightest timidity upon being approached and had no hesitation in taking the offensive.

If slightly wounded by a ball, a female cat would scream and fight like a young tiger.

Day after day, as we crossed and recrossed the river, we found the country full of game. If one place had the advantage over others, it was around Rocky Point. From there we passed through the May Queen Channel; shot over Wade Island, which was full of deer; again took to the banks, miles inland; and finally finished about ten miles above the island.

The weather was bitterly cold at night, cold and bright through the day—grand weather for shooting, and just the temperature for keeping game. The boat now, at the end of three weeks, began to look very much like a poulterer's shop, carrying over eight hundred head of pheasant; two long lines of wild pig and deer; a choice selection of wild cats, civet cats, and otters; and about thirty wild swans, bitterns, geese, ducks, and other birds. Truly Chen-chiang and Shanghai reveled in game for many days after our return.

The river, here more than two hundred and fifty miles from the sea, is a noble stream, about a mile to a mile and a half wide. With a wind blowing against the current, there soon rises what a sailor would call very lumpy water, which on two or three occasions made me prefer to pass the night in a mud shelter ashore, miserably cold, rather than trust myself to the incessant pitching, rolling, and groaning of the cruiser.

If I were to begin to describe the incidents connected with this trip, I would fill a volume. There were constant pleasures and excitements, with few annoyances. We had daily difficulties with the natives. They objected to our passing through the few mud huts they called a village, and to our crossing a creek, until a dollar or two, judiciously and privately passed over to the head man of the village, caused him suddenly to discover that we were most respected and important strangers, traveling under the special protection of the Emperor, the Son of Heaven and the Brother of the Moon. This was quite true; our passports showed that this was the case. He would urgently advise, or rather order, the country people to be civil and obliging and to assist us in every possible manner, or the supreme displeasure would be heavily visited upon them in the form of fines

and possibly in the loss of a few heads. A speech of this kind was generally sufficient to secure our freedom from molestation for the remainder of the day.

On another occasion our yacht became the object of what was evidently a piratical attack from a large number of junks and boats that completely surrounded her. It soon became clear that, if we were to save our boat, there was no time to be lost.

Then a good notion entered into our skipper's brain. He hoisted to the masthead a brilliant yellow dragon flag, fresh from the Imperial stores. The sight of this flag created more consternation among our visitors than any other means we could have adopted; they quietly sneaked off, vanishing in twos and threes, and, although we remained another ten days near the same place, they never disturbed us, and we never saw them again.

At the end of the twenty-fifth day we returned again to Chen-chiang and passed the boat over to the customhouse officers. The following morning we left on ponies for the Wuchow Shang Hills, about ten miles off, where we had arranged to finish our trip by spending four or five days among the boars and deer, with a possible chance of a leopard.

I had four beaters with me, thrashing the tangled scrub, while I kept to a small track about eighteen inches wide, which was much easier walking. This was our second day out, and it was near the summit of one of these hills that I bagged the largest pig I ever saw. It was within an ace of reversing the order of things, for it nearly bagged me instead.

The habitat of these animals is on ground exceedingly difficult to travel over—thick, tangled scrub three to four feet high, with holes and hidden dry ditches that in the wet season are rapid watercourses. Large and small boulders, visible and invisible, are constantly cropping up. The tops of the hills are barren rocks with caves and holes into which all animals retire during the wet season. The pigs commit a great amount of destruction among the crops lower down in the valleys. The country people are only too glad to get rid of them at any cost, and willingly turn out as beaters for Europeans bent upon slaughtering the pigs.

Suddenly one of the beaters called out, *"Yah-chue!"* and a huge pig crashed through the scrub and trotted along the narrow path before me. I had a heavy 12-gauge double rifle weighing close to twelve pounds, which threw two-ounce flat-headed conical balls propelled by six and a half drams of the best rifle powder. Some twenty yards in front of me was the monster, the largest I had ever seen: a splendid driving shot, and I knew there was sufficient power in the gun to rake the boar from stern to stem.

It was too easy a shot, and I suppose I was careless over it, for a worse shot I never made. The ball struck the pig five inches higher than I had intended and ran along its spine, tearing the skin along its back and cutting away half an ear, inflicting a mere scratch that did not in the least disable it. With something between a yell, a grunt, and a roar, and with a look of most vicious wickedness in its eyes, the boar, quick as thought, wheeled left about and charged straight, at a gallop. In a moment we were at close quarters. I knew, if I could not stop the boar, it would make things extremely unpleasant, and I had no desire to take a prominent part in the proceedings that would be held on the morrow before Her Britannic Majesty's Consul, acting as coroner.

The direct line for the boar's brain was too risky, since its head was at such an angle that the ball was certain to glance from its forehead, and its head completely covered its chest. There was no alternative but to wait and watch for a more favorable opportunity before disposing of my last chance. This long description passed in less time than it has taken to write two words. There was no time to take out the empty cartridge and insert a live one, and I knew perfectly well that my keeping a whole skin depended upon the one remaining shot. As the boar passed, it made a vigorous dig with its tusks, but the instant before it made this thrust I had sprung to one side, off the track, into the scrub, and, as it passed, it just grazed me near the thigh. The impetus of the beast carried it two or three yards farther, before it quite realized it had missed. Then it came around for another charge, but, as it exposed its broadside, I planted the second ball well behind its shoulder at a distance of no more than six feet. The boar stopped instantly and favored me with another of its wicked glances; then, slowly, its head dropped, and it fell over on its side and died.

A loud whistle soon brought St. Croix to me. We gralloched the boar, slung it over a bamboo, and sent it with four coolies down to

Chen-chiang, where we afterward heard that it turned the scales at 501 pounds. Its tusks, which were in perfect condition, were six and a half inches long.

My second shot had made up for the first one, for the ball entered its left side and passed through the center of its heart, smashing its right shoulder before burying itself in the side of the hill.

I have heard of much larger boars than this one, which roam the hills in the Yuetchow District of Chekiang Province. They are reported to be very savage, causing great devastation in the rice fields and sometimes eating children. The country people are very much afraid of them, as the boars attack them and have no fear. They are black-and-white in color and are commonly reported to have teeth like saws and to weigh from eight to nine hundred pounds. I should like to see them before I rely on this description.

For the next two or three days we had some excellent sport; then, picking up our ponies at the first temple where we had stayed, we quietly rode back to Chen-chiang. Within twenty-four hours I found myself on board the *Peking*, bound for Shanghai.

CHAPTER TWO

ERNEST HENRY WILSON

European and American scientists from various disciplines have journeyed through China, studying bird life, collecting rare plants, and observing small and large animals of all species. Among these noted naturalists was Ernest Henry Wilson. Born in Gloucestershire in 1876, Wilson achieved fame as a horticulturist, eventually serving as keeper of the Arnold Arboretum at Harvard University and as a fellow of the American Academy of Arts and Sciences. A prodigious writer, Wilson wrote numerous articles and books recounting his searches for and examinations of plants, flowers, and exotic gardens. Among his notable books on horticulture were The Romance of Our Trees *(1920),* Plant Hunting *(1927),* The Lilies of Eastern Asia *(1929), and* China, Mother of Gardens *(1929).*

Wilson spent eleven years in China, receiving the sobriquet "Chinese" Wilson. Spanning more than a decade of war and rebellion in the region, his travels often put him in harm's way, but he commented: "I was in interior China during the Boxer outbreak and the Russo-Japanese War, and visited places shortly before or after antiforeign riots, but never experienced any incivility meriting the name." Scientific pursuits remained paramount for him. On one expedition from 1907 to 1909, he and his party paid special attention to collecting the fauna of the region. They collected over 3,100 birds, as well as the skins of 370 mammals, reptiles, and fish. On one leg of the expedition, Wilson, accompanied by his associate Walter R. Zappey, embarked on bamboo rafts to hunt waterfowl on the tumbling streams that fed the Yangtze River. The rafts were of the type used by native merchants and wine peddlers to carry their wares to riverfront villages and towns, but the scientists nicely converted them to duck-hunting craft.

In this passage from a chapter in his first book, A Naturalist in Western China, *published in two volumes in 1913, Wilson describes the bamboo rafts, travel on churning streams, and shooting waterfowl in the region.*

RAFTING FOR DUCKS ON THE YA RIVER

Wildfowl in great variety abound all over China, and the west has its share, though a lesser one. In that great alluvial plain and swamp bordering the Tungting Lake in central China, they occur in great numbers during the winter season. The same is true of the lower Yangtze Delta. Throughout the region of the Gorges, wildfowl are comparatively rare for the simple reason that steep cliffs and deep water are not to their liking. Above Kuichou-fu they are more common, but not nearly as common as farther west. On the lower reaches of the Min River and its tributary the Ya, which unites with the Tung at Kiatingfu, they are very plentiful. Sandbars difficult to reach and stony places near the rapids and races of the shallower parts of the rivers are their favorite daytime haunts. At night they freely visit the farmers' wheat and pulse fields near the rivers. The wildfowl that frequent western China in the winter season probably breed in the Koko Nor region, whereas those that visit the eastern parts of China breed in the tundras of eastern Siberia. The mountains of western Hupeh, eastern Szechuan, and Shesi constitute barrier ranges demarcating the lines of migratory flight. Regarding this boundary, it is noteworthy that geese have never been shot or observed resting west of I-ch'ang, according to my own records and observations. Yet to the east of this point they are probably more abundant than any other family of wildfowl.

The annual slaughter of wildfowl in China is enormous, but the birds are as wary as others of their kind anywhere else in the world. On bright, sunny days it is easier to catch them "napping," but, in my experience, the man with a 12-bore earns all the wildfowl he bags in a season. I have no intention of entering deeply into this subject, since this type of sport is no different elsewhere in the world. There is, however, a novel form of duck shooting obtainable on the Ya River, in western Szechuan, that affords both excitement and good sport, and it is not to be missed.

The Ya, which unites with the Tung River a mile or so beyond the western gate of the city of Loshan, is a swift-running stream thickly strewn with boulders, shingle, and sandbanks. Boats are in use at the various ferries, but the river generally is unsuited to navigation, and merchandise is conveyed up and down on rafts. The latter are specially built for shallow rivers, and ply principally between Yachou-fu and Chong-peh-sha via the Ya River to Kiatingfu, from there on the Min to I-pin, and from there on the Yangtze to Chong-peh-sha. With the exception of Luchou, Chong-peh-sha is the largest town between Chungking and I-pin, although it has no official status. It is a great and famous wine mart, and rafts carry the wine in large jars from the town to the inland markets situated on the shallow rivers farther west.

Although they are fragile-looking affairs, these rafts are quite unsinkable, and are the best of their kind in existence. They are built entirely of the culms of a giant bamboo known as "Nan chu" *(Dendrocalamus giganteus).* Each raft is about sixty-six feet long and eleven feet wide. The canes are laid side by side in one plane and are securely lashed to numerous crossbeams; not a single nail is used in the whole construction. Several unequal lengths of bamboo are used so that the end-to-end joints occur at irregular intervals. The stern of the raft is square, the prow bent upward to serve as a fender against rocks and shoals. The outer siliceous "skin" of the canes is removed and the nodes hardened over a hot fire. The bending of the canes to form the upturned prow is done by heating and weighting with heavy stones. A narrow wicker platform is carried down the center of the raft; it is about a foot above the floor, and the merchandise is placed on this to keep it dry. Wine jars are lashed to it.

These rafts are capable of yielding both transversely and laterally, so they can pass over any slightly submerged obstruction. Fully loaded, one raft carries freight weighing about thirty thousand pounds, and then draws only about six inches of water, because of the great buoyancy of the hollow cylinders of bamboo. Downstream, a crew of four men manipulates each craft, propelling it with an oar on either side and steering with a scull aft and another forward, but the latter is only used in the more difficult places. The sculls and oars are fitted to alder stumps, which serve as oarlocks. Men attached to bamboo lines haul the rafts hauled upstream, and several usually travel in company so that the crews can assist one another over the more difficult rapids.

The Ya when not in flood is a clear stream, and from the raft the stony river bottom is plainly visible; often the boulders look so dangerously near the bottom of the raft that the passenger expects a bump every few minutes. A curious hissing and crackling noise

accompanies the raft's progress over the shallower places. This noise comes from the movement of the boulders and stones in the streambed, the hollow bamboo tubes acting as sounding boards. There are many angry and dangerous rapids and whirlpools on the Ya, and the current is very swift, so shooting in these places is most exciting work. There is very little possibility of an accident unless the raft is overloaded, but every rock and stone is visible in the clear water, so the uninitiated feel the presence of danger and are alarmed.

In the winter season this stony river is the haunt of thousands of wild ducks, which congregate in the daytime in the vicinity of rapids, races, and boulder-strewn shoals. It is an excellent and highly exhilarating sport to engage a raft at Yachou and shoot wildfowl from it while descending the stream. A little noise will scare the birds on the approach of the raft, and, while the raft successfully shoots the rapid or race, it is up to the man with the gun to bring down the ducks. The size of the bag depends largely upon the steadiness of nerve, but it takes a few cartridges before one can fairly well judge just how much to "lead" a bird when pulling the trigger. The movement of the craft, both forward and sideways, considerably increases the difficulty of aim. Two guns are best, one forward and the other aft. One can easily retrieve the dead birds at the foot of the rapids; the wounded ones are carried on the current and can then be finished off. Those falling on land are difficult to mark down and retrieve. With a little practice, a steady shot can make a good bag of duck from these rafts.

Early in December 1908, my companion, Mr. Zappey, accompanied me on a journey by raft from Yachou to Loshan, which occupied a couple of days. The weather was boisterous and wet, and wildfowl were comparatively scarce. We shot and retrieved fifty-three ducks and probably killed in addition about a third that number. Although the bag was not large, the excitement and fun was immense.

The wild ducks commonly found in the west are mallard, waxbill, and ordinary teal. Others occurring in lesser numbers are falcated teal, spectacled teal, goldeneye, pintail, goosander, smew, pochard, shoveler, grebe, and ruddy shelduck. Three species of gull—two large gray types and a kittiwake—ascend to this region, two thousand miles inland from the coast. I never saw wigeon, mandarin duck, swan, or geese in the west. At Loshan the harsh cry of a very large kind of crane may be heard day and night during November, and on dull wet days small flocks may be seen flying south. Very seldom, however, do they alight in this neighborhood, and still more rarely are they to be seen resting during the daytime. These birds winter around the lakes in Yunnan and apparently make a posthaste thousand-mile flight there from their breeding grounds in the Koko Nor region.

The goosander, smew, pochard, and one or two others are diving, fish-eating ducks. If skinned they lose their fishy flavor and become palatable but even then are inferior eating in comparison with mallard, waxbill, and common teal.

CHAPTER THREE

HENLING THOMAS WADE

Perhaps the best book to describe the types of small game and methods of hunting along the Yangtze River is Henling Thomas Wade's With Boat and Gun in the Yangtze Valley. *Originally published in Shanghai in 1895, the 1910 edition was nearly one hundred pages longer. The work was an immediate success among Anglo-American sportsmen traveling to the Middle Kingdom. Wade, with the help of sporting companions, compiled numerous observations and experiences of shooting waterfowl and upland game along the Yangtze. He described landscapes in great detail, to aid sportsmen in choosing the area and types of game they preferred. In addition, he provided considerable detail on the building and use of houseboats to ply the Yangtze. These served as shooting quarters for hunters who were afield for weeks at a time.*

Houseboats generally accommodated four hunters with appropriate canine companions. Steered by a native captain called a lowdah, *the vessels relied both on sail power and the use of a large, stern-mounted sweep (*yuloh*) as a means of propulsion. Their shallow draft enabled houseboats to maneuver close to shore or on smaller streams.*

Wade, a longtime resident and tea inspector for the firm of Shaw Brothers & Company, in Shanghai, kept a detailed diary of his hunting excursions dating to 1867. He recounted the abundance of game in the region, as well as his social intercourse with Chinese villagers and the hazards of river travel. In this passage from With Boat and Gun in the Yangtze Valley *(1910), he relates the vagaries of riverine travel and episodes of hunting the creeks and backwaters of the great Yangtze.*

THE HOUSEBOAT UPCOUNTRY

Precautions Against Losing Your Way. It is no easy matter to put in writing suggestions that will prevent a sportsman, especially if he is new to the country, from losing his way occasionally. Some men find their way about by a species of instinct, often working miles inland, and are never at a loss to discover the shortest way back to their boat. Other men lose their way within gunshot of the boat, and are completely puzzled if the flag is temporarily hidden from their view by a tree or copse. It is anything but pleasant, even to an old hand, to spend a night in a farmhouse or in a native boat (especially if the thermometer is below freezing), so, on the principle that it is easier to prevent than to cure, I offer a few precautions, which may perhaps be useful to beginners.

First: Be sure that you, and the coolie who accompanies you, know the name of the place where the boat is at anchor, and make sure the flag is properly hoisted. If the boat is lying under a high bank, have the flag made fast to a long bamboo fixed securely on the top of the bank, or, if the tree is near, fasten your bamboo flagstaff to one of the top branches.

Second: On starting, take note of the direction of the wind, which usually is quite steady in the northeastern monsoon season, and, if you can manage it, get to accompany you a beater who is a native of the place where the boat is anchored. Ascertain by your compass the bearing of the creek where the boat is anchored, and note the general direction (as compared with the position of the boat) of the line of country you propose to work over. Keep this in mind, and from time to time, while in sight of the flag, look back and see if your idea of your position is correct.

Third: Take note of any conspicuous tree, mound, house, or other object that is likely to assist you in finding your way back. In fact, keep your eyes open.

Last: When uncertain of your position, sit down and think for a moment or two. Calculate coolly how long you have been walking, and when you last caught sight of the boat flag. Allow 2½ miles per hour for the distance traveled, and call to mind whether you turned to the right or left after losing sight of the flag. Consult your compass, and then walk in a direction, as nearly as you can ascertain, at right angles with the creek, the bearing of which you took before starting. In nine cases out of ten, you will discover the flag before you have walked any great distance, or you will come to some object you recognize as having taken note of on your outward journey, and which will assist you in shaping your course for the boat.

Losing the Boat. If, notwithstanding the foregoing precautions, you lose your way in the country and find darkness coming on and no boat in sight, make for the nearest rising ground, if any is in the neighborhood, and if the flag or light is nowhere visible, fire two shots in rapid succession, count thirty, and then fire two more shots, keeping a bright lookout for a rocket, a blue light, or a return signal from the boat. After waiting for a few moments, if there is no response to your signal, repeat it at intervals for a quarter of an hour. If there is no result, walk to the nearest village and have your coolie ask the way to the boat, or use sign language if you cannot muster sufficient Chinese words. If you can obtain the desired information, walk in the direction of the boat, firing your gun every now and then, until you have exhausted all hope of finding her.

There is nothing for you to do but to make up your mind to pass an uncomfortable night in a Chinese village or on board a native boat. Pick out the most respectable house (a farmhouse is the best choice), and ask for a night's lodging. It will seldom be refused, and a few small coins will speedily cause the production of some tea, eggs, rice, or other "chow-chow," which, though not so tasty as "pot" or so satisfying as a "rumpsteak and onions," will be helped down by that best of sauce—hunger; lucky will you be if you can find a little whisky in your flask and a "baccy" in your cigar case. A few bundles of clean straw for a shakedown and a game bag for a pillow will give you a taste of "roughing it," which, if not exactly pleasant, will at least be something to talk about when you once more get your legs under the mahogany. But take a native boat if you can.

Signals. When it is evident to the party on board the boat that one of their number is missing at nightfall, they should signal by firing their guns from time to time; if they receive no reply, they should send up a rocket, and at the same time burn a blue light, continuing these signals at intervals until the return of the lost one is hopeless. These signals must all be prearranged and understood.

A trip upcountry is an outing in which people so commonly indulge nowadays that it would be superfluous to say anything about the provisioning of the boat. Usually the arrangements are left to the "boy," but it can do no harm to overlook the list of stores, wines, etcetera, a couple of days before starting. Sometimes, in the case of a couple of men going away together in the same boat, it is simplest to order from the well-known establishments here provisions and wines to last a given time. One can always return any surplus. The tendency generally is to take far more commissaries than is really warranted.

****

I shall never forget a trip I made with Mr. George Butler in the winter of 1868. At that time he was tea inspector to the firm of Petrococchino & Company, and I was ditto for the firm of Shaw Brothers & Company. We had long been bent on having a good shoot. The boat was well provisioned for a trip of three weeks, and we started off for Chiahsing with a fresh northeasterly breeze and a strong spring flood tide. We were soon bowling along at the rate of eight miles an hour, and to occupy the time we began quite early to overhaul our things. When we had barely cleared the settlement, Butler let slip a very short but emphatic monosyllable. Inquiring its occasion, I learned that he had forgotten his cartridges. Here was a pretty state of things. Chafing at the knowledge that we should lose both wind and tide—there were no steam launches in those days—there was no alternative but to tie up the boat at the Tungkadoo Dock and hail a sampan. Poor Butler got into it, and then I watched the boat struggling against both wind and tide. She ultimately fetched opposite the Roman Catholic cathedral of the city, and Butler had to make his way to Mackenzie & Company and wait while they loaded five hundred cartridges for him—a longer operation than it is today. He did not return to the boat till late in the afternoon, and we had to wait for the next flood before we finally started.

For days we had varying sport, mostly good, until we struck the broad waters around Eshing, and after sailing across these we landed some distance from the city. As evening closed in, Butler wisely made his way to the boat, but I, more venturesome, stayed out longer. When I tried to return later on, I found that I was cut off by a bridgeless creek. There I was on a cold, dark evening—it was around eight o'clock—the boat's masthead light flickering tantalizingly near and a deep creek intervening between me and comfort. There were but two alternatives:

to seek shelter in some native farmhouse, for there were no boats about, or to make a dash for home. I chose the latter. I shouldered my gun muzzle downward and swam the creek. Landing on the opposite bank was no easy matter, for the foothold was slimy, greasy mud, and a pocketful of wet cartridges and half a dozen pheasants made my progress uncertain and slow until I got on firm ground. Once on board the boat, it was not long before I was sipping something hot with sugar in it beneath the blankets. And as I became suffused with a gentle glow, I realized to the full what a heaven a houseboat could be.

****

"But ships are but boards, sailors but men. There be land-rats and water-rats, water-thieves and land-thieves. . . ." [from Shakespeare's *The Merchant of Venice]*

In October 1901, I was Mr. James Craven's guest, and we went to the Zhengdong marshes in his boat, the *Wharfe,* to see what the marshes would yield and how his newly acquired pointer Gip, derived from my own imported strain, promised to shape. The bag was modest enough, but my host had good reason to be satisfied with his purchase, for, on the first time it was asked, the dog crossed a creek after a wounded cock pheasant its master had dropped, and brought the bird back in first-rate style. In the evening the boat brought up between Monksijow and Zhengdong, and, since it was very hot and close, we left the windows open. When Craven looked for his watch in the morning, he discovered that it had disappeared, together with his khaki coat and two bottles of sherry, all of which were on his side of the boat. From my side I merely lost a pair of spectacles, my braces, and a silk handkerchief. My loss was nothing, but Craven's was a serious one, for his watch, chain, and seal, the gifts of his brother, had cost over forty pounds. We reported the theft to the Kading authorities, who sent some runners to make inquiries, without results, and also to the British consulate and the municipal police. The latter promptly took the "matter in hand," and there it remains unto this day. Doubtless the robbery was the work of creek sneaks. These gentry in their shallow, silent punts can with ease sneak noiselessly alongside a houseboat, scoop up its portable contents with their hooked bamboos, and as silently steal away. To follow them would be useless, for these punts are very fast and, when occasion requires, can be carried across country or hidden away with consummate ease.

****

A very pretty little waterway is that which breaks off from the Maychee Creek at Donkow, passes Lezar and Changshin and finds its exit into the Taihu at Capoo. The country to the west of the creek is strongly suggestive of Wu-na-mu—long dikes with creeks on either side, beautiful lagoons well margined with sedge, many and long bamboo copses. It was in this neighborhood, when shooting with S. Daly in 1879, that I had a startling experience. I had wandered away, my dog boy being my sole attendant. The country was inviting-looking enough, and I was passing from a small tea plantation to some grassland beyond when all of a sudden, without any warning, I found myself ten feet below the level of the land. It was some moments before I realized my position and that I had walked into a pig pit whose presence had been artfully and artistically concealed with branches, bracken, and grass. Happily, the pointed stakes usually driven into the bottom of these pits were on this occasion absent. The base of the pit was half again as wide as its mouth, and to get out unaided was impossible. So I shouted as loudly as I could, but my dog boy, who had gone to the far side of the copse with the object of driving anything it might hold in my direction, heard not the *vox clamantis*. I fired a few shots, which finally succeeded in bringing him to the scene. But how to extricate me was the trouble. I handed him my gun, but I could not get a grip on the sides of my prison. A happy thought then occurred to him. He took my shooting knife and, with the saw that it contained, succeeded in sawing through a pretty thick bamboo. To this he fastened his girdle, and then he laid the bamboo across the mouth of the pit. It was not long before I was above ground once more, but the dread of a second edition of pig pits robbed the morning's shoot of much of its pleasure. These pits are so deep that they drain all the surrounding land and often become nothing but wells. Imagine yourself in six or seven feet of water with no one near to lend a hand, and imagine an old sow with her farrow blundering in on top of you!

****

In the winter of 1873, I was at Chiahsing with my Quaker friend John Blain, at one time president of the firm of Blain, Tate & Company.

The country was white with snow, and those who know Chiahsing and have seen it robed in its spotless mantle know how dazzlingly, brilliantly white the long stretches of plain can look. Blain had been shooting without any luck by himself, and, since the birds had all been driven into cover for warmth and food, I suggested that we work together. We found that nearly every snowbound covert had its tenants. As a hen pheasant broke back over a rather open bamboo copse, I dropped her. A shot from Blain immediately followed, and I saw him running hard after the bird, which he fondly believed he had knocked over, a belief that it would have been sheer cruelty to have shaken. The bird made for a solitary holly bush, and Blain went after it. I could see him dodging from side to side as he got an occasional glimpse of the runner. Then came a shot, followed quickly by Blain's calls for me in muffled tones. What I then saw was as ludicrous as it was dangerous. Blain had an exceptionally heavy moustache, and he was following the movements of the bird with his gun at his shoulder all the time. Suddenly the chance to fire came, and the right hammer fell, locking the moustache to the barrel. And there was my friend with the gun his master, pointing seemingly wherever it wished. A weird but impressionable picture it was: the dark-green leaves of the holly, the brilliant scarlet of its berries, the dusky garment of the swarthy Blain, all in their setting of spotless white. He was afraid of raising the right hammer in case he should inadvertently touch the left trigger. My difficulty was to get near him, for, as he moved, his gun constantly pointed at me. However, I got the prisoner to stand still, went up behind him, raised the right hammer, and set free my friend. An eight-pound gun suspended only by one's moustache must have left a painful impression and certainly was as terrifying as Damocles's sword of the ancient story.

Many a time afterward did we laugh over this incident, and Blain himself rejoiced in telling the tale. But it was no laughing matter at the time, either for him or for me.

CHAPTER FOUR

LT. CHRISTOPHER CRADOCK, R.N.

Sir Christopher George Francis Maurice Cradock, K.C.V.O., was only a lieutenant in the Royal Navy when he was posted to duty in the Far East in the 1880s. While stationed in those waters for three years, he managed to visit a number of hunting grounds, not only in China but also in Korea and Japan and on the Siberian coast. He often traveled by houseboat up China's numerous river systems in search of waterfowl and upland birds. He noted that the hunting was demanding, but if sportsmen did not "object to long hard days, and are also content with a moderate, and in some cases a most varied bag, you can have great fun to make up for all the undoubtedly heavy work."

Cradock was a career navy man, rising through the ranks to become an admiral. A contributor to numerous journals, he also wrote three books. His first, Sporting Notes in the Far East *(1889), ably described his experiences hunting the Asian coastline. Other works of naval interest include* Wrinkles in Seamanship *(1894) and* Whispers from the Fleet *(1907).*

In Sporting Notes in the Far East *(1889), he provides hints to sportsmen on where to hunt and where he encountered species of game. The book also contains chapters on hunting dogs and treating the tropical ailments that often afflicted them.*

THE SPORTING DOG IN CHINA

In order to make good bags anywhere in the East, the services of a sporting dog are quite indispensable. They are necessary not only in finding game but in picking up dead birds.

For good all-around work, I would recommend a strong, long-legged Clumber spaniel—the long legs for the heavy undergrowth one invariably finds up north. The dog should be under perfect control (many a hunter has missed a shot at deer through shouting and hollering at a useless dog) and ought to be at least two years old before it is brought out from England. The dog should in no case be subject to attacks of mange; dogs that work in bad or putrid water suffer greatly from this miserable disease and, by drinking this water, are often seized with a dreaded and almost fatal illness known as "worms in the heart."

Once a dog has developed the latter affliction, the case is more or less hopeless, and this is most distressing for the owner. He (the master) probably looks upon his "tyke" almost in the light of a mess-mate, or in some cases as a tie from the "old place at home." He sees the poor beast dying by inches before his eyes, and he can do nothing to relieve its suffering until death itself intervenes.

The same disease sometimes acts in quite a different form. Dogs apparently in full health will suddenly drop dead in their tracks, and a postmortem examination reveals their hearts are perforated with white worms, some as long as nine inches.

I have also heard the origin of this affliction ascribed to feeding on bad rice—it may be so; all I can say is that I have never yet met the individual who could tell the exact cause of the disease and then cure it. However, a European sportsman in Nagasaki, Japan, has given me a recipe, and the reader can take it for what it is worth. It consists of administering to the dog, immediately on its return from shooting, seven drops of liquor *arsenicalis* in a cup of milk or any liquid that it will readily drink, and repeating the dose on the following two days.

Especially up the Yangtze River, dogs also suffer from deafness that arises when the seeds of certain grasses work their way into the ears. In the districts where these grasses abound, a light linen canker cap over the ears, which is then tied under the jaws, is a good protection.

These same seeds will occasionally enter the feet between the toes and, by working their way up the legs under the skin, will cause acute inflammation. It is a most difficult task to locate these seeds, and there is no remedy but fomentation, with the hope that they will work their way to the surface before long. Fortunately, they nearly always do.

In some parts of the East, the vegetation in the autumn is swarming with ticks, and these persistent little brutes will cause an intolerable amount of worry to a dog left in its coat, even for a few hours. Therefore, if shooting in these more or less infested parts, extract the insects immediately on your return home; otherwise, they will get fixed: that is, their head and shoulders will be well buried, and they will have commenced to suck. Hundreds of these ferocious little beggars, filling themselves out till they reach the size of small acorns, will in a single day completely destroy a dog's condition. The females absorb the most blood and reach by far the biggest proportions.

They say that a solution of strong tobacco juice and water will effect a cure. But I have found that nothing can be applied with safety to a dog's coat that will at once destroy these insects. Whatever you do, never forget to examine and remove any ticks from the inside and crevices of the ear.

In a climate like China, when days are hot and nights are cold, it is always good to have a roughly fitted blanket or "fearnought" coat made for your dog, to button under the belly and across the chest. Putting this on when the animal is damp and chilled after shooting will keep it from catching a cold on the journey home.

In hot weather it is necessary to clip a long-haired dog. Avoid shortening the hair on its back, as the long coat forms a natural and efficient protection from the rays of the sun. Never give a dog a hot bath after severe exercise, and do not forget that good grooming—that is, combing and brushing—does more to cleanse a dog's skin than any amount of washing.

Now we address the kennel on board ship. Naturally, the dimensions of the kennel depend to a great extent on the build of the dog, but for an ordinary-sized animal—say, a spaniel weighing between thirty and forty pounds—order a simple rectangular kennel with a sloping roof. These are the dimensions I find best:

Length of kennel	2 feet, 9 inches
Breath of floor	8 feet
Height of sides	3 feet
Height of apex of roof	2 feet, 1 inch

It must stand on four stout legs at least four inches long to keep the kneel floor clear of salt water and the dampness of the deck, and, as further prevention against damp, the entire inside should be lined with fearnaught.

The kennel should have two floors, the upper one capable of being withdrawn, like the false bottom of a birdcage; this will enable you to dry it thoroughly after a wet animal has lain on it.

Build the roof with well-overhanging sides, like a Swiss cottage, and construct it so that in hot weather or after wet weather it will completely lift off to cool or thoroughly air the inside. Last, make the kennel out of teak or some other close-grained wood that will not readily retain moisture.

In conclusion, build a kennel as you think fit, but it *must* be a dry one, for it is easier to raise a flock of one hundred young turkeys on shore than it is to keep one highly bred dog in perfect health afloat, and wet and damp are its chief enemies.

And here let me say one word regarding victuals. I think the best food for a sporting dog when in this part of the world is good boiled rice mixed with vegetables and gravy and a few bones, but on no account solid flesh, cooked or otherwise. The "beef block" is one of the greatest banes to an owner of a dog on board ship. Tie up the dog as you will, when the beef is being cut up for distribution, it will find its way there somehow.

CHAPTER FIVE

THOMAS R. JERNIGAN

Thomas R. Jernigan, a member of the American consular staff in Shanghai, was as respected for his scholarship as for his diplomatic expertise. An ardent student of economics, he studied Chinese trade and commercial laws in detail, penning two well-received books: China's Business Methods and Policy *(1904) and* China in Law and Commerce *(1905). In addition, he attended Chinese courts, observed the Manchu judicial process in action, and was a regular customer at Chinese shops and businesses.*

Jernigan also received recognition as a sportsman. Particularly adept at bird shooting, he traveled through eastern China in search of sport. In 1908 he published Shooting in China, *a kind of vade mecum for novice sportsmen entering the region. He not only described the varieties of game to be encountered but made note of proper clothing, guns, dogs, and local customs. One fascinating chapter even described Chinese traditional methods of hunting. In addition, he included passages from Henling Thomas Wade's diary of sporting trips.*

In this passage from Shooting in China, *Jernigan had embarked on a bird-hunting trip near the Ningpo lakes when he suddenly encountered wolves, a terror for local farmers.*

WOLF HUNTING IN THE NINGPO LAKES DISTRICT

My first shoot in China was on these lakes. The lakes are about twenty miles southeast of the city of Ningpo, which is situated on the Yangtze River, fifteen miles from its mouth.

If the shooter starts out from Shanghai, the journey should be comfortable all the way, and there will be no delay if, after arriving at Ningpo, he arranges for a houseboat before he leaves for the lakes.

Every day, Sundays excepted, large and comfortable steamers leave Shanghai for Ningpo and Ningpo for Shanghai at 4 P.M., and the distance is only a twelve-hour run. But after arriving at Ningpo it will be necessary to secure a houseboat in order to travel to the lakes, and, therefore, one should take the precaution of engaging the boat a day or so ahead. With this arrangement, the shooter will find at the steamer's wharf a properly outfitted houseboat with a competent crew ready to leave at once. After he has put his equipment aboard, the crew rows[1] the houseboat a short distance up the river, and, by means of a most primitive windlass, pulls it over the river embankment into the creek that leads to the lakes. If the shooter starts from Ningpo immediately on the arrival of the steamer, he should reach the lakes at 11 A.M., which will leave time to prepare lunch and spend the entire afternoon shooting.

If the shooter wishes to take his houseboat into the lakes, the *lowdah* (chief boatman) will inform him which branch of the creek to travel, but unless the weather is warm it is advisable to stop the boat near the lower end of the lakes and in the creek, and he will be within a few hundred yards of the best feeding grounds for ducks. The lakes are small, and in reality make but one sheet of water, so the houseboat looms quite large in contrast to the small canoes used by the fishermen and farmers of the surrounding country.

All around there were high hills and mountains, and, as there had not been much rain, the water in the lakes was clear, and the bottom, clearly visible, was covered with the grass the ducks are so fond of. The sides of many of the hills and mountains were terraced and beautifully cultivated, and the industrious farmers were busy at work. Sometimes I could see an entire hillside, green with vegetable growth, reflected in the water. So clearly could I see all this that it looked as if the farmers who were moving about between the turnip and cabbage rows were walking on the bottom of the lakes.

There are several villages built on the narrow plains that separate the hills from the water, but the inhabitants are peacefully disposed, and the shooter can easily buy all the vegetables, eggs, and chickens he may need. I have been shooting on the lakes for several seasons

1. The Chinese use a blade-heavy oar, called a yuloh, *made of two or three straight pieces set at an angle so the blade curves down into the water. Unlike western oars that use a notch, lock, or socket on the boat, the* yuloh *has a socket cut or let into its bottom, and it rests on a pivot. (www.woodenboat.net.nz/Stories/Sculling/sculIthree.html)*

and have always found the natives friendly. The best sweet potatoes I have seen in China were grown on a small island in the lakes. The principal products are vegetables, which are sold in the Ningpo city markets, and early every morning the creeks leading from the lakes and the surrounding country are covered with small boats loaded with vegetables, bound for the city markets. A large number of natives work in the granite quarries, and the rock slabs they produce there are readily sold in any market.

Since I first came to China I have visited the lakes at least once during each season. I love to go there, because the bright waters and beautiful scenery seem to shut one out from the noise of the great outer world, and are so restful to look upon. It is true that shooting there is not on any grand scale, but it is sufficient for genuine amusement, and when the shooter tires of shooting wildfowl he can look for pheasants on the hillsides. If he has been thoughtful and brought his bird dog, he should bag a couple of brace of strong mountain pheasants on his way to his houseboat. The pheasants I have shot in mountainous places are larger and stronger than those found on the plains. They are quicker in flight, and to bring them down requires a steady nerve and clear eye.

One of my most pleasant trips to the lakes was in company with another friend. Each of us owned a new 8-bore Greener gun and was anxious to put it to the test. We had left Shanghai at 4 P.M. on one of the regular mail steamers but did not reach the lakes until about 2 P.M. the following day. The crew pulled our houseboat over into the lakes and had not rowed far toward the lower end when we saw that the water in that direction was almost covered with geese and ducks. We at once took the 8-bores out of the cases and cleaned them of oil, and each had his small boat ready for the evening shoot. I was the first to fire and, with a right and left, brought down two large geese. My friend had never stalked wild geese and did not get any the first afternoon, but on the second he made a good bag of geese and ducks. The weather was favorable, and we had been fortunate in arriving at the lakes at the proper time. Our bag during the two full days we shot counted 120 large ducks and 30 geese. It was the largest bag ever made by any shooter on the lakes within so short a time. It was larger

than any I had made previously or since, and a pleasing feature was that the count to each gun was practically the same.

In February 1906 I was shooting on the lakes in company with a friend. The ducks were scarce, and neither of us was in a pleasant humor when we returned to the houseboat one evening with scarcely enough game to satisfy our appetites. I was suffering from a neuralgic pain in the face, and on retiring for the night I remarked to my friend that he could have all the lakes to himself the next day; I would remain aboard the houseboat and would not expose myself to the cold wind. Early next morning he equipped himself, and I said goodbye and wished him better luck.

Around eight o'clock my Chinese servant came to my bunk and said the sun was shining brightly, and he thought I would feel better if I took some outdoor exercise. I dressed, drank a cup of coffee, and took my light 12-bore gun, loaded with No. 5 shot, and walked toward the dikes that hold back the waters of the lakes and prevent them from overflowing the little fields of the Chinese farmers. The particular dike toward which I was walking connected two mountain ranges; it was quite high and nearly half a mile in length.

I had just reached it and was looking across the lake when my servant boy, who was walking behind, shouted out at the top of his voice, in Chinese, the name of the animal to which he wished to direct my attention. I knew something was going on, and, as I turned to see what it was, I saw a large wolf on top of the dike, running directly toward me. The animal did not see me until it was within a few yards of where I stood, and then it increased its speed and, with a vicious growl, attempted to jump past me, but when it touched the ground it fell stone dead. I do not know whether I had hit it when I fired the first barrel, but I took no risk and followed quickly with the second.

In the meantime, the boy was near me with a heavier 12-bore, used for duck shooting, and I heard him shout out again the same Chinese sound. As I looked up, there was another wolf, larger than the first, coming toward me from the same direction. I could see that the wolf I had shot was a female, and the one coming toward me was the male. I exchanged guns and awaited his coming; he was a daring fellow and approached, plainly showing his teeth, but I knew he could not escape. He made a similar jump but on the opposite side of the dike from where his mate lay dead, and when he touched the ground he rolled over also stone dead. I consumed no more than half a minute in killing the two wolves, and both lay dead on the ground, about ten yards apart. I did not have any scales convenient and can only approximate the weight of the male. My friend and I estimated that, from the tip of the tail to the nose, the male measured 62½ inches, and the skin across the body measured 25 inches. The color was light brown, but a darker shade along the middle of the back.

As soon as word spread that two wolves had been shot, a great many natives came to the houseboat to see them, and there was much rejoicing that we had killed two of the enemy of their flocks of sheep and goats. Of course, a wolf should be shot in any condition, but I became somewhat sympathetic when I observed what appeared to be the true condition of the female. The day was rather warm, so I decided to have the entrails taken out to preserve the hides the best I could. When the female was cut open, half of a young goat rolled out. She had caught and eaten it probably not more than a few hours before she was shot. When the natives saw that the wolves had been shot so soon after the killing and eating of the little goat, their expression of gladness at the just retribution was intense. They walked around the carcasses again and again as if to say, "You remorseless tyrants of our meadows, your nights of pillage are ended."

I do not know the moment the neuralgic pain left me, but I did not feel it again after I saw the first wolf. The male wolf had looked as if there might be some fight in him. He must have heard the two barrels fired into the body of his comrade and seen her outstretched on the ground, and still he did not change his course but seemed intent upon facing me. Somehow I was perfectly calm and collected, and, with a Greener gun that had often proved trustworthy, I felt as if my aim would be sure.

After the wolves had been put on board the houseboat, I was feeling so much better I got aboard a canoe and had the boatman push it to one of the islands in the lakes where I thought I might find

Thomas Jernigan (right), shown here with his shooting companions, explored the hunting grounds of eastern China in the early twentieth century.

a pheasant or a woodcock. Almost immediately after going ashore, my dog put up a large cock pheasant, which I bagged with the first barrel. I then looked up the lakes and saw my friend returning from his morning shoot, and I pushed out meet him. He had shot a hen pheasant and one or two ducks and felt the need of a cup of strong coffee. I told him that I had shot two large animals but would not name them, which excited his curiosity, and he proposed that we return to the houseboat and rest until the hour for afternoon shooting.

A few years ago the Ningpo plain was an excellent shooting ground for pheasants, and the small ponds in the fields were favorite places of wild ducks, but now the game is not so plentiful. The foreign population of the port in recent years has materially increased, and the breechloader has proved as destructive there as it has been elsewhere in China.

CHAPTER SIX

ERNEST HENRY WILSON

*Ernest H. Wilson, as I have already noted, was a scientist of questioning mind and a sportsman of considerable shooting skill. His China travels began in 1899, as he sought new plants with the idea of introducing them to Europe and North America. During his expedition to central China from 1907 to 1909, Wilson collected numerous species of pheasant, including the Lady Amherst variety with its exotic caparison, as well as various waterfowls, partridges, and snipes. Although he did not personally hunt any of the larger species of wild goat or wild sheep, leaving that sport to Walter Zappey, he did pursue the Chinese water deer (*Hydropotes inermis*), an inhabitant of marshes and riverine lowlands. This little deer had once been common in many locales along the Yangtze, but a thriving market-hunting industry had thinned local populations and had driven many of the animals away from their former habitat. Fortunately for water deer, their does produce three to six young at a time.*

Though Wilson notes in this excerpt from A Naturalist in Western China *(1913) that he considered this species to be trophy material, many other sportsmen did not. There is no mention of trophy water deer in either the Seventh Edition (1914) or the Eighth Edition (1922) of* Rowland Ward's Records of Big Game, *the bible of trophy hunters. There was, however, plenty of excitement to be had in hunting them.*

IN THE SHANGHAI LOWLANDS FOR RIVER DEER

It is customary to write disparagingly of this interesting little animal *(Hydropotes inermis)*, both as to the sport it affords and its value for the table. This attitude may be attributed to "familiarity breeding contempt." Certain kinds of venison are certainly superior for the table, but this water deer is wholesome, palatable, and very much superior to the beef obtainable in most of the riverine ports of China. When it is properly kept and properly cooked, there are many worse things than a cutlet of this much-abused water deer.

Formerly, this animal was extraordinarily abundant throughout the fluviatile regions of the lower Yangtze basin, and it is still very common in many places. The Chinese hunt it mercilessly, and they sell several thousand annually in the markets from Jinsha downriver to Shanghai and elsewhere. The low hills that commence some thirty miles east of Yichang mark the western boundary of this animal, as they mark the boundary of the ringneck pheasant. The home of the river deer is the great alluvial plain of the Yangtze, which extends from the point mentioned above eastward one thousand miles to the sea. Any cover is sufficient to hold river deer, and though it is not averse to water and swamps it prefers the drier land afforded by any rising ground. In winter an ideal spot in which to find this animal is longer grass on rising ground near reed-clad marshes. When the cover is mostly cut (in midwinter), water deer are to be found in open fields, lying in the furrows and hollows.

Small shot is usually recommended as sufficient to kill this deer, and it is sufficient at fifteen to twenty yards. A charge of No. 8 shot will kill almost any thin-skinned animal a few yards from the muzzle of the gun if it happens to strike a vital spot. A famous big-game shot (the late Mr. H. C. Syers) once killed a black panther with a charge of No. 9s when returning at dusk from snipe shooting. It was a snapshot at something that crossed the path and entered the brush immediately in front of him. The next day, when he discovered what animal he had shot, he realized the foolishness of his action and the terrible danger in which it might have involved him. But this is an aside.

There is no danger to apprehend from a river deer, wounded or otherwise, though it is courageous in its own way. I have seen one beat off and wound a pointer dog almost its own size. There is certainly no sport in killing deer at fifteen to twenty-five yards. Beyond this distance no true sportsman would fire using small shot on the off-chance of bringing the animal down. The sportsman is out to kill mercifully and not to maim game.

The only time I have really hunted water deer was during the winter of 1907–1908. Mr. Zappey wanted specimens, and we made a trip downriver below Jinsha in quest of them. In this flat country a rifle is out of the question; otherwise, some excellent sport could be enjoyed. Using BB shot, we had good sport, bagging every deer at which we fired but one. We had men to beat the likely places and to

drive the deer across. We killed most of the bag at around forty yards, but several fell at over fifty-five yards and one at seventy-four yards. Two or three of them shot square through the heart ran fifty to one hundred yards before they dropped dead in their tracks.

We limited ourselves to twenty but could have killed many more had we been so inclined; on our best day we bagged nine. A couple of mounted heads in my possession make a pretty trophy and are a pleasant memento of days spent in the Chinese wilds. Though so abundant, this water deer is quite rare in museums, and it was this knowledge that induced us to kill so many.

Water deer stand about twenty to twenty-two inches at shoulder, with a total length of forty inches; length of tail, three inches; and heel, eleven inches. The body is tawny grey; the legs and belly are buff; the top of the shoulders and rump are somewhat chestnut in old males. The hair is coarse and bristly and easily pulls out. They develop no horns. In the males the upper canine teeth protrude downward, forming scimitar-shaped tusks two to two and a half inches long. These tusks are said to develop in old females, but I never met with this phenomenon. The tusks are brittle and easily broken, at least after the animal is dead. The legs are lightly but muscularly built, and the animal can cover the ground at good speed, running great distances and taking to water like a duck. The deer are prolific, dropping four to six fawns annually in May. The average weight is twenty to twenty-four pounds; the flesh is dark-colored. Swinhoe, who described this animal, gave it the generic name *hydropotes*, signifying "water-drinker."

CHAPTER SEVEN

ARTHUR DE CARLE SOWERBY

Without a doubt, the most prolific contributor to the literature of sport in China was Arthur de Carle Sowerby. The son of a British Baptist missionary, Sowerby was born in Taiyuan in China's Shanxi Province in 1885. Well versed in the culture of the people, and skilled with a rifle and shotgun, the young man made a name for himself as a hunter. His love of sport was coupled with a keen interest in natural history and in identifying and collecting Chinese art.

His breakthrough as a naturalist occurred in 1908, when he joined Robert Sterling Clark's scientific expedition through northern China. Sowerby and Clark coauthored their adventures in Through Shên-kan *(1912), a detailed work that also featured Sowerby's watercolors. The young Briton received additional recognition when he led a relief expedition to evacuate missionaries threatened by widespread revolutions in China in 1911. He also became a fellow of prestigious scientific groups such as the Royal Geographical Society and the Royal Zoological Society, and he was a member of the Biological Society of Washington.*

Sowerby wrote a host of books relating his hunting and collecting experiences. Fur and Feather in Northern China *(1914) featured a chapter-by-chapter analysis of various species. In* A Sportsman's Miscellany *(1917) he bagged game, from pheasant and snipe to takin and goral. His* Sport and Science on the Sino-Mongolian Frontier*—completed in 1913 but not published until 1918 due to the outbreak of World War I—described his adventures in northern China and the Manchurian border country. Sowerby's literary tour de force was his five-volume* The Naturalist in Manchuria *(1922), which not only recounted his travels and explorations in the region but provided detailed accounts of the species collected. In addition, he wrote* A Naturalist's Holiday by the Sea *(1923), a study of the natural history of Britain's Cornwall region, and* A Naturalist's Note-book in China *(1925).*

By the 1930s, Sowerby's attention had turned to art. He served as editor of The China Journal of Art and Science, *continued writing articles for scientific and art journals, then wrote* Nature and Chinese Art *(1940), which was published both in Britain and the United States. His final work was a study of his family's lineage. Sowerby died in 1954.*

In this excerpt from A Sportsman's Miscellany, *Sowerby hunts his beloved hill country in Shanxi for that most famous of all Chinese game birds, the pheasant.*

PHEASANTS AROUND TAIYUAN

In the summer of 1911 we returned to China with the idea of carrying out extensive explorations in Mongolia and Manchuria. We reached Taiyuan in July, when, at the height of the rainy season, it was impossible to start our contemplated journey for some time.

I tried one short trip into the mountains of the Ningwu District, but it ended in disaster when my head servant was accidentally shot by one of his companions. Subsequently, disquieting rumors about the impending outbreak began to circulate, so I decided to wait a while to see how things were going, before starting on a long journey northward.

In view of the general unrest in the country, we had decided that my wife should not accompany me on this journey, but I soon found a pleasant and able companion and assistant in Mr. F. W. Warrington, son of Professor A. W. Warrington of Shanxi University.

For the time being we contented ourselves with short excursions around the city and into the adjoining country, and were very successful.

September, in China the best month of the year, arrived, and with it the thought of the pheasants and other game, only waiting for the sportsman's gun. We decided therefore to try our luck in the mountains west of Taiyuan.

Hiring mules to carry our stores, and accompanied by one of the railway officials—a Frenchman and a very good fellow—we left the city in high spirits. It was just the right sort of day for travel, and our ponies, fresh from a good summer's rest, curvetted and careered in their anxiety for a gallop across the flats.

After seeing our mules across the swollen river in safety, and traversing the low-lying loess terraces on the western side of the valley, we entered a deep gorge in the limestone formation. Being well mounted, we had long since outstripped the mules, so, when we found a clear stream a couple of miles up the gorge, we dismounted to have lunch and await the slow-moving train.

We finished our lunch and then put in time searching for fossils. The hours slipped by, but brought no sign of the mules, so that we began to wonder what had become of them. Finally we rode back to the nearest village, some three miles along the road, and made inquiries of the natives. No, the mules had not passed through the village, and no one had seen them. This was awkward. What had become of those mules, or where to go in search of them, we were entirely at a loss to know. We did not want to return to Taiyuan and spoil our trip, and yet to go on into the mountains without any prospect of food or shelter did not commend itself as a much better alternative. Finally, through much questioning, we learned that there was another path up to the spot where we wished to camp. Putting everything on one cast of the dice, we decided to make for our original goal on the chance that our outfit and servants had already arrived there by this other path.

As night was fast coming on, we borrowed a lantern and set out to make the twelve miles of mountain path as fast as possible. Daylight lasted another half-hour or so, allowing us to get well into the gorge. Our plucky little ponies kept up a sharp trot, even in he darkness, till we reached the end of the boulder-strewn gorge. We then began a steep and, under the circumstances, somewhat dangerous ascent. For more than two hours we climbed, sometimes zigzagging up the steep face of a mountain, at other times winding along the edge of a precipice. Once we missed the path and found ourselves at the end of a narrow ledge, looking down into the inky depths of a yawning chasm. Carefully retracing our steps, we regained the path, which, owing to numerous landslides caused by recent rains, was obliterated in many places for yards at a stretch. It was with the utmost difficulty that our surefooted ponies picked their way over these masses of jagged rock.

At last, however, we reached the village of Sheng-yeh, and to our great relief found that our mules had arrived in safety and had put up at a little temple. We soon forgot our trying experiences in anticipation of a good week's sport amongst the pheasants.

We got a campfire going and were soon comfortably enjoying a good dinner, followed by a smoke, a chat, and bed.

Early the next morning we were astir, and after a hasty breakfast we set out over the brush-covered hills. It was not long before we began to flush pheasants, and had excellent shooting. As we traversed the ridges and intervening ravines, bouquet after bouquet of fine young birds, led by magnificent old cocks, rose in front of us, and our guns rang out incessantly. Now and then a hare, breaking cover, would form a little diversion; once or twice great excitement reigned as a fat woodcock burst out of some thick coppice of young pines and went rocketing away, sometimes falling to one or the other of the guns.

Presently, as we worked down a long ridge, the unearthly and awe-inspiring cry of the brown-eared pheasant (*Crossoptilon mantchuricum*) rang out from a clump of pines on the opposite slope, to be taken up and thrown back from several other points in the underbrush. To my companions the peculiar noise was new, but to me it was a familiar sound, though I was surprised to hear it in this locality.

How well I remember my first experience of that fearsome call or, rather, series of calls. I was at the time away in the high mountains of western Shanxi and was stalking a deer through a dense forest when the noise rang out within a few yards of me, echoing through the dark arches of the pines and sending cold shivers down my back. I did not then discover the perpetrator of the discordant cries. Later, when I was out in Gansu and was traversing some dark and wooded gorges high up in the Liupan Mountains, I was again startled by the same indescribable sound, which seemed to issue from the throat of some fearsome beast of prey lurking in the gloomy depths of those mountain gorges. It was not till the winter of 1909, while on the expedition I described in the foregoing chapter, that I discovered it was the brown-eared pheasant's challenge that had so startled me. Thus the sound, which now caused my companions to look around in something approaching trepidation, was to me the sweetest of music, as I remembered the fine sport I had already had with these birds.

We hurried around the top of the ridge, and, having arrived at a point above the spinney whence the calls had issued, we worked slowly down through the young pines. We had not gone far when three fine birds broke cover and went gliding across the valley. The trees prevented anybody from shooting, but we carefully noted where the birds settled. One lighted in a pine tree near the bottom of the ravine, while the other two settled higher up the slope and in their usual manner began to run upward at top speed. Hurrying down, we approached the tree in which the bird had settled but saw no trace of it. Suddenly it broke cover once more, and I managed to get in a shot that made the feathers fly. The bird continued, however, and reached the opposite slope. Again we hurried across to the spot where it stopped, but could find no trace of it. Jimmy, our pointer, soon picked up the warm scent, however, and there ensued a long and exciting chase through the underbrush. None of us could see the quarry, which was running with wonderful speed through the dense hazel scrub. At last Jimmy caught it and held it till we came up. It turned out to be a magnificent cock, which must have weighed six or seven pounds. The other two birds made their escape.

It was indeed a surprise to me to find this bird, which usually inhabits the highest and wildest regions of the country, so close to the thickly populated country around Taiyuan.

Our time, regulated by the duration of our friend's leave, was almost at an end, so we decided to finish up with a grand drive, in which we hoped to settle the vexing question—who should claim the honors of the chase.

Unfortunately for me, it proved to be my off-day, so that, but for a nice right and left at the commencement of the drive, and a bird here and there throughout the day, I missed everything. Warrington, on the other hand, did particularly well, and the Frenchman increased his total bag by several brace of pheasants. The result of the day's shooting was a win for Warrington. This finished our little trip, and we returned without adventure to Taiyuan.

We found that the revolution had just broken out in Hankow and that the general unrest and excitement was increasing. Loath to risk my outfit, and knowing that if the North joined in the rebellion against the Manchu power it would be impossible to travel with any safety, I decided further to postpone our intended journey into Mongolia, and we spent the time instead in a short camping trip down the river. Thus it was that on 12 October we found ourselves comfortably settled under canvas upon the bank of the Fen River, about five miles south of Taiyuan.

Around us the farmers were busy harvesting rich crops of beans and sorghum. The weather was superb, with just sufficient nip in it to make a stove at night pleasant, and to send the blood coursing through one's veins as one tramped along in the early mornings, watching the sky for the long lines of migrating geese or beating the scrub and underbrush for quails and hares.

Thus we continued day after day, hunting, riding, and trapping. Still the province remained quiet, till at last we began to think that after all we might venture upon our proposed expedition, and we were just finishing up at camp on the river when an urgent letter reached us from Taiyuan, advising us to come in at once, as an outbreak was about to occur.

A few days later the Shanxi soldiers revolted and, raising the revolutionary flag, declared in favor of a republic. This effectually interrupted our work for many months to come. Advice, which amounted to orders, from the legations in Peking, resulted in all Europeans taking their wives and children to the coast.

Subsequently, news of the murder of some missionaries and children and rumored peril of the Europeans in the adjoining province of Shaanxi, led to the formation of the Shaanxi Relief Expedition, which was placed under my leadership, and which kept Warrington and myself very busy throughout the winter.

CHAPTER EIGHT

JOSEPH CLARK GREW

Joseph Clark Grew (1880–1965) was not only a hunter extraordinaire but an esteemed member of the American diplomatic corps. After his graduation from Harvard, he embarked on an eighteen-month tour of the world, which combined travel and big-game hunting. In 1910 he wrote Sport and Travel in the Far East, *relating his experiences in India, Baltistan, New Zealand, and Kashmir. A year later he entered the U.S. Foreign Service as a junior diplomat with appointments to Berlin and Vienna. After the United States declared war on the Central Powers in 1917, Grew was sent to Vienna to close the embassy.*

Through the 1930s, he served as the U.S. ambassador to Japan, a post he still held when the Japanese bombed Pearl Harbor on 7 December 1941. Grew had tried to warn the government of growing Japanese militarism. He published two books after America's entry into the war: Report from Tokyo *(1942) and* Ten Years in Japan *(1944). After World War II, he aided in the rebuilding of Japan and warned of the rise of Communist China.*

Though his diplomatic duties precluded much leisure time, stalking big game remained one of Grew's favorite activities. His story of tiger hunting in the caves near Xiamen (Amoy) is undoubtedly one of the most vibrant passages from Sport and Travel in the Far East. *This hunting was not like stalking "stripes" in the style of shikar in the Indian jungle, but it features a close encounter in the dark, narrow caverns of the Chinese coast.*

HUNTING THE CAVE-DWELLING TIGER OF CHINA

Along the coast of China, midway between Hong Kong and Shanghai, there lies a tract of country quite devoid of any growth, where the barren hills that roll back from the sea to the rice-cultivated country inland are strewn with the gigantic boulders of some prehistoric glacial moraine, and it is in the numberless caves and subterranean passages formed by these great confused masses of rock that the sole wild occupant of the country, the Chinese tiger, finds its lair.

Accordingly, the sport of tiger shooting here is quite a different proposition from that in India and other tropical countries, where the methods of shooting are adapted to the jungle—that is, one hunts from the backs of elephants; on foot on a jungle path; by driving, beating, or sitting up over a kill. Here in China the sportsman must track the animal to its cave, and, if he finds it in such a position that it cannot be driven out to the gun, the tiger must be blocked in so that the sportsman can enter with comparative safety. In India the excitement is generally over in a few seconds; in cave shooting in China, a sportsman is frequently in a state of high tension for several hours. Having located the game, he is still uncertain whether it will charge out before it can be successfully blocked.

I had had my fill of the jungle. Rains, flies, and fever had convinced me that tiger shooting in the tropics had its distinct disadvantages, and had made me wish for a healthful country and a respectable atmosphere, where one could enjoy living and shooting at the same time—a paradox in the jungle. I was unwilling to return without a tiger; I had heard glowing tales of this cave district. Here, then, was the very thing for which I had been waiting.

It was with the keenest anticipation that I finally found myself rolling down the coast of China toward Xiamen on the little *haitan*. Over our pipes and coffee in the evening, the old Scotch engineer told me stories of lighthouse keepers along the shore watching the tigers play at night on the beaches below, and of natives carried away from the rice fields within shouting distance of their villages, which made me feel that at last I was in for some sport. So, though I was alone except for my old Sinhalese servant, Thomas, who had shared with me many adventures, I was not at all loath to take my goods and chattels and transfer myself to the care of a yellow pirate in a dilapidated junk, and set sail for the shore.

It was a few days later that I found myself in a snug little village named Chi Phaw, tucked away at the foot of the hills. Flooded paddies skirted it on one side, and to the west a pagoda-crowned mountain towered like a sentinel—far too peaceful a scene to suggest the sport for which I had come.

As the guest of the village, expected to do my best in ridding the inhabitants of a nuisance, I was led up the central path through a staring and wondering crowd of peasants, who were unaccustomed to seeing white men and had no modesty about showing it. We walked among innumerable black hogs enjoying undisturbed slumber along the highway, and past rude hovels within which hens, babies, dogs, and kittens sprawled promiscuously. At the end of the village we came to a remarkable-looking building—a sort of large shed with an arched roof and a paved floor. One side opened to a courtyard flanked by a ten-foot wall. This was ordinarily a temple sacred to the common ancestor of the village, but now, I learned, it was to be my habitation for as long as I cared to remain. On inspection it proved to be a filthy lodging: I had to sweep much debris from the floor and drive away several huge black spiders before I could make up my mind that it was at all habitable. I shook down a pile of straw in a corner for a bed, and I spread my dressing articles on the altar, after which the seven Chinese hunters who from now on were to escort me presented themselves.

They stood grinning in a row, their almond-shaped eyes sloping upward, their yellow skins burned to bronze and wrinkled like old parchment from work in the rice fields. With one exception they were under five feet tall—hardly the imposing individuals I had pictured, who were to walk into the tiger's den with only their torches to frighten it and their spears to stop a charge. Their weapons, however, looked sufficiently businesslike, for each carried a sort of trident with three iron prongs and a heavy wooden shaft. They carried with them also, in a small, sand-filled basket, an exact miniature of a hunter like themselves—a little Chinaman who held in his hand the identical trident. Around him in the sand were burning joss sticks. This, I discovered, was their idol, whom they worshipped fervently and regularly, and never in our subsequent hunting were they without him, for, as they told me, it was he who gave them the courage to hunt and the strength to fight the tiger. They had promised, if I were successful, to take the idol to see a play on their return to Xiamen, so it seemed certain that he would grant their prayers without delay.

My interpreter was a young Chinaman named Lim Ek Hui, who had learned English at an American mission school in Fuzhou. He was to prove invaluable in communicating the directions of the Chinese and was to be a most interesting companion in discussing things Chinese during the long, lonely evenings. We arranged between us the rate of wages, and, having satisfactorily decided this matter, we repaired to our respective suppers—I (to the great delight of the admiring throng in the courtyard) to knife, fork, and plate; they to their chow bowls and chopsticks. The ten Chinamen who were to share my temple then stretched themselves in various positions about the floor, lit their opium lamps, and smoked themselves into oblivion. The interior quickly filled with the pungent but not unpleasant odor of the drug. Thomas found a position at the other end of the temple, as far removed as possible from the Chinamen, while I, repairing to my bale of straw, was quickly asleep amid these novel surroundings.

At dawn the courtyard was filled with the same admiring crowd of the night before. Men, women, and children watched the processes of bathing, dressing, and eating breakfast much as we might observe the Wild Man of Borneo taking dinner at the dime museum. This was embarrassing, and before many days it became extremely irritating, though it was a rather difficult matter to drive them away. The hunters had procured long, slender bamboo poles and were winding strips of cloth about their tips. The tips then were dipped in oil and would serve as torches to light up the interior of the caves we explored. After chow, we started out in single file. I followed the head hunter, quite ignorant as to where or into what he would lead me.

Knowing the lay of the land, the hunters chose without hesitation the most likely caves to explore. A tramp of some four miles brought us up into the rocky hills, and here at last, with the openings of caves and passages all about us, I felt the first pleasant realization that game might be near. The hunters soon stopped above a cave that led directly down into the earth, while one of them led me a few yards down the hillside to station me at the mouth of another opening below. Lim translated that they would move through the passage and drive the tiger, if it were there, down to the exit I was guarding. They quickly oiled their torches, shed their great umbrella hats, and dropped one by one out of sight into the hole.

Lim had scruples about accompanying me on the hunt, but he gave in to protests that he was indispensable and assurances of perfect safety: He was necessary, not only to interpret directions, but to hold my extra gun and pass it to me, should the two barrels

of the .450 cordite-powder express prove ineffectual. I had fair confidence in the stopping power of the express but in case of emergency thought it best to take a second gun. This gun, which was a double-barreled 10-bore, I gave to Lim, loaded but uncocked. Stationing him behind me on a suitable rock a few yards from the cave opening, I awaited results.

Probably few forms of sport afford greater interest than watching the opening of a cave, knowing that at any moment one or more tigers may charge out and aware that, if they do, one must shoot both instantly and accurately. Under such circumstances an ordinary hole in a hillside becomes a distinctly fascinating object. A year before, in the same spot, Perry and Wheeler had seen four tigers break cover simultaneously, and two days later Perry had found and shot a fifth in another cave nearby, so I was confident of success. We saw no results from our work that day, however, or for many days to come. The smoke of the torches appearing through the fissures in the rock, and the sound of the spears feeling about near the exit, betrayed the men's passage. We explored several other caves before returning to the village, but to no purpose.

I now decided, and the men agreed with me, that this wholesale exploration of caves was a poor thing, since, if a tiger should happen to come to one of them later, the smell of the torches would prevent it from entering, and it would doubtless move to some other part of the country at once. The animals are continually roaming and may appear in a certain district at any time, so that there is nothing to do but wait. Accordingly, in the evening I purchased from a shepherd six small goats and placed them around the country within a radius of a mile or so, attaching each before the opening of some promising cave, and as we returned to camp we could hear their bleating coming from all directions. If a tiger came within reach of that sound, I knew we would have something to work on.

The next week was a monotonous one. Every evening we attached the goats, and every morning at sunrise we brought them back untouched to the village; these were the only events of the long, hot days. Occasionally I crossed the hills to the shore and had a swim, or had a sail in some fisherman's junk, but I spent most of my time under a tree behind the village, where, with a pipe and a book, I did my best to make the days seem shorter.

The village life was that of the peaceful peasants of any country. At sunrise the men put on their great pagoda-shaped hats and trudged off to the rice fields, where they worked, knee-deep in water, till dark. The women remained in their huts, spinning, or chatted on the paths while their babies made mud pies and played with the somnolent hogs. Then, at sunset, when the men returned from work, my courtyard became the gathering place for the evening, for the novelty of watching a white man eat, smoke, and read did not in any way seem to pall on them.

The hunters were next in importance and always held an admiring circle about them as they squatted over their chow. This was a sort of soup, brewed in a big black kettle, into which any number of ingredients, from shellfish to sweet potatoes, had been thrown, and they ate it with some kind of herb on the side as a relish. Tiger hunting is nothing new to them; the profession is handed down in the same family from father to son. They attack the tiger in its cave, killing it with their spears, and sell the meat, bones, claws, and skin at a high price, as the natives believe possessing the claws or eating the meat gives them strength and bravery. The men are undoubtedly courageous. Although some of them are killed from time to time, they walk into the caves without hesitation, and many were the stories they told through my interpreter, over their opium pipes in the evenings, of adventures and hairbreadth escapes.

Bruce and Leyburn, businessmen in Xiamen, are the names most prominently connected with the sport of tiger shooting in this district. Whenever the hunters located a tiger, Bruce and Leyburn would pick up their guns from beneath their office desks and come over posthaste to the cave where the tiger had been marked. Generally they would return home the same night, successful. Leyburn is credited with over forty tigers.

The village, as did all the small towns of the district, regarded itself as one large family, descended from the common ancestor to whose memory my temple was built. So closely do they adhere to this idea that intermarriage among the villagers is forbidden, and a man must choose his wife from elsewhere. They are a simple, trusting lot and have great faith in the medicinal powers of the white man.

One morning a woman stalked into my temple on her diminutive feet and pulled me by the sleeve to her house nearby. Her husband was lying groaning on his straw bed and wooden pillow. He had fallen out of a tree and evidently had hurt his spine. It was clear that I could do nothing more than to ease the pain, so I ordered hot water to be applied and rubbed some salve on the injured spot. The next morning the woman returned and thanked me profusely, saying that the pain had ceased. Later, I was called in to see a fever patient and gave him a few grains of quinine. He appeared the next morning to thank me, evidently restored to health, more by the mental help than by any physical good I had done him.

These were the peaceful surroundings in which I found myself, and I watched the days pass slowly by until the first event that told me game had arrived at last. I roused all my energies to bring the hunt to a successful close as speedily as possible.

Two days earlier I had moved to a nearby village called Kilai, and was awakened at one or two o'clock in the morning by the loud barking of a dog, in which all the other dogs in the village immediately joined. It was seldom that anything disturbed the silence of the town at night, and I was vaguely wondering what could be the matter when the men in the temple all got to their feet, some running for their spears and others going to get my gun out of its case. In a minute we were out in the village street in the moonlight, where the dogs were bolting up and down, barking furiously and evidently much disturbed at something, though the cause was not apparent. And just then I distinctly saw, off in the rice fields, a shadowy form sneaking away—a dog, perhaps, or a pig, though it looked like something larger, and though my first impulse was to follow I saw at once that it would be useless. The barking of the curs soon subsided, and we returned to the temple.

In the morning great excitement prevailed in the courtyard. The whole village had apparently gathered there, talking and gesticulating violently. Lim translated that a dog had been taken away in the night and that a tiger was undoubtedly about. The hunters had meanwhile gone out to inspect the goats, and returned with the news that one had vanished. The rope had been severed cleanly, and the animal had completely disappeared without a sign of blood. I was on the spot immediately and verified the report. There was no vestige of a track to work on; there was nothing to be done. To smoke up the caves by exploring them was clearly inadvisable, so we returned to wait patiently till nightfall. The anticipation of sport near at hand made that day seem endless. The morning blazed wearily till tiffin time, and the afternoon hours dragged till evening. Then, finally, the sun sank, and by seven o'clock I had the five remaining goats at their posts, and, as nothing more could be done, I prepared to sit up over the fifth, which was the loudest bleater, in the hope that the tiger would pick that goat for its night's kill.

Some five yards from the goat we found a suitable rock, which shaded us from the moonlight, and waited. The animal was crying lustily and was answered continually by one of the others that was within call. The first hour or two of this sitting up was not bad, but eventually one's eyes became strained from peering through the moonlight and, with the help of a sharpened imagination, pictured a moving form in every rock and shadow. The goat had by this time quieted down, the moon had waned, and the hunters were fidgeting, so it seemed better to give it up, and silently and in single file we covered the three miles to the village.

But the discouragement of the evening was not to last. The men had gone out to the goats at sunrise, and I was awakened on their return by a tremendous clamor. They were all shouting at once, running about the temple for their spears, and preparing the torches in a way that looked like business. Lim himself was so excited that he could hardly translate, but I finally quieted him enough to learn the news. All five remaining goats, including the one by which I had sat up, had been killed; the surrounding country was covered with blood tracks; and only one head and one body had been found. I vainly endeavored to repress a war whoop.

The preparations that ensued would have convinced an observer that the village was about to make a sally against a hostile tribe—the villagers sharpening their knives to cut down the bushes should the tiger have to be blocked in its cave; the hunters arranging their torches and getting the oil; and the sportsman making sure for the fifteenth time that his gun barrels were spotless and his cartridges in pockets quickly accessible.

At eight we were at the spot where I had kept watch the night before. The string that tied the goat had been cut off short, and ten yards away was the head of the animal, torn roughly from the body. The men then brought up for my inspection the body of still another goat, untouched except for two distinct tooth marks in the neck, as clean as if made by a vampire. This was excellent news, for the tiger had clearly killed more than it could eat and must have retired for the day to some cave nearby to sleep off its gorge. But to track it to its lair was no easy matter, for we quickly lost the trails of blood leading in several directions, and in a few minutes we had to abandon the idea. To search all the large caves in the vicinity and to trust to fortune to find the tiger seemed the only thing to do.

Then followed a scene that was thoroughly amusing under the circumstances, though at that time I was too impatient with the delay to appreciate it. The hunters set the idol, which they invariably carried with them while hunting, on a rock, and, gathering about, they lighted joss sticks and proceeded to worship in the usual manner: clasping their hands, waving the joss sticks three times up and down, and then placing them in the sand before the image. This done, they asked the idol if the tiger was in a certain cave, which opened within a hundred yards of us, while at the same moment they threw up two pieces of wood, each with one smooth and one rough side. If they came down even, the answer would be affirmative; if odd, negative. In spite of the fact that the blood trails all seemed to lead in other directions, the answer, *mirabile dictu,* was "yes." The men immediately picked up their spears and ran downhill to the cave, which, like most of the caves, was formed of immense boulders, with a crevice running straight downward. Then, stationing me at its mouth, with warnings to be ready, they entered.

Five minutes passed. A hunter reappeared and said something that caused the crowd of villagers who had approached to scramble back up the hillside. Lim's eyes bulged as he whispered excitedly, "Get ready, master, tiger inside."

The sport was now on in earnest. The hunters made announcements at regular intervals from below. At first they could see but one paw of the animal; then it moved and showed itself in full—"very large tiger," Lim translated. They were trying to drive the tiger out; it might charge from any of the three openings, and I was to watch them all carefully, for it would be quick shooting. A half-hour passed. Then came up the announcement that the tiger had got into a small passage and could not be driven out; they would block it in, after which I must enter. The villagers immediately set to work gathering bushes, which they bound together and threw down to the opening, while the hunters came to the cave's mouth and dragged them in. They worked quickly and quietly, but with a subdued excitement that kept my interest at highest pitch. My finger was on the trigger for four hours, and I didn't dare take my eyes from the openings during this entire time, for the men had cautioned me that, until finally blocked, the tiger might charge out at any moment.

It was past midday when the seven men emerged and beckoned me to enter. I slipped down into the crevice, landing in a sort of small chamber that was partially lighted by the torches, though my eyes, fresh from the sunlight, could not see where it led. They directed me to one side and pointed to a narrow shelf or ledge from which a hole seemed to lead straight into the face of the rock. Lim, who was behind me, translated that I was to crawl into it until I came to the tiger. This did not sound reassuring, but, knowing that the men were trustworthy and would not send me into a risky position, I scrambled in quickly, dragging the express behind, as I was too cramped by the smallness of the hole to carry it with me.

One of the men held his spear ahead in the passage, though he himself stood behind. I crawled slowly in for some ten feet; it was quite dark, and I did not know where the animal was or how the hole ended. Then there was a loud *aughr-r-r* within a few feet of my face, and I knew by the sound that the tiger was in another cavern into which my passage opened. It appeared that this cavern broke off and turned abruptly downward. My eyes were now becoming used to the darkness, and by the light of the torches that had been thrust into the tiger's cavern through the chinks in the rock I could see it in full.

It lay on a ledge of rock, facing me, its green eyes shining and blinking sleepily in the light, its great striped back moving up and down as it panted from fright and anger. Its face was not four feet from mine when I came to the end of the passage, but there was little danger, since it was too cowed by the light to charge, and, had it done so, my opening was too small for it to enter. Had it tried to get at me by tearing away the stones at the mouth of my passage, I could have warded it off with the barrel of the express.

I lay fully five minutes watching the tiger. At the end of that time I moved the express slowly into position, being badly cramped; the tiger snarled angrily as it saw the barrel approaching and drew back restlessly, still roaring. This was not pleasant to hear. I then fired without being able to see the sights, trusting I would hit a vital spot. In the darkness that immediately ensued—for the report had extinguished the torches—it was impossible to tell what the tiger would do, though I could hear it roaring and leaping around its cavern. The hunters were in a frenzy of excitement behind and were calling me loudly to come out, though for the moment this was a physical impossibility because I was firmly wedged in the passage. I fired two more shots. The tiger lay panting, and was still.

Once in the open, it was evident for the first time in what high tension my nerves had been kept during the four hours of watching. In another hour we had dragged the tiger up to the mouth of the cave, which was no easy matter, owing to the big rocks that had to be replaced before we could get at its cavern. We photographed the tiger and then carried it suspended from a pole to the village, while the peasants ran alongside, laughing, shouting, and generally showing their delight.

I skinned the body on a flat rock in the village and found to my satisfaction that the pelt measured 10 feet, 6 inches, from nose to tip of tail, which the hunters said was a record, though I have no means of verifying this assertion. I then adjourned to the temple, where a feast of triumph and tiger meat was held throughout the evening. Indeed, within two hours of the shooting the meat was being sold in the village streets and the peasants were voraciously eating it.

This ended my tiger shooting. With the prospect of a visit to Japan before returning to America, and realizing that I might stay for weeks in this region without having the fortune to find another tiger, it seemed unwise to remain longer. The following morning I returned to Xiamen, where the skin was thoroughly coated with alum and rolled up to be taken to Hong Kong. The Englishmen at the club were so fired with enthusiasm at my luck that they immediately began to plan trips for themselves, and I do not doubt that several eventually went to the village I had just left.

Unfortunately, it was two days before I could get away from Xiamen. A typhoon came up the coast and burst on the town with full violence, preceded by that black silence that seems to me the most terrifying of natural phenomena. No steamers would put out, while some twenty ships entered the harbor for refuge. When finally I did get away, it was on a little tub called the *Thales*, whose passenger list consisted of ninety-three Chinese and myself, to say nothing of the livestock on board in the shape of a full complement of fleas, cockroaches, and rats. Stopping at Shantou and arriving at Hong Kong two days later, I had the tiger skin cured at the museum. The claws, which I had inadvertently left on my hotel windowsill to dry, were all stolen by the room boy, except two that I fortunately had placed elsewhere. The skin was well prepared on my return to America, and now lies before the fireplace as a pleasant reminder of an interesting hunt. The head is mounted on the rug with an expression of such ferocity as to seem scarcely true to life.

CHAPTER NINE

NIKOLAI A. BAIKOV

Nikolai Apollonovich Baikov's career as a hunter and trapper in Manchuria spanned the era of Imperial Russia through the rise of the Communist regime. Born in 1872, Baikov learned at an early age the craft of trapping and stalking wild game in the heavily forested taiga and river valleys of the fluid border region between Russia and China. In this rough-and-tumble frontier he survived capture by bandits, an epidemic of bubonic plague that killed over one million people in the winter of 1910–1911, and being stalked by a man-eating tiger.

Although it is difficult to determine Baikov's formal education, he proved to be a prolific writer. Among his books were nearly a dozen works of fiction that often referred to his experiences in the taiga zone. Most of his books were published in Russian; the only one translated into English was Big-Game Hunting in Manchuria *(1936), a work popular enough to warrant two printings and a French edition.*

The following passage from Big-Game Hunting in Manchuria *recounts Baikov's almost mystical experience of stalking a man-eating tiger.*

HUNTING THE MANCHURIAN TIGER

In the primeval forests of southeastern Manchuria, customs of old-world cruelty still survive. A man has still to fight, in a ceaseless struggle, to defend every hour of his existence, not only against nature, but more particularly against relentless superstitions.

The forests, covering vast tracts of Girin Province, extend for hundreds of miles. They reach across mountain ridges and river valleys and over endless miles of tableland. Forest dwellers call these vast tracts of forest Shoe-khay (Forest Sea), and indeed they resemble a shoreless sea, ever roaring, ever moving, and singing its song—the song of the taiga.

A man who seeks to make his living in the depths of the forest must be stouthearted and ever watchful. There is no room for the idle or careless man: Idleness would weaken his strength, and carelessness would lead him direct to death. The taiga has evolved its own code of laws, unwritten laws, based on customs of bygone days. These laws are severe and merciless. The capital crime is theft, not murder, and the punishment for theft, throughout the Manchurian taiga, is death.

In the section of Girin Province crossed by the railway, life is made easier for forest dwellers. The coming of the railway has brought a certain civilizing influence. It is in the faraway corners of Shoe-khay, where few civilized men have penetrated, that the old heathen gods of the virgin forest still hold sway. Cruelties, heart-sickening to think about, are practiced in all good faith that the god of the forest wills them.

The taiga trial is a quick one, and there is no appeal. The plaintiff is also the witness, and the decision of the court is carried out immediately. The convicted person is usually buried alive (members of the court fulfilling the duties of gravediggers), though in winter, when the earth is frozen two or three yards deep, making the digging of a grave impossible, the condemned man is given to tigers. He is tied to a tree and left there to be devoured alive. Sometimes the condemned man is allowed to have a cup of *samshu*, a drink that induces some degree of merciful oblivion. This is considered very humane treatment.

Queerly enough, the tree where a man has been tied and eaten alive is regarded as sacred by Shoe-khay dwellers. They build nearby the tree a small temple, dedicated to the service of Great Van, the Mountain Spirit.

A trapper, hunter, or other forest man, coming upon one of these temples, stops and offers a prayer to the Mountain Spirit. He also lights a candle by the temple altar and places a stone at the foot of the tree. One finds frequently, in the remote corners of Shoe-khay, piles of stones circling the trunks of trees and telling their tale of tragedy. Nowadays, when civilization is working its way into the country, this terrible custom of martyring thieves is gradually dying out.

During my many years of wandering in the Manchurian mountains and forests, I came in close contact with the inhabitants, thereby learning much of their mode of life and sometimes actively sharing in it. An incident illustrating this cruel practice of taiga justice remains very fresh in my memory.

It happened in January. We had been hunting boars for nearly two weeks in the thick cedar forest of Khailin-khe. The short winter day was drawing in, and we were hastening westward along the rocky hills. A hunter, Akindin Matrosov, was with me. He walked ahead along the narrow path, leaving behind him a heavy odor from his well-primed pipe.

We were nearing our goal—the hut of my trapper friend Toon-lin—when we came upon fresh tiger footprints in the snow. The marks showed that tigers had gone up to the tree-clad hills, where we expected to find the boars. We hurried along, wishing to get to the hut before complete darkness shut out our path. It was a winding, zigzagging path, difficult to follow, and darkness had overtaken us before we reached the hut.

Toon-lin heard our footsteps on the crackling snow and recognized our voices. He came out to meet us, pleased to welcome visitors to his lonely log cabin. It was pleasantly warm in the cabin, and Matrosov and I enjoyed the coziness as we sat at the low table drinking tea and eating hot pelmenis. We were both dead tired, and we soon made up our beds on the narrow benches and went to sleep.

Not long before sunrise, I awoke, disturbed by movements about the cabin. I looked around and saw Toon-lin standing by the door, listening intently to some outside noise. It was still dark in the valley, and the moon was fast disappearing beyond the black range of hills.

"What is it?" I asked him, "*Shina?*"

The old man waved his hand nervously and whispered gravely: "Don't go out! Very bad. Two Governors-Van! Been listening all night. Van is angry; if we disturb him he will eat up the Chinaman."

He pointed in the direction of an outside sound. "Listen," he said in a low voice.

I heard sinister cracklings of the snow; the heavy steps of tigers were coming very near. The creatures were now wailing around the cabin; we could hear them approaching the door, and it seemed as if they intended to break through. I snatched up my rifle.

The old man was horrified at my action; he shook his head disapprovingly at me: "Don't, don't!"

Matrosov now wakened, but remained silent. He stretched himself and yawned; then, leaning on his elbow, he peered through a small opening in the wall.

"No use going out now! It's too dark," he said. "We won't see him. It's better to wait until there is more light."

Toon-lin, his slanting, Mongolian eyes unusually wide-open, was listening to the heavy steps of the beasts. He knew that the terrible Van, the man-eater, wanted an offering. A man must be sacrificed. If one human body isn't given voluntarily, it will take ten men of its own accord. This was the reason, Toon-lin was explaining, why Van and his wife had been prowling about the cabin for the last two nights.

Toon-lin told us that, a few miles away, a tiger had recently been watching trappers' posts. Regularly, every night, it came scratching with its paws on the walls of their cabins. The panic-stricken trappers knew what it wanted: a human body. They decided it was necessary to comply with the demands of the Great Van, but, as none of them wanted to be the one given to the tiger, the Chinese trappers had to look for a victim elsewhere. Fortunately for them, they found a victim in an outlying district, on the western slope of the mountain range of Tatuindzi. He was one of the Chinese peasants who brought food supplies from the village: He had stolen sable skins from the trappers' hiding place. He was caught, tried, and condemned to be given to the tigers. Toon-lin told us this gruesome story, looking worried and awestruck, and listening, always, to the noises outside the cabin.

When the first rays of the January sun began to penetrate the thick growth on the tops of the hills, Matrosov and I stepped out of the cabin. It was still very cold. We shivered as we held a short council and examined the footprints. We agreed to follow the trail and go at once in pursuit of the two tigers. After a march of ten miles, we stopped at the foot of the steep, granite range of Lao-e-lin. There the trail disappeared among inaccessible rocks. We could not climb the rocks, and the only alternative left to us was to follow the path to the valley and hope to find a passage over the mountain farther down.

For two hours we tramped on, only to find ourselves faced again by another inaccessible wall of rocks. We realized that we must give up, at least for that day, our plans of having a scratch with the tigers we were after.

We were standing, debating what we should do, near a spot where the snow was ruffled and dirty. There was evidence that boars had

passed this way, so, thinking that "a bird in the hand is worth two in the bush," we decided to stalk them.

We separated, and Matrosov went off to make a detour of half a mile. Our arrangement was that he should wait for my shots to signal that I had disturbed the boars, and then he was to attack them from the top of the hills.

I went along the border of the wood for about two hundred yards and was pleased to hear the loud and joyful squeals of young pigs. I stopped and listened. The squeals were very near me and mingled with the gruntings of old pigs. I moved stealthily from tree to tree, keeping myself under cover, until I arrived at an open space near the top of the hill. And there they were: nearly two hundred pigs of all ages—the elders carrying menacing white tusks, the infants tuskless and joyful. A strong wind was blowing from their direction, and the pigs did not scent my presence.

The dark bodies of pigs lying here and there, and of young pigs gamboling round them, struck an effective contrast with the vast white background. Magpies, the only intruders into the peaceful domestic scene, ran familiarly over the pigs, picking insects from the animals and chattering loudly to each other. In the distance a woodpecker was working hard at its interminable tapping.

I stood admiring the peaceful picture of taiga dwellers at home and inhaling the mingled aroma of pine wood warmed by the sun and of wild beasts. The pigs looked very contented, and I regretted that we needed to replenish our stocks. But man must eat, and I leveled my rifle at the nearest animal, which was leisurely scratching its back against a tree. The report of my rifle echoed sharply in the hills. The pig jumped forward a few yards and fell on the snow, reddening it. In a split second the whole herd was on it feet and, as if following an order from a chief, ran at full speed toward the summit of the hill. It was a most orderly and silent retreat.

A few minutes later I heard two shots, and I knew that Matrosov had accounted for two more pigs. Matrosov never missed. I went to inspect my trophy. The boar was lying on its side, its powerful tusks protruding grotesquely from the open mouth. It was dead.

Judging by the size of its head, I guessed its weight to be not less than six hundred pounds. I began to skin the boar immediately, a job to be done before the body got stiff. I was about two hours at the work. When I had finished skinning, I buried the carcass in the snow and covered it carefully with branches and old leaves. I put more snow on the top to protect it against small forest plunderers.

I then joined Matrosov, whom I found completing the skinning of his kill.

"You know," he said, wiping blood from his hands with dry snow, "tigers are not far from here." And he pointed at tigers' footprints and the beaten path crossing the top of the hill. There could be no doubt that the beast had gone this way, passing the spot where we were standing, quite recently—perhaps this morning. Together, Matrosov and I buried the two carcasses in the snow and started off again, following the old trail. It went zigzagging on the snow amidst scattered masses of rocks, disappearing in the hills behind the steep cliffs and coming down again into the valley. Then, unexpectedly, we saw our two tigers high on the hill. They were lying on a protruding crag and surveying the woods and the valley below them.

The distance between us and the tigers was still considerable, and, as it was nearly sunset, we decided to spend the night in one of the caverns so common in the Manchurian mountains. We made our beds quickly, using pine branches and dry leaves, and prepared to have a good rest. The tigers made it difficult to sleep. There were many of them in the hills, all of them very restless that night. Their continuous roaring, echoing in the mountains, kept us awake for most of the night. It was one of those "tigers' nights" when the whole taiga is stirring, pulsating, and when male tigers square their differences.

At dawn we were up, and after having our tea we set off once more along the trail. Toward midday we ascended another steep mountain, and at the top we came upon a dreadful sight. The snow, ruffled and trampled by the paws of gigantic cats, was stained with patches of blood. Fragments of Chinese garments were scattered about the place. A Chinese pigtail, looking like a writhing serpent, was lying beside a fur cap under a cedar tree. Pieces of thick cord were hanging from the trunk of the tree, and the trunk itself was smeared with blood.

A few yards away from the tree, we saw a frozen pool of blood, with a human skull and some bones gnawed of every vestige of flesh. A ghastly tragedy had taken place here. We remembered the words of Toon-lin. This horrible mess was all that remained of the unfortunate Chinese peasant who stole the two sable skins. He had been given to the tigers by his superstitious and unmerciful judges. Tied tightly to the tree, he was gradually torn to pieces by the beasts.

We stood in silence, horrified, sickened by the dreadful scene. Even Matrosov, who could not be called a sentimentalist, gave way to his feelings of disgust; he swore violent and terrible curses on the trappers who had sent the man to such an appalling death.

We resumed our march in pursuit of tiger. We were now warmed by the bright Manchurian sun, shining from a cloudless sky, intensely blue. The stillness of the morning was broken by the croaking of hungry ravens hastening to the cedar tree. We kept our pace and continued along the trail. Soon we came to a spot where tigers—evidently there were two of them—had separated. The female had gone into the thicket, and the male had headed straight toward the temporary camp of Chinese workmen who were felling trees along the route of the railway line. Two men from this camp and four of their horses had been killed recently by tigers, so it was no wonder the panic-stricken Chinese were refusing to go to the forest!

Well, we tracked the tigers down, and the Great Van knew that we were following him.

A short way ahead of us was a flock of ravens, circling and croaking, as if anticipating a good feast—a sure sign that a tiger was near. With our nerves strained to a high pitch we advanced noiselessly. My fiercely beating heart seemed to be knocking against the bones of my chest. The decisive moment was at hand.

Matrosov and I separated, he going to the right and I to the left. Keeping well within sight of each other, we moved, inch by inch, toward the croaking ravens. The ravens, disturbed by our approach, left the tree and flew away to another point of vantage. We rounded the tree and came unexpectedly upon our quarry, the Great Van, lying behind the tree. He was lying on his belly and nervously lashing the snow with his long tail.

Nikolai Baikov and a pair of tigers bagged in the Manchurian taiga.

We stopped instantly. We were about thirty paces from him. The tiger looked at us attentively; apparently he was calculating the distance between himself and us, and planning his attack. This was a vital moment. Then the tiger, flattening his ears close to his head, stretched his lithe body, ready to spring. He stiffened for the leap, and Matrosov and I discharged our rifles almost simultaneously. The beast, checked in his leap, fell near us but rose quickly, snarling and ready to attack. Two more bullets finished him off. With relief we saw him lying on the white snow, blood flowing freely from his wounds. Another deep gasp, a last convulsive movement, and the Mountain Spirit was dead.

"Well, Great Van!" said Matrosov. "That's the end of you! You have had your share of human blood, and now you have paid with your life."

The tiger was one of unusual beauty. He measured nearly four meters, and Matrosov lovingly stroked the fur with his rough hand, humorously commenting on the expensive fur worn by the Mountain Spirit.

CHAPTER TEN

HARRY CALDWELL

Harry Caldwell, a native of Tennessee, admitted that while growing up he was more comfortable with his squirrel rifle than with his slate in the classroom. The call of his Christian faith was great, however, and he left his beloved mountains to serve as a Methodist missionary in China in the early twentieth century. After a year of preaching among the Chinese and battling bouts of depression, the young American was sure his commitment to evangelizing was over. His bishop counseled him to mix leisure activities with his work and take up hunting as he once had in Tennessee. Caldwell did so with appreciation.

A friend and hunting companion of famous explorer Roy Chapman Andrews, Caldwell hunted in a variety of venues in China. When not stalking tigers or climbing after bighorn sheep, he studied plant life and insects, contributing several scientific articles and monographs to scholarly publications in the United States. But he felt most comfortable in pursuit of large game with his favorite Savage lever-action rifle in hand.

In this passage from his only sporting book, Blue Tiger *(1924), Caldwell recreates his efforts to bag an elusive, slate-hued tiger that had been raiding the countryside in southern China.*

BLUEBEARD OF THE BIG RAVINE

The first time I ever heard of "Bluebeard," or "Black Devil," as the Chinese call him, was in the spring of 1910. The many stories I had previously heard of tigers and their doings had little interested me, as I was busy, and it seemed useless to entertain the thought of a real tiger hunt. But when I began to hear of the periodic visits of a "black tiger," I began to sit straight up and take notice.

I desired, of course, not only to see but to secure one of these peculiarly marked animals, the existence of which I could no longer doubt. They were moving about between the villages, wreaking havoc among both the cattle and goats, and were most daring in attacking human beings. So mysterious were the movements of this animal that many people declared it was some evil spirit abroad. The animal definitely had been reported as having been seen at points a considerable distance apart at about the same hour, so it was uncertain where I would be able to connect with it.

I selected for my hunt the largest of a number of heavily wooded ravines, staking out a goat in what was known to be an oft-frequented lair. I knew that man-eaters of the regular type were almost constantly found in and around this lair. When I started on the enterprise I realized that it was an undertaking fit to try the nerve of any man, for the only possible chance for a shot was to clear a place with a jackknife where the goat could be tethered and then conceal oneself in the grass to await an attack.

Armed with a .303 Savage rifle, I made an attempt to lure into my presence the wonderful tiger about which I had heard so many interesting stories. I did not meet with success this time, though it was an interesting experience to brave a tiger right in the lair under hazardous conditions. A couple of weeks later I decided to combine another hunt for this tiger with an evangelistic trip into the region adjacent to its habitat. Arranging with my burden bearer to meet me on a certain day with supplies, and with my rifle, I set off on my extended itinerary, armed only with my shotgun, upon which I depended in supplying the larder with fresh meat. Arriving at the point on the day agreed upon, I found my burden bearer had not turned up, so there was nothing for me to do but forego the pleasure of the attempt to get the prize upon which I had set my heart or else to undertake the task with a shotgun.

I had previously had an experience in shooting a tiger at a few yards' distance with a shotgun, so I hesitated to go after this animal thus armed. But, being pressed for time, I decided to make an attempt with the gun in hand. I molded some sticks of lead by melting birdshot and pouring the metal into a small bamboo. I cut these into slugs and rolled them quite round between flat stones. This furnished a formidable load. I then secured a goat and led it into the ravine, tying it at a point where two trails crossed. Taking my seat in the bushes a few yards from the goat, I settled down for a long wait, if necessary.

Long before the sun had set behind the rugged peaks overhanging the western rim of the ravine, my attention was summoned by that mysterious something—which the woodsman is unable to explain—that directs the eye to a point where something has moved without the conscious realization of having seen it move. My eye was immediately fixed upon the object of my hunt—"Bluebeard," lying like a great domestic cat with head erect in a perfectly open place crossed by the trail.

The animal was all I had pictured, and far more. No more than twenty yards away, the great beast lay motionless except for the nervous whipping of the end of the tail. I could easily have had it with a popgun, yet I would not venture to fire with my shotgun, for I did not intend to send the animal wounded into the brush. In order to attack my goat, the tiger would have to pass within eight yards of my hiding place, and it was my purpose to permit it to reach the nearest point before I fired.

Instead of attacking the goat as I had expected, the big cat slowly arose, sat for a moment in the trail, then stood erect for a few moments as if about to advance. Instead of doing so, it turned around three times, as if undecided what move to make next, and showed signs of great nervousness. Then it gracefully bounded up three terraces and disappeared behind the flowering wild pear bush. I waited almost breathlessly until dusk, but the tiger did not appear again. I worked my way out of the ravine in the darkness with the satisfaction of having seen at short distance the trophy I was seeking, so that I could no longer doubt the actual existence of what seemed to be a new species of tiger.

A number of weeks elapsed before I could again devote any attention to Bluebeard. It happened that on the eleventh of May I was passing through the same region when the villagers met me and informed me of the sad news that a boy had been killed and eaten by a tiger the day before. I suspected the blue tiger, of course, and felt sure that it was in the ravine where I had seen it. Yielding to the entreaties of the villagers, I decided to spend the night in the community and try to get a shot. Again I secured a goat and led it into the ravine, tethering it in exactly the spot where the blue tiger had lain on the trail.

After waiting in a cramped position for three hours, my cook, who was crouched beside me, nudged my elbow, whispering, "Tiger," and, glancing in the direction he was looking, I saw a huge tiger watching the goat.

I was very much disappointed upon seeing that the animal responding to the bleating of the goat was not the blue trophy I so much desired. As I was now armed with my rifle, one shot dropped the cat where it stood. I was pleased at securing such a fine specimen but far from satisfied.

In September of the same year I was again passing through this region when I heard that the blue tiger had rushed into a home the evening before and attacked a child. The child had fallen asleep at its play under the family table, around which men sat smoking and conversing. Everything was normal in the home when the "Black Devil" rushed in at the open door and dashed at the sleeping child. The Chinese declare the gods protected the child, for instead of seizing the head of the child the tiger grasped the leg of the table against which the head was reclining and bolted out the door with the table into the open court. The child slept peacefully on until awakened in the arms of its terrified mother.

Again I tried for the strange animal. This time I selected a point on a ridge between two lairs, clearing away a few yards with my pocketknife and tying a goat in the center of it. It was necessary to take our stand within ten feet of the goat because the cover was so dense. The unexpected happened, and the tiger approached along a path from our rear.

Again my cook saw it first, calling my attention to what he declared was an animal. I glanced at the object, which appeared to me to be a man dressed in the conventional light blue garment and crouching as if picking herbs from beside the trail. I simply whispered to the cook "Man," and again turned my attention to watching the goat.

Again the cook tugged at my elbow, saying, "Tiger, surely a tiger," and I once more looked at the object, this time to see what I thought was a man still upon his knees in the trail. I was about to turn again toward the goat when my cook excitedly said, "Look, look, it is a tiger," and, turning, I saw the great beast lengthen out and move cautiously along the trail a couple of rods and then come to a sitting position near a clump of grass. Now focusing upon what I had altogether overlooked in my previous hurried glances, I saw the huge head of the tiger above the blue that had appeared to me to be the clothes of a man. What I had been looking at was the chest and belly of the beast.

The tiger had followed a trail along the side of a hill and I suppose was advancing in response to the bleating of our goat. I noiselessly turned around and sidled up to a little pine tree, leveling my rifle upon the chest of the brute.

As I was about to tighten my finger upon the trigger, I noticed that the animal was interested in something below it in the intervening ravine. Without removing the gun from the limb upon which it was resting, I leaned forward to look into the ravine to see what was attracting the attention of the tiger. To my horror I saw two boys gathering up bundles of dry ferns and grass.

I dared not fire at the tiger. I preferred to give up ever getting a shot at it than to have it roll down wounded upon the defenseless boys. Instead of firing, I stood up and moved to attract its attention. Upon seeing me, Bluebeard crouched low in the path behind the grass. I waited, moving back and forth to keep its attention directed my way, until the boys gathered up their fuel and moved out of danger.

The tiger crouched behind the tussock of grass, motionless, for half an hour. I suggested to my cook that the only chance to get a shot was to steal away and stalk it from the flank. This maneuver required longer than we had anticipated, and when our heads came up over the level of the trail the tiger was gone. There were tracks in the trail showing where it had hurriedly retreated when we withdrew. Thus had come and gone the opportunity for which I had been waiting a full year.

I had met this strange tiger face to face and had deliberately permitted it to go at large, to continue its depredations throughout the neighborhood, but I felt quite satisfied in having seen so plainly and for so long a time the cat about which many strange and almost uncanny tales had been told. The markings of the animal were marvelously beautiful. The ground color seemed to be a deep shade of Maltese (blue-gray), changing into almost deep blue on the underparts. The stripes were well defined and, so far as I was able to make out, similar to those on a tiger of the regular type.

I made the above notes several years ago. I moved away from this coastal region in 1915 and, with the exception of two short visits, have not been back since. I have thus not been able to make further firsthand studies of this wonderful animal, though many appeals have come to me far inland to return and devote some time to hunting this vicious man-eating member of the cat family.

CHAPTER ELEVEN

A. E. LEATHAM

A. E. Leatham, a noted cricketer in England, traveled to various parts of the British Empire not only with cricket bat but also with rifle and shotgun. His seemingly nomadic existence took him to such exotic ports of call as the river valleys of New Zealand, the tiger jungles of India, the mountains of British Columbia, and the African veld.

In the first decade of the twentieth century, he traveled to coastal China, where he enjoyed sport with a smoothbore. Continuing up the Yangtze River for one thousand miles to Ichang (Yichang), he successfully stalked goral and hunted pheasant. He also noted the Chinese hunters' method of firing their primitive muskets. While in the snow-covered hill country around Ichang, Leatham encountered the little-known tufted deer of central China.

This chapter from his only book, Sport in Five Continents *(1912), reflects the somber climate of a Chinese winter coupled with the excitement of hunting an unknown species.*

THE TUFTED DEER OF CENTRAL CHINA

It does not fall to the lot of every big-game shooter to get a new and hitherto unknown, and therefore unnamed, variety of wild animal, and it follows that I was very pleased when Mr. Lydekker of the Natural History Museum at South Kensington told me that the little dark-grey skin, which I had taken there to ask its name, belonged to a new variety of tufted deer. Although the officials had already received, some years before, a skull and an imperfect skin that had been bought from a Chinaman on the Yangtze River, they had been unable to identify the species, but on receiving mine they had no doubt that it was a new variety of tufted deer and therefore named it after the locality of China where I had shot it.

This is part of the account entitled "Ichang Tufted Deer," by R. Lydekker, that appears in the *Proceedings of the Zoological Society of London,* Vol. II, published 1 October 1904:

> The genus *Elaphodus* has been hitherto known by two species—the typical *E. cephalophus* (from Tibet) and the perfectly distinct *E. michianus* from the Ningpo District, province of Chekiang, on the eastern coast of China. A few days ago Mr. A. E. Leatham called at the Natural History Museum, bringing with him for determination the skull and skin of a young male tufted deer (*Elaphodus*), shot by himself last January in the mountains near Ichang, province of Hupei, central China. Ichang, it may be mentioned, is fully a thousand miles from Ningpo, and the deer killed by Mr. Leatham was shot high up in the mountains far away from water, whereas *E. michianus* is reported to inhabit the reed breaks on the Ningpo rivers.

Mr. Lydekker goes on to explain the difference in the color and the markings on the skins, and also several differences in the bones of the skulls, from which he concludes: "There is no doubt as to the specific distinctness of the Ichang tufted deer, which may be named '*Elaphodus ichangensis*.'" And he says: "It is characterized, as compared with *E. michianus*, by its darker and more uniform color, white tail, smaller antlers, larger tusks, shorter nasals, and more evenly circular preorbital fossa, while it is smaller than *E. cephalophus*."

I had gone out to Shanghai, and had spent all the autumn of 1903 shooting from houseboats up the Yangtze River and the neighboring canals, which are the highways of China, when a keen ornithologist invited me to join him on a trip in the mountains of Central China. He had started a few days before me from Shanghai, so I followed him up the Yangtze River by steamer to Ichang, just a thousand miles from the sea and only 129 feet above it.

There is a tide running up all the way, and the innumerable boats and junks make use of it in coming up the river when the wind is against them, anchoring when the tide is coming down and drifting up when it is favorable. It took ten days to get up to Ichang from Shanghai, and on the way we passed the big towns of Chen-chiang and Hankow and many smaller towns. We saw quantities of small game and the little yellow deer with long pointed teeth, and we encountered huge fleets of Chinese junks, which do most of the trade of the country, bringing down tea, rice, maize, raw cotton, silk, and reeds for firing, and taking up on their return loads of salt, opium, and cotton goods.

I saw also some little grass huts perched on top of some thirty- to sixty-foot scaffolding, with one man in each. The man spent his time plaiting long strips of bamboo into ropes, which he let hang down to the ground. These ropes, I was informed, are extremely strong, and with them the ships are towed up the rapids that begin above Ichang. The men who drag the ships up, sometimes 100 to 150 on a rope, often have to climb around the precipices on such tiny paths that they occasionally fall off into the river.

I had one little excitement on the way, at a town called Jiujiang, where we stopped for a couple of hours. I had taken my two dogs ashore to give them a run, and after walking through the city I came to a village. There were some rushes and rough ground, so I encouraged the dogs to hunt by way of giving them a little exercise. Presently I heard a terrific squealing in the rushes about two hundred yards off, and, running up, I found my pointer shaking a tiny pig, like a rat, in a most ferocious manner. I collared hold of him, and he let the pig go, and by the help of a strap I did my best to persuade him that little tame pigs were not fair game.

Meanwhile, the Chinamen of the village came running up from all directions, so I asked for the owner of the pig and at once fed him with a dollar. He was quite satisfied, and so the matter ended, for, if a Chinaman once takes money offered, it is always recognized that he is satisfied, and he will never claim more. In the same way, if once a Chinaman engages to do a thing, it is quite certain that he will do it, and no signature is necessary.

The land on each side of the Yangtze up to within thirty miles of Ichang is dead flat and covered with high reeds, which in the winter are dry and are cut and stacked for firing; they grow ten to twelve feet high and are hollow. In the summer, when the river overflows its banks, there are miles of flooded ground on each side of the river, and sometimes the ships run ashore and are left high and dry a long way from the river when the water subsides in the autumn.

The ring-necked—or, as we commonly call them, "Chinese"—pheasants breed on high ground, and as the river goes down in the autumn they wander down into the reeds to feed on the seeds. They go for hundreds of miles, which easily explains the wandering habits of our ring-necked pheasants at home, but the birds without rings, which breed in the hills, stay in the hills where they are bred all winter.

At Ichang I was the guest of the commissioner of customs, a most delightful and keen sportsman, and he introduced me to several other Englishmen, also in the I. M. Customs, who helped me to collect my stores, coolies, etcetera, and also to obtain a boy who could speak English and cook. I had five coolies to carry my kit and four to carry a chair, which the commander of the gunboat sent me, telling me I must take it to impress the natives with my importance, as all mandarins travel with a chair. I also got my Chinese visiting cards, which are far grander and more imposing than ours. They were made of bright red paper cut into an oblong shape about nine inches long and four inches wide, on which my name was stamped in black Chinese characters. I also got 50,000 cash, which cost 70 dollars Mexican, and ten shillings' worth is one coolie's load. Chinese "cash" or copper coins are about the size of a halfpenny, with square holes in the middle, and are threaded on strings of 1,000 cash to each string, looking not unlike strings of ten sausages, with 100 cash in each sausage. The boy got 400 cash, each chair coolie 350, and the load coolies 250 per day.

I crossed the river above Ichang, escorted by the two very kind Englishmen who had helped me with my outfit. They walked with me for a few miles just to see that everything was right, and when they left me and returned to Ichang I went on alone with my little party of Chinamen. It was far too cold to sit in the chair for more than a few minutes, and it soon began to snow. I passed several high conglomerate cliffs, and the scenery improved all the way till I got to the stopping place 50 *li* (or 17 miles) from the river and put up at the village inn.

A small Chinese inn is not what we Europeans generally consider luxurious, as the guest accommodation more often than not consists of a single room with a mud floor, which, of course, it is not possible to wash, and through which liquids soak when spilt. There are no windows and chimneys but holes in the roof, and walls serve at once to let in plenty of fresh air and light and let out the smoke of the fire, which is on the floor in the middle of the room. Every Chinaman snores; the animals that belong to the household all sleep under the same roof, and the big wooden bolts of the front door are perpetually slid backward and forward to let men in or out, so, needless to say, the night is not very still. Pigs, dogs, cats, goats, ducks, and fowl all have their own little ways of letting the weary Britisher know that they are pretty handy and keeping him company, and there is no fear of his feeling lonely.

The next day it snowed hard, and we had an uphill tramp up miles of stone steps, but in the clearer intervals the scenery was very fine—high-peaked hills with bush and trees in the hollows up the craggy sides. I saw no game, but one golden pheasant skin was hanging on a string as a scarecrow in a garden.

I met several lots of pigs being driven down at the rate of one mile per hour, with one man walking in front with a basket at each end of a long pole over his shoulder, in which he put any little pigs that fell out from being overtired, and he chanted a dull, monotonous, funereal dirge to encourage them, while a man behind drove the bigger laggards on with a switch. There were also bands of small ponies hopping gaily down the steep steps, and some goats and small cattle, all bound for the Ichang market, to be shipped from downriver from there.

We passed through several villages, where our arrival was heralded by all the dogs, or "wonks," as they are called, and although they made a tremendous noise and threatened to tear us and my two dogs to pieces, they were quite harmless. It was really amusing to see the contempt with which my dogs treated them, not even deigning to look at them when they were barking within a few inches of their ears. The word *wonk* is a corruption of the Chinese word *wong*, which means *yellow*, and most of the wonks are yellow, or white and yellow.

The men with the pigs were not hillmen, as shown by their baskets at the end of long poles. The coolies on the hills carry their loads in baskets or on baskets called *pei-tse*, on their backs, and not on bamboo poles called *pien tang*, as they do on the plains: Of course, wheelbarrows on the hills would be useless. Babies, pigs, and in fact everything that can be put into a basket are carried in this way, and I have seen old men and women in *pei-tse*, but big fat pigs, eight to ten score pounds in weight, and large white blocks of vegetable tallow are carried on boards on the top of the baskets across men's backs, and I also saw trains of men carrying indigo, maize, furniture, and coffins down from the hills to Ichang.

I slept well the second night, as the cock that had crowed incessantly close to my head the night before had not come along with us.

The next day was a long one, and the coolies did very well, as we marched 70 *li* (23½ miles) and got to Pusi-li at six o'clock dead tired. I found my companion in a nice inn, and he had just got his first cock Reeves pheasant, 6 feet, 1 inch long, and also several small birds which he wanted. We had only stopped once on the way for the men to get their lunch of rice and beans. The price of rice at an inn is twelve cash per bowl, and four cash for a bowl of beans, which is a sort of white porridge often eaten with the rice. A hungry man can eat three or four bowls at a sitting, but probably a coolie eats about that quantity in a day.

My companion had a room to himself, and I got one opposite him; there were no windows, but the light came in though paper on the doors. Chinese houses are not built with the idea of making the most use of the ground covered, and in winter there is far too much exposure to the air, as they generally have an open court in the middle. In the center of the court is an open pit, which catches the water off the roof, and the only fires are charcoal or wood braziers, or an open wood fire in the center of the room. We each paid five hundred cash (about eighteen pence) per night for our rooms, and our landlord was a cheery old fellow and often came to have a chat with us. He was delighted when I said that, since his name was Lee-wong, he must be a relation of mine because all Lees are related, although it may have been a bit remote. He thought it a splendid joke, and I furthermore took pains to explain to him that my hair was so precious that I kept my tail at home for fear of losing it.

Next day and for several days we shot the woods on the hillsides, using the coolies as beaters, and my two dogs, a German pointer and a retrieving spaniel, were of great help. We got Reeves, golden, and ringless pheasants, and common hill partridges with dark tops to their heads, not gray like the ringed pheasant. We also got a forked-tail pheasant *(Pucrasi macrolopha darwini),* a pretty, short, grey bird with a dark-green head, a long crest, and a silver-spangled breast.

One day we arrived with some Chinese sportsmen to have a deer drive. There were two shooters and five men who were armed with matchlocks with pistol grip. All were posted up a very steep mountainside, on bush-covered ledges, while several men with seven dogs drove the ledges around to us. The beat took two hours, and nothing came, but the view was glorious, and although it was rather cool I enjoyed sitting up there in my shirtsleeves. My coolie, who had my coat, either could not or would not follow me up.

The native matchlock is a wonderful weapon. The barrel is iron, and it tapers toward the muzzle like the original chokebore gun. The Chinese sportsman has his own system of loading this weapon—simple, perhaps, but I would not recommend imitating it. In the first place, the loader pours the powder into the barrel, the quantity varying according to his taste, discretion, or ambition. Whether the powder reaches one, two, three, or four inches up the barrel is a matter of minor importance. He uses no wad, but on top of the powder he drops three oblong slugs if he is to be hunting deer or goat; where birds only are the destined prey, he substitutes a modicum of iron shot for the slugs. Again he uses no wad, with the result that he must always hold the gun with the muzzle pointing upward, and shooting downhill is out of the question. A small hole punched in the barrel connects the powder inside with a pan outside, into which he puts another small stock of powder. And the latter is ignited by a piece of rope, which is always kept glowing and is attached to the iron hammer. The shooter, at what we will hope to be the extreme psychological moment, presses the hammer with his thumb onto the powder pan. There is a slight fizz, and the gun goes off with a terrific noise and so much recoil that all the sportsmen have deep indentations on their noses and cheeks from the shock. In place of a shoulder stock there is only a pistol handle, so one can readily gather that the recoil must be fairly potent, and that Mr. Tupman's laudable ambition "to discharge his piece without injury to himself" is seldom realized. With such a weapon, however, the Chinaman often shoots pheasants flying, although he prefers them sitting or running. Still, no doubt, he must be written down a fine sportsman, for, although he sometimes shoots from the hip without putting up the gun at pheasants, he always puts the gun up to his nose to aim at a deer, and, since he does not waste many shots, he has to get within twenty or twenty-five yards of his deer before he shoots.

We found a cave on the face of a huge rock, with ladders going up to it, and on inquiry we were told that the villagers used this place as a retreat when an enemy came, and on one occasion three thousand people had saved themselves by staying in it for weeks.

The people we met were all nice and polite, though very poor as a rule, and whenever we asked the way, they insisted on coming with us to show us and never had any idea of being rewarded for coming. When I passed houses I sometimes accepted their invitation to go in, and we would all sit around the fire. They would make a place for the dog to sit on his haunches with his chest to the warmth, and they would prepare tea and the best provender they had, generally a white, sticky sort of sweetmeat made of beans and sugar, and they always cooked some maize for the dog.

We had a chat about ordinary everyday topics, all by sign language, at which they are adept. They are great travelers and speak a different language every two or three hundred miles, so they get lots of practice. When I thought that I had stayed long enough, I would produce a couple of little ten-cent pieces, which I gave to two of the small children. Everyone would hand them around and examine them as great curios. I would tell them that it was Shanghai money, and the father would return them to me, and it would be a matter of some difficulty to persuade him to let the children keep them. We invariably parted great friends, and the whole family would come out to see me off, although it was bitterly cold. They were a charming and simple people, infinitely more intelligent than the same class of rustics would be in England and much more pleasant to the foreigner who came to visit their country.

The Chinese mind could not grasp the Englishman's reason for coming so far to shoot the pheasant, or wild chicken, as they call it. One tame fowl is worth about two pence up there, and, as they think a wild fowl is not worth nearly so much, they decide that the

Englishman must either plan to sell the fowl at an enormous profit when he gets home or else must be a lunatic, as certainly no reasonable man would go to so much expense and trouble unless he was sure of making a lot of money. One man brought me a live golden pheasant in a long funnel-shaped basket made to fit the pheasant, with its head sticking out of a hole at one end and its tail though a hole at the other end. In this way they often keep a pheasant for weeks, and when let out the bird cannot walk at all from being so cramped. The would-be vendor asked 2,400 cash—about a fortnight's pay for an ordinary coolie—for his bird, and was much surprised when I declined to buy it. Another man asked 2,400 cash for each of three little fox skins, which, needless to say, we did not buy.

On 15 January we moved about 50 *li* to a farmhouse 1,500 feet higher. We found it quite nice and cleaner than the inn; it was from here that I got the little tufted deer. I was out with one coolie looking for pheasant one very cold morning when the snow was quite deep on the hillsides and the streams all frozen over, and on walking down a ridge and looking into the scrub on the opposite side of the valley, I saw a small beast distinctly against the white snow in the bushy undergrowth. I had only my gun with me, so I went back to the farm for my Mannlicher rifle, and on my return I saw the little deer in the same place. There was no chance of getting nearer; if I had crossed into the scrubby bush where the deer was harboring I certainly could not have seen it. Accordingly, I took a longish shot and missed, but with the second shot I hit it. It did not fall dead immediately but gradually slid down the steep bank for five hundred yards into the valley, and on going down to it we found it dead. We carried it home and skinned it, leaving the shin bones in the skin.

My old coolie no doubt very much exaggerated the distance of the shot. It soon grew from the original 250 yards or thereabouts to several *li*—nay, even a few miles, and I had the gratification of seeing my attitude, both in squatting and in the act of aiming, in fact the whole performance, graphically reproduced to an admiring audience of rustics, who kept shouting with delight.

Another day I was fortunate in getting two yellow-throated goral, which are also rather rare. On my return to England I found there was no specimen in the Natural History Museum and presented one of my own.

Evidently people do not often shoot chamois up where we were; Europeans never do, as no European sportsmen visit this spot. When the villagers heard that my coolies were carrying these two little Chinese chamois home, they crowded out to meet us and expressed great admiration at the rifle, which I graciously permitted them to inspect.

My barometer at the last place we stopped at, Quam Pau, registered 4,800 feet, and the highest pass we crossed to come back was 5,800 feet above the sea, so no wonder it was cold in the middle of winter.

We got back to Ichang on 28 January, after a twenty-five-day trip. The whole trip had cost twenty pounds, and our bag of 105 head included Sclater muntjac; Ichang tufted deer; yellow-throated goral; Swinhoe hare; Reeves, golden, Pukras, and common pheasant; quail; and pigeon.

CHAPTER TWELVE

ARTHUR DE CARLE SOWERBY

As noted in chapter 7, Arthur de Carle Sowerby mixed a love of studying fauna with a passion for hunting big game. In this chapter from his book Fur and Feather in Northern China *(1914), Sowerby describes his pursuit of the goatlike goral in Shansi (*Shanxi*) Province.*

GORAL HUNTING IN NORTHERN CHINA

North China, except for the great alluvial plains adjoining the seaboard, is essentially a mountainous country. From east to west and north to south the mighty ranges run. Massive spurs and castellated peaks rise from the ridges, their ribbed and naked sides often falling sharply away for thousands of feet. Down through the strata descend deep chasms, hewn by the eternal passage of mist-fed waters, whose many voices rise from the shadowy depths, so far below that they come only as a gentle murmur. In many places these walls of rock, sheer and precipitous, are scarred across with light grass-covered ledges, upon which one would think an eagle could scarcely find foothold, far less a wingless quadruped.

Here and there caves, wide crevices, or water-worn hollows beneath overhanging crags give shelter from the warring elements, while, at intervals among the precipices and rugged cliffs, occur gentler slopes, covered with rich grass, dense brush, and sometimes stunted trees.

He who would hunt the goral must be prepared to face the most difficult climbs, involving the hardest kind of work and calling for a cool head, steady nerves, and an active body. Often he will find himself hanging on by his nails with nothing but space beneath him, and a seemingly unattainable shelf his only hope of safety. All this, however, only lends zest to the sport, which ranks very high among the different kinds to be had in this country.

The goral has been called the chamois of Asia, and it would be difficult to find a more appropriate name. In build, size, and habits the goral, or good-antelope, as it is sometimes called, has the same short goatlike feet, the same soft though fuzzy hair and mane, the same large ears, and the same wonderful agility and climbing powers. The goral's horns, though of the same type, are straighter and do not have the sharp hook of those of the chamois. The chamois goes about in herds; the goral is more of a solitary animal. The chamois inhabits the mountain summits and open ridge tops; the goral keeps more to the steep, precipitous sides.

The goral, together with the chamois, the serow, and the remarkable takin, form a connecting link between the true goats and the antelopes. All are mountain inhabitants and are mainly characterized by their smooth, cylindrical horns, usually annulated at the base; their goatlike forms; and their absence of beards. Two species occur in the Himalayas. These are *Urotragus goral* and *U. bedfordi*. In eastern Tibet two others occur: *U. cinereus* and *U. griseus*. Heude has described several species from different parts of China, but the status of some of these is questionable, so we will not bother with them. In this chapter we need be concerned with only two distinct species: *U. galeanus* from southern Shansi and *U. caudatus* from northern Chihli. Milne-Edwards originally described the latter as *Antilope caudata*.

It is just possible that *U. cinereus*, one of the Tibetan forms, may extend into western Kansu and so may come under our heading of North China fauna.

U. galeanus is a dark grey-brown animal that has a broad cream-colored patch on the throat; legs cream-colored from the knee and hock joints downward; a slight suggestion of a median dorsal line; and a long curled, black tail. The insides of the ears are also cream-colored. It stands about thirty inches at the shoulder and has horns from four to six inches in length. These slope back sharply and are very pointed, with a slight curve.

The length of the tail is due chiefly to the great length of the hairs, which protrude five or six inches beyond the last vertebra and have a strong upward curl. The long tail, arched shoulders, and head held low, together with the stealthy catlike movements or the quick, erratic bounds from rock to rock, give the goral a most peculiar appearance.

U. caudatus, so called on account of its unusually long tail, is much browner in color than the foregoing species. It has a less conspicuous patch on the throat, a more pronounced median dorsal line, and the same cream-colored legs. It inhabits the mountains of northern Chihli and is found as near to Peking as the peaks surrounding the Nankou Pass. It is also common in the mountains to the west of the capital and extends for a considerable distance south. In Shansi it occurs only in the extreme north, where, in certain places, it is very plentiful indeed.

Here, as elsewhere, the natives remorselessly hunt the goral, and it is rapidly becoming extinct. The goral's skin is very pretty, the fur soft and strong, so it fetches a good price. Doubtless, with the opening up of the country to increased trade with Europe and America, the goral is another fine sporting animal to add to the list already doomed to extermination.

In hunting the goral it is particularly important to learn as much as possible about its habits. It is by far the most elusive of all the larger game animals in this country, and it is only by knowing just where it may be found, and what it is likely to do when bayed, that one can hope to secure it. Native hunters can help a great deal, and when hunting goral the beginner would do well to pay strict attention to what his shikari tells him to do.

The goral feeds early in the mornings and late in the evenings, often before and after daylight. After the morning meal, it clambers down to the streambed to get a drink and then hurries back to the cliffs. Here it chooses a sunny spot, often on some spur or ledge of rock in full view of the passerby, and lies down to rest. In summer it prefers the shade of the caves and overhanging rocks. One must not imagine, however, that it is easy to see the goral because of the exposed positions it chooses for its siesta. On the contrary, so perfectly does it resemble its surroundings, and so still does it lie, that it is absolutely invisible, even to the keen-eyed natives. Sometimes, however, its nerves get the better of it, and it betrays

its presence by a flicker of the ear, or even by a sudden precipitous rush for a safer vicinity.

When bayed it is by far the hardest animal to hit. Its small size and quick erratic movements, combined with its constant appearance and disappearance as it dodges among the boulders and through the brush, and its remarkable protective coloring, render it a most difficult mark. Also, it is usually bayed under the worst possible conditions for accurate shooting. Not infrequently it happens that, just at the critical moment, the hunter finds himself perched perilously on the edge of some yawning chasm, when the loss of balance would mean certain destruction, or he is struggling to recover his breath after the exhausting climb when, with a rush, the quarry breaks cover, and he finds himself unable to draw a bead upon it.

This elusive little quadruped often beats the best shots, and I know of more than one sportsman in this country, with long a list of big game to his credit, to whom it would not be safe to mention the word *goral.*

Nevertheless, that the goral can be secured, and just how this may be done, the following narratives will show.

I gained my first experience of the goral in the Chinling Mountains south of Sianfu, Shansi. Here I camped in a little temple in a deep ravine while I scoured the neighboring peaks and ridges for specimens. One day I was shown a pair of goral's horns and was told that these animals were very plentiful on a certain peak not far away. Accordingly, I set off the next day, accompanied by my boy, and after a stiff climb reached the summit of the peak in question. There we found a little temple, the inmates of which told me that we would find a goral in a certain small cut on the east side of the peak. With great difficulty—owing to the dense scrub, matted trees, and steep slopes—we made our way to the cut, and sure enough, as we reached it, out jumped a large goral. I was in a very awkward position for shooting, and the animal escaped me and was soon out of sight.

We followed the trail, however, which led us around the shoulder of the peak, ending abruptly on the edge of a precipice that fell away almost sheerly for some hundreds of feet. I decided to climb down after my quarry and had not gone far before the goral broke cover and, climbing rapidly upward, vanished over the top as my rifle rang out. Fortunately, my boy was ready with the shotgun and brought the animal down with a well-directed charge of buckshot. Though I could not claim the honors of the chase, I was more than pleased to secure this fine specimen for my collection.

It was some years before I got another opportunity to shoot a goral. This was in the mountainous country of northern Shansi. Here, with three companions, I hunted several days for goats, as we called them. We had all done very well with sheep, roe deer, and wapiti, but we failed to secure a goat. On one occasion two of the party went out specially to get one of these animals. After a hard climb up some precipitous slopes, the native hunters stationed the two men on narrow ledges. From these giddy perches they could command a view of two or three other ledges and, incidentally, an uninterrupted view of the stream and boulder-strewn bed a thousand feet below them. The natives, repeatedly enjoining the sportsmen not to move, then made a detour to the head of some adjacent cliffs and began heaving over rocks and shouting. Very soon two goats broke cover and came scrambling along toward the watchers. One of the sportsmen opened fire, and immediately the goats sought cover and were lost to view. The hunter then started to climb down to where he thought the quarry were hiding, and he had not gone far when they broke cover again. Raising his rifle, he commenced to fire, regardless of the fact that his foothold had given way and he was sliding down a grassy slope toward the brink of the precipice. His shots went wide, the goats got away, and he was barely able to save himself by digging the butt of his Winchester into the grass roots. The other sportsman had been unable to get a second view of the goats.

On another occasion a hunter bayed a goat and actually headed it off from the high cliffs, and it kept dodging about the lower slopes for fully half an hour. The sixteen shots he fired at this one all went wide, and, after having worn its pursuers down to a state approaching prostration, the goat managed to get back to the high peaks and safety.

During my last trip the party bagged several goats, but it was only by driving, the method Chinese hunters invariably employ, that my companion got his.

This form of sport is really enjoyable. Choosing, if possible, a bright, warm day, the party, consisting of two or three guns and as many beaters, makes for a likely spot. A stiff climb is always necessary for the guns to get to their posts. They are assigned certain positions along the probable lines of flight of the quarry. Here they make themselves as comfortable as possible, while the beaters go to drive out the goats. Presently the long shouts of the drivers commence. After a while these change, and the anxious listener can distinctly make out the words "*yang doe ke la*" (a sheep has gone over), indicating that the game is afoot. If luck is with the sportsman, he will soon see a goat passing within easy range, and a careful shot will bring the drive to a successful close.

Though I spent a couple of days driving, I secured my only goat on its way back to its haunts one morning, after its daily drink from the stream in the valley bottom. I had started out earlier than usual that morning and so got ahead of the grass cutters who, on their way to work, usually disturbed the game in the valleys. Within a mile of camp we suddenly came upon the goat, which offered the usual tantalizing mark as it scurried up among the rocks. It had gained an altitude of some two hundred feet above the streambed before I was able to get a good aim. My second shot hit it in the shoulders but did not disable it, and it continued upward with wonderful agility. At last, however, a bullet found its heart, and with a few convulsive struggles it rolled off the shelf and came flying down through space. I expected to find my prize hopelessly mangled after such a fall, but, strange to relate, except for a slight injury to one horn and the two bullet wounds, it was undamaged.

I saw several more goats in the same way but succeeded in hitting only one. I lost this one as it got away, and picked up its remains the next day after the wolves had been at it.

My driving was a complete failure. I bayed only one goat, and, though I managed to hit it at unusually long range, it escaped in the

Arthur de Carle Sowerby was not only a noted naturalist, but a keen sportsman who pursued all manner of wild game in China. Here he poses with a trophy Gobi argali. His rifle is a Winchester Model 1895.

labyrinth of rocks and boulders of a mighty amphitheater of towering cliffs and jagged scarps.

My companion had better luck, securing three goats altogether. Two of these had good heads. He very nearly lost one of them as it took refuge in a cave with a deep shaft going into the bowels of the earth. In its dying struggles the goat fell into this shaft but fortunately was caught on a small ledge, from which one of the natives rescued it.

CHAPTER THIRTEEN

W. N. FERGUSSON

W. N. Fergusson, a fellow of the Royal Geographical Society, traveled extensively in China during the early twentieth century. During one such excursion, he joined fellow Britons John Weston Brooke and C. H. Meares on a trek through western Szechuan and eastern Tibet. It was during this journey that the three hunters enjoyed many sporting excursions and, ultimately, experienced tragedy.

Lt. John Weston Brooke, like Fergusson, was an experienced adventurer in China, gaining recognition for his explorations of eastern Central Africa and for his service during the Boer War (1898–1900). He arrived in the Middle Kingdom in 1906. He crossed from Shanghai to the inner reaches of Tibet and back in an attempt to study the upper streams of the Brahmaputra River. Meares and Fergusson accompanied him on a second expedition to the region of Wassu and Lololand in southern Szechuan. They hunted serow and goral in the area's mountainous terrain and also pursued takin. It was in Lololand that Brooke, after separating from his companions, was murdered by local tribesmen.

Fergusson eventually retrieved the body of his friend from Chinese authorities. His book, Adventure, Sport and Travel on the Tibetan Steppes *(1911), combined his own experiences of the ill-fated journey with the diaries left by Lt. Brooke. This excerpt captures the difficulties of hunting serow and goral in the rugged hill country of Wassu.*

AFTER WILD GOATS IN WASSU

Next morning we were up early, but by 8 A.M. no hunters had arrived, so we went over to the chief to ask if they were coming. A little later two hunters appeared. They looked like ruffians, dressed in skin coats and armed with long gas-pipe guns, with coils of fuse made with bamboo fiber. They all wore bamboo or hemp sandals, and we did the same; leather boots were quite useless, not to say dangerous, on the crags where we were to hunt. After leaving the village behind, we followed a small path that zigzagged up the precipitous side of the mountain and, after some more climbing, found six other hunters with their dogs awaiting our arrival.

We climbed still higher to take our positions, while some of the hunters with their dogs remained below to drive the game. Before we reached our positions we heard the dogs barking, and the hunters shouted up to us that a musk deer had got away.

After a tremendous struggle up the precipitous cliffs—scrambling over them, dragging ourselves up by catching hold of the brushwood and shrub bamboo that covered the face of the mountain—we finally reached a position far up the mountainside, where we had a most wonderful view of the surrounding country. Here we halted for a while to catch our breath and enjoy the panoramic view unfolded before us. Away to the west a great snow range seemed to blend its glistening peaks with the clear light blue of the western sky. The lower slopes were dotted with the dull gray stone dwellings of the Wassu and Changming peasantry, and the great towers erected in these villages looked like church spires in the distance. Above the cultivated fields rose green forests of bamboo, white fir, birch, shrub, and prickly oak, and just below the snow line rose the rhododendron forest and, higher yet, the grassland topped by great craggy rocks, their peaks covered with eternal snow.

In the valley beneath us, four thousand feet below where we stood, the Min River, like a little stream of silver, glistened in the sunshine. To the south the view was not as extensive, but it was no less beautiful and interesting—the mountain wooded almost to its base and, far up its sides, small openings in the forest where one could see the perpetual smoke of the charcoal burners where the potash makers were at work; the trees bending under their load of snow.

We looked northward to see if we were nearing the summit of the mountain, toward which we had been toiling the last two hours, but, on looking to the valley from which we had just come and then toward the top of the slope that contained our hunting ground for the day, we decided that we were not more than one-quarter of the way up. We had climbed three thousand feet already, and the valley from which we had started was five thousand feet above sea level, so our position was about eight thousand feet above the mighty ocean.

Our hunting ground was covered with shrub bamboo, but there were many open spots and runways here and there, so, by choosing good positions, we had command of a considerable stretch of mountainside.

Prince So's head hunter allotted us our position, and we were all in place by noon.

It was bitterly cold, for a strong wind had sprung up, and the heat of the sun did not seem to have much effect.

We knew from the barking of the dogs that game was moving, but no shots had yet been fired; everyone was expectantly waiting, for there was no telling where the game might pop out.

The dogs kept zigzagging back and forth up the mountainside, at times coming near, then turning and apparently driving the game away, around the farther side of the mountain. It was then the cold wind seemed to pierce us, chilling us to the marrow, and my own hands got so cold that I don't think I could have held my rifle steady if the dogs had brought something to my feet.

For a long time they had not come near my side of the mountain, and their bark became almost indistinguishable from the murmur of the wind. One second I imagined I could hear them coming nearer and nearer, then the sound would die away. Knowing that the game in this part of the country are not afraid of smoke because they are used to the charcoal burners, with their camps everywhere in these mountains, I gathered at last some dry wild grass and bamboo and made a fire in a little nook under a rock near my station.

Finally, just as we were giving up hope of seeing anything coming our way, we heard a shot around the corner of a hill, and Mr. Meares rushed around just in time to meet a large wild boar and give it a charge of buckshot at ten yards. This bowled over the boar, but it recovered sufficiently to scramble down the steep hillside for a distance. Mr. Brooke glided down the hillside after it and gave it the *coup de grâce*—rather dangerous work, as a steep hillside covered with thicket, in which a wounded boar is taking shelter, is not the safest place in the world.

The hunters soon gathered around and were very pleased to see a mass of pork, which they cut up and packed on their backs. We then descended three thousand feet back to the riverbed by one of the steepest tracks we had ever traversed. We found it as difficult to safely descend the mountainside as it was to ascend it. The path was narrow and covered with small round pebbles that rolled under our feet, and we all took turns unwillingly and suddenly sitting down.

We had not yet got used to our new footwear, and the coarse hemp ropes of our sandals seemed to find tender spots on our feet, especially as we found our way down the steep mountainside. Our toes would insist on finding their way through the strands of rope, which felt as though they were cutting ruts into the bones. We were glad when at last we arrived at the inn and found a good supper of boiled rice and curried chicken awaiting us, and I am sure the cook was pleased with himself, for we licked the platter clean that night.

We all felt quite proud of our first day's hunt, for, although we had not got anything remarkable for our arduous climb, we had found there was something in the neighborhood worth hunting, and our first day was not a blank. The carcass of the wild boar, which we had divided among the men, had put them all in the best of spirits, and they all joined in earnest expectation for good success on the morrow.

When the hunters gathered the next morning, they brought the report that a *ngaelu* (cliff donkey), which we afterward discovered was a serow, had been seen near where we had hunted the day before. We set out early; it had snowed during the night and the paths were quite slippery, but it was wonderful how our hemp sandals gripped the rock. By 10 A.M. we were all in our places, for we did not go quite so high as on the previous day.

Meares and I were posted in the riverbed, and Brooke went higher up the mountainside with the hunters. Old Wang, the head hunter, stayed with Brooke, and they took up their position on a little ledge of rock with cliffs on two sides of them. The serow might at any moment appear on the cliff, should it be pressed hard by the dogs.

They had hardly got to their places when some of the dogs began to bark, and in a short time the beaters sent down the cry that a serow had gone to bay on one of the crags on the opposite side of the cliff from Brooke and old Wang. But before any of the beaters could get close enough to get a shot, the serow broke through the dogs and started up the mountain in the opposite direction from what those experts had expected, and, getting into the deep snow, escaped.

Another pack of dogs that had been started simultaneously raised another serow and brought it around the lower end of the cliff. It was too far away from Meares and me to get a shot, though we could see it like a little speck on the mountainside.

Old Wang rushed down the mountainside by leaps and bounds, calling to Brooke to follow. Endeavoring to keep up with Wang, an expert mountaineer, Brooke soon found himself in a sitting position and came sliding down, rather to the damage of his trousers, but he got off without a scratch. The serow turned just as it was about to enter the open ground, crossed its track, and went off in pursuit of the first serow. It was now getting late, and we thought the sport was over for the day, but old Wang said there was still a chance, for when the hunters had come up in the morning they had heard a goral blowing on the mountainside. Wang declared these creatures did not travel far at this season unless they were hunted and that they would be out feeding at this hour of the evening.

They called the dogs in by a shrill, long cry, followed by several shorter cries that echoed and reechoed through the mountainside, and we soon saw the weary, disappointed little creatures coming slowly back from three different directions. The men had all collected in the valley where Meares and I were posted.

The beaters had begun to grow anxious that one little stray dog had pursued the serow too far up the mountain into the deep snow and had got eaten by a panther, but it now appeared. Just before it, far up the mountainside in the clearing, we could see a little colored creature hopping along, almost like a rabbit. This, the hunters declared, was a *chitze*, a chamois. It was over one thousand yards from us, and though we sent a few shots after it, it escaped without injury, and the dog left it in order to answer the call of its master.

One of the hunters sent the dogs home and took us along on the other bank of the small stream. We followed a narrow path leading up to a potash burner's hut, then went around the face of the cliff and crossed over a precipice bridged by rotten logs pinned to the side of the cliff by wooden pins that were just as rotten. They had been placed there many years before by some venturesome charcoal burner to enable him to collect suitable sticks for burning in his kiln farther up the mountainside. Any timber suitable for this purpose had now been cut down, and the road had long since been abandoned. Now only fearless hunters passed over it. It would bear one person at a time.

Old Want said, *"Siaosin, siaosin"* (carefully, carefully), but there was no need for this advice. In places there was a sheer drop of five hundred feet, and the only footing was a single rotten log that had been no more than six inches in diameter when first placed there but had now wasted to half that size, and we never knew just how sound the remaining portion might be. There was some snow lying on the logs in places, which added to the treacherousness of the situation, and there was nothing to hold onto but the side of the rock or a small piece of brushwood here and there that had grown out of some crevice on the cliff's side, and one could hardly rely on that.

The only thing was to look aloft, keep steady, and try not to think of the danger, for if one's nerves were to go for a second, one's head would begin to swim, greatly increasing the danger.

After about five hundred yards of this, we came out on a more sloping hillside, but it still was not a place to slip, for it was a long way to the bottom. We soon came to a flat place where there had been an old hut. Here we stood still to scan the rocky cliff on the opposite side of a small ravine just in front of us; it was here the hunters had heard the goral in the morning.

The keen eye of Wang soon picked out something he declared was a living creature, but, though he tried to point it out to us, we could see nothing but rocks and trees, even with the aid of a good binocular. Some of the men were sent to beat the side of the cliff and drive the goral our way. How they were to make their way was a mystery—in fact, it seemed impossible—but these men are like flies; they stick anywhere they set their feet.

We were a long time waiting. At length some of the beaters got to the area where Wang kept telling us the animal was; we saw an object move. It started to come toward us. Suddenly it disappeared into a hole in the rock. The hunter followed but could not find where it was hidden; he threw a stone into the hole, and out came the goral within a few yards of him. It went sliding along the face of the cliff across the gully from us, more like a panther than a goral.

When the goral came opposite us, it stopped; the light was failing when Brooke fired at about two hundred yards, and he wounded it badly. The goral fell straight off the cliffs and turned several somersaults before reaching the rocky streambed, and we expected to find the beast a mangled mass at the bottom. With great difficulty we got down the face of the cliff, but when we came to where we expected to find the goral, up it jumped and escaped undamaged by the volley of shots that followed. After running about five hundred yards it halted, and Mr. Brooke bowled it over again, and now we thought that it really was killed and sent up a hunter to carry it down. No sooner did the hunter approach the spot where it lay than it jumped up again. We had given our guns to the hunter to carry, and it escaped.

It was now getting very dark, and the paths were terrible, so we thought that we had better get down to the level as soon as possible. The hunter put a dog on the track of the goral, saying the dog would drive it down, but we saw nothing more of it that night. When we got safely back to the main road, we could still hear the faint sound of the dog baying the goral in pitch-darkness, right on the face of the perpendicular wall of rock two thousand feet above us. We never expected to see the dog alive again, so we sat down to await events. Suddenly, from the face of the cliff shot out a flash of sparks and a bang, then silence; then the dog barked again, then another flash and bang, then a final silence. After waiting some time, the other hunters said we had better get home, though there was neither sight nor sound of the companion who had gone after the goral.

The brave little hunter had followed the goat along the face of the cliff in the dark and had shot at it by hearing. Then he had returned safely along those terrible tracks in the dark. Few foreigners would have cared to undertake so much in broad daylight.

On returning to the town we spoke to the chief about what had happened, as we were very anxious about the man, but he only laughed and said, "My men are not Chinese."

The goral was brought in next morning, badly bruised from its fall over the cliff. It had stuck in the brushwood on a narrow ledge,

some five hundred feet below where the hunter had given it the *coup de grâce* the night before. To get the beast, one of the men was roped and suspended over the side of the cliff, and he attached the rope to the dead goral, which the men drew up, and again they let the rope down for the man, who clung to the narrow ledge by the few bushes that grew out of a crevice in the rock.

We found that three shots had entered the beast—one through the intestines, which also broke a hind leg, the other not far behind the heart, and one of the little hunter's buckshot, which hit it in the head and bowled it over the cliff. The vitality and agility of these animals is incredible. The horns were so badly broken from the fall that the skin was useless as a specimen.

The next day Meares and I went out on the other side of the river. The road was much better, but the game was not so plentiful. Just as we were giving up—for we had patiently waited for some hours—the dogs drove a chamois down to Meares. It came out of the undergrowth just behind him but turned before Meares got a shot and came toward me. The dogs were hard after, one of them not more than ten paces behind. I let drive at the chamois at about seventy yards, while it was on the run, and shot it through, breaking a front and a hind leg. It did not go far but managed to get down the mountainside a distance before the dogs got it.

One of the hunters and I were soon at the spot and recovered our prize from the dogs, who would have torn it to pieces. We had each now bagged something and felt that we had also gained some experience in shooting in a mountainous country.

CHAPTER FOURTEEN

SAMUEL J. STONE

Samuel James Stone, Deputy Inspector of Police, Western Circle Northwest Province, was typical of many British civil servants laboring in India during the heyday of the Raj. His duties carried him to remote locales in the districts of Kashmir and Jammu, where he met with the inhabitants and studied the terrain. Such visits also brought him into contact with numerous species of Indian game animals. As with many Anglo-European civil servants stationed abroad, he chose to use his vacation time in search of game among the mountains and valleys of northern India and beyond.

Stone made seven trips into the Himalayas during a period of twenty years in the last quarter of the nineteenth century. Though he hunted in the more familiar regions of Kashmir and Gilgit, he also stalked abroad to the lofty recesses of Ladakh and the Sino-Tibetan border. Like many Victorian-era sportsmen and travelers, he kept a detailed journal of his treks, editing them on occasion for publication in India's primary sporting tabloid, The Asian. *In 1895 he collected his articles and notes, publishing them as* In and Beyond the Himalayas: A Record of Sport and Travel in the Abode of Snow *(1896), his only book.*

Among the mountain game Stone hunted was dong, *the Tibetan name for wild yak. Noted for its huge mass of long hair covering its shoulders, flanks, and thighs, the yak also sports horns that often span over thirty inches on the outside curve. As Stone and his native shikari, Paljour, found out, a wounded dong could become a formidable foe.*

In this chapter from In and Beyond the Himalayas, *the author and his companion picked up the trail of wild yak at an altitude over fifteen thousand feet.*

STALKING THE WILD YAK

On 10 August we started for Keipsang, with four yaks and fifteen days' provisions, for a long search after wild yak. We crossed the valley and went up gradually to what is called the Konka-la on the map, a name that is not known locally. The path runs just under the conical red hill that is visible from Kiám camp, the "pass" is just under it, and the Keipsang Valley opens out to view as soon as one reaches the crest. The ascent is hardly perceptible. Just as we topped, Paljour spied nine antelope on the stony plain below, and we went after them at once. They were below the bank of the stream, and we got very close, but just then the biggest buck topped the bank about a hundred yards away. There was hurry and confusion, and I missed the big one. A second shot, however, broke its foreleg, and a third shot bowled over a smaller one at over two hundred yards. I was using the Winchester again. We followed up the wounded antelope for a long time but could not find it.

The sun was hot, I was blown and tired—and the usual thing happened. How often it is the "usual thing"! The wounded buck had hidden itself somewhere so effectually that I gave up the hunt and handed the rifle to Paljour to carry. He went along the ridge, and I lazily followed. Suddenly, the antelope appeared on the skyline, on a level but at some distance from Paljour and about a hundred yards from me. The buck stood for some time motionless and had a good look at us. We all three stood like statues. As the buck went over the ridge, I rushed up for the rifle and had six shots, missing every time; nothing under six shots would have relieved my feelings. The wounded animal made for another slope higher up, and I had two good hours' further toil in the hot sun before it was mine. The moral is always obvious, but *cui bono?* Like other fellows, I shall do the same thing till the end of the chapter.

Next day was my red-letter dong day. We left camp at six to explore the upper Keipsang Valley for traces of wild yak, but with little hope. We had not gone very far along a kiang track when Paljour noticed the broad hoofprints of a large yak leading up the valley. He decided that they were four days old but worth following, especially as the animal was traveling in the direction we were going. After a short distance the track bent toward the stream flowing at the bottom of the valley, and the marks showed distinctly in the damp earth. Paljour began to think the footprints were more recent and quickened his pace. Presently, he came to some droppings and exclaimed, "It is only two days old!" Farther on we passed more dung, and Paljour with great animation declared that the animal had passed along here only the day before. We carried on the tracking with great diligence

now, for we were evidently on the track of a very large bull, and it could not be far off. As we got farther into the folds of the valley our caution increased, and old Paljour, who led the way, became the embodiment of circumspection.

At 12:30 we reached the opening of the Lúngún side valley, our intended camping place, and were making eagerly for the opposite side, where there was a stream, when, looking up the valley, Paljour made out a dark object about a mile off. The glasses showed it to be a dong. Here was a fix! I was dead tired with seven hours' tramping and had had no breakfast yet, and now we had to undertake a tremendous stalk (the wind was wrong, as usual) at once. We went back on our tracks a bit, and, after a hurried snack, began to ascend the hill. We had to get to the very skyline before we could cross over to the proper side for a safe and close approach. The ascent took us fully two hours, and when we got into position, about a hundred yards from the bull, it lay down, facing us straight! I did the same, glad of a little rest to pull myself together, while Paljour kept watch.

Half an hour had passed when the shikari said, "He is up." I raised myself and saw the bull going fast up the side valley in which it had been sleeping—no doubt it had got a puff of our wind and was alarmed. I ran as fast as I could and had a snapshot at 150 yards with the Winchester as the bull climbed the hill in front. The shot turned the bull, and from its sudden change of course I made certain it was hit. It then turned suddenly and came in a curve to our right and above us. I imagined that it could not long ascend on account of its wound. As it made the curve, I had time to put in four more shots with the double express, but at very long ranges. One took effect and broke its right hind leg below the knee. This crippled the bull, but it made a regular bolt around the steep and stony hillside above us, evidently with the intention of getting into the upper part of the valley. We ran, too, in the same direction, but lower down the slope, to cut off the bull. Its progress, however, was slow, as I could see from the dust—the bull was out of sight owing to a curve in the hill.

I slackened my pace, but Paljour, not noticing this, went on and got above me; he was thus between the bull and myself. As the bull turned the swell in the hillside, it suddenly came in sight of Paljour, and, instantly changing its course, charged furiously at the old man, straight down the hill. Paljour retreated toward me at his best pace, shouting to me to fire, but at first I could not see the bull, and when it did come in sight the shikari was directly in line with it. I shouted to him to get out of the way, but he was too flustered to understand. Fortunately, above me and about ten yards off, a small rock jutted out of the hillside, and Paljour screwed himself under it, into the smallest space. The infuriated bull stood above the rock only a few feet from the man, evidently at a loss. It could hear its enemy distinctly, for Paljour was shouting continuously, at the top of his voice, for me to come and hide under the rock beside him. It was clear that both man and animal were unconscious of each other's proximity: One was mad with rage, and the other was off his head with funk.

There was no time, however, to admire the tableau, for the monster above me was bent on mischief. I put a .500 Express bullet into its chest, and down it came straight for me. I backed up a few yards to get out of its course and fell into a stony hole, cutting my legs severely—the hand of Providence again! In the hole I was out of sight of the furious animal, which thundered past about three yards off. I had just time to twist myself into a sitting position and deliver my second barrel into its shoulder as it rushed by. That finished it. The bull fell twenty yards below me, sprawling on its belly with its legs spread out, thus checking the otherwise inevitable roll downhill. Its head was raised, and it was bleeding copiously from the mouth.

The scene, though it lasted only a few moments, has left an indelible impression on my memory. Our respective positions in this transaction were, I should say, unique: the blazing sun behind the bull as it stood over Paljour, setting off its grand proportions; Paljour jammed under the rock, bawling at the pitch of his voice; and myself quivering with excitement on the stony hillside. It seems a laughing matter now, but at the time we were all desperately in earnest. At any rate, Paljour thought the situation critical, for when the bull rolled over he came down to me and put his head on my feet, crying, "You have saved me; you have saved me!" He patted the rifle affectionately, exclaiming, "*Bahút achha bandúk, bahút achha bandúk*!" (a very good gun, a very good gun), and was altogether hysterical for a time.

After we had recovered somewhat, we went down to the *dong*, which was still alive, and I was debating in my mind whether I would spend another cartridge to put it out of pain when Paljour shouted something at it—abusive, I suppose—in Tibetan. The sound of the human voice roused the savage brute's fury again; it moved angrily, but that was its last effort. The poor beast rolled over and went down the stony hillside over and over for a hundred yards, stopping at a level place at the bottom, on the flat of its back, dead. The camp came up presently, and we pitched near the carcass.

Next morning we cut up the bull. It was a compact, sturdy beast of immense power. Its horn points were worn away and chipped, but thick at the base. When Paljour noticed the condition of its horns, he said, "This is a Khúni," meaning that the animal was a murderer and must have killed a man. He related the story of a Tibetan who had been attacked by a wild bull the year before, beyond Lanak La. The bull tore open the man's stomach and killed him on the spot. Wild yaks whose horns are worn and battered are always vicious and dangerous; they are constantly fighting and attack everything they encounter. This bull had all the appearance of a morose old rogue; it probably was the identical brute of Paljour's story, for I shot it within two days' march of the place where the Tibetan was killed. The wild yak's face was greatly grizzled; its teeth were worn down, and one was missing. Paljour said its age could not be less than twenty years. As it lay, it gave me the impression of a well-trained prizefighter.

The chest and shoulder shots were well placed and made short work of the huge beast. I fired both within ten yards' range, and the result was only natural. The bullets were solid .500s and had 135 grains of powder behind them. The penetration was great and the effect inside tremendous. Both lungs were torn through from right to left, and the chest shot had gone through the body so far that we could not trace the bullet. There was mystery in the first shot I fired from the Winchester. It had seemed to disable the animal—or was it pure cussedness that had caused the bull to change its course when it heard the shot and come around the hill toward us?

Next morning we went up Kiamgo-Traggar in the direction of Lanak La. We reached the opening of the Kalúng Valley at nine

In this illustration from S. J. Stone's In and Beyond the Himalayas, *artist Charles Whymper captures the danger of hunting wild yak.*

o'clock, and at the same time Paljour discovered the tracks of a large dong going in the same direction that we were. We followed them for two hours, first down into the plain, where there was water, then through grassy plots and over stony plains. There were two, a large bull and a smaller one. I gave up the search at that point, but Paljour followed the beasts up a small valley and then returned, saying the dong had gone up very high. We proceeded farther to find a good place for camp, and when turning a spur Pámber, the boy, pointed out two black spots near the skyline, which the glasses soon resolved into the bulls. We backed around the corner at once and made camp under the hill, well concealed from the dongs above.

At 2 P.M. we began the stalk, passing up the Kalúng Valley until we got past the point where our game was. We had to go this distance to get the right side of the wind, which was blowing up the valley. It took us an hour's steady climbing to get near the top of the ridge. As we approached the point for which we were making I thought to myself that if the bulls appeared on the crest above we should be fairly caught, and that we ought to uncover and load the rifles, but such is the perversity of human nature that I only thought, and put off action until the very thing I had been imagining occurred.

When we were eighty yards from the ridge, an immense black form rose slowly above the sharply defined skyline and came slowly along the crest, looming twice its actual size against the deep blue above. We flattened ourselves among the stones in an instant, I tearing madly at the cover of the .500 Express while Paljour presented two cartridges with a trembling hand. The bull, however, did not see us, and the wind for once moved along very slowly and gave me a splendid chance. The first bullet told loudly and was answered by a flourish of the bushy tail, but the second shot missed. I just had time to reload when the other bull came along, but only the top of its back showed above the crest, and the bullet passed over it harmlessly. We rushed over the ridge and followed the tracks till we had the two animals again in sight in a small valley below, about a mile away. The big bull, standing with its head down, seemed hard hit, and the smaller stood close to it in an attitude of inquiring sympathy. We stalked down and found they had gone on, but very slowly, so we followed the tracks around a couple of side valleys and at last came on the bulls standing quietly in a narrow depression. It seemed as if they were trying to hide the best way they could in this fold of the barren hillside, for the smaller one turned its head and looked in our direction in the sly fashion of a wild animal trying to escape notice. The big bull was twenty yards ahead of the youngster, who was the more alert and was evidently looking after the safety of its older companion. I fired at the wounded animal with the Winchester and missed, and missed twice again as they bolted.

The distance was over 150 yards, and I did not have a clear view. I now put up the second sight, and my fourth shot, at certainly not less than three hundred yards, rolled the big bull over like a rabbit; the fifth shot did exactly the same to the other. Here was luck! Old Paljour was surprised out of his stolidity; he raised a shout, waved his greasy headgear, and salaamed me several times. I was certainly elated myself at the sight of the two bulls kicking up the dust on the hillside below me. We had not gone fifty yards toward them when the smaller one got up and limped along the level track with its leg hanging useless from its shoulder. It fell twice, and I thought it could not go far so did not fire again, but it mended his pace by degrees and ran around the valley and over the dividing ridge before I realized that it was getting out of my hands. That was the last I saw of it. The escape of the wounded bull haunted me and made me unhappy for several days, though I spent some precious time trying to retrieve it. It crossed the range of mountains to the north and must have made its way to the Great Plain beyond and died.

CHAPTER FIFTEEN

ROY CHAPMAN ANDREWS

Born in Beloit, Wisconsin, in 1884, Roy Chapman Andrews decided at an early age that he wanted to work for a museum. After graduating from Beloit College in 1906, he traveled to New York, where he hoped to find a job at the American Museum of Natural History. When he was told that no positions were available, he offered to scrub floors for the museum, and so began the career of one of the world's greatest explorers, sportsmen, and scientists.

By 1909, he had been promoted to the field staff of the museum and began his studies of whales and other marine mammals, traveling to Asian and Alaskan waters to collect specimens. In 1916 he published his first book, Whale Hunting with Gun and Camera, *which went through several printings. Andrews married Yvette Borup in 1914, and she accompanied him on the Asiatic Zoological Expedition of the American Museum of Natural History to China, Burma, and Vietnam in 1916. They chronicled the results of their journey in* Camps and Trails in China *(1918). Two years later, Andrews left Peking (Beijing) on another zoological expedition, this time to the unknown reaches of Mongolia. In his book* Across Mongolian Plains *(1921), Andrews admitted that he preferred writing from the sportsman's standpoint. During this trip, he collected specimens of argali, goral, roebuck, wapiti, and gazelle.*

In 1920 Andrews assembled a small army of cartographers, zoologists, and other scientists to search the Gobi Desert for fossils. With a fleet of Dodge trucks and a caravan of 125 camels, the expedition entered the forbidding landscape. Bones of ancient Baluchitherium (Paraceratherium), *an ancestor of the rhinoceros, were discovered, as well as dinosaur eggs and flint implements used by prehistoric man. He recounted the epic findings in* On the Trail of Ancient Man *(1926). During his later journeys to northern China and Mongolia, Andrews ran into difficulties with bandits, canceling further expeditions when civil war threatened the region.*

Andrews continued to churn out books about his travels, discoveries, and big-game hunts. In 1929 he published Ends of the Earth, *followed three years later by his monumental* The New Conquest of Central Asia, *which detailed his five expeditions from 1921 to 1930. But the toll of constant fieldwork and exposure to danger affected his marriage. After his divorce in 1930, he served as the director of the American Museum of Natural History and wrote* This Business of Exploring *(1935). In 1943 he published his autobiography,* Under a Lucky Star. *An anthology of his stories that had originally appeared in* True: The Men's Magazine *was published in 1951 as* Heart of Asia. *His work also appeared in other anthologies, and throughout the 1950s he wrote books for children.*

To generations of readers, Roy Chapman Andrews represented courage, stamina, and the romantic image of rugged individuality. It has been suggested that Andrews—with his battered hat, the ever-present pistol on his hip, and his aversion to snakes—served as the model for Hollywood's popular explorer-hero Indiana Jones. Andrews died in 1960.

The following account of hunting Mongolian gazelle (Gazella gutturosa) *is adapted from* Across Mongolian Plains *(1921). Accompanied by his wife, Yvette, and a handful of native guides, Andrews encountered vast herds of the swift antelopes.*

ANTELOPES ON THE TURIN PLAIN

On Monday, 16 June, we left Urga to go south along the old caravan trail toward Kalgan. Only a few weeks earlier we had skimmed over the rolling surface in motorcars, crossing in one day as many miles of plains as our own carts could do in ten. But it had another meaning to us now, and the first night, as we sat at dinner in front of the tent and watched the afterglow fade from the sky behind the pine-crowned ridge of the Bogdo-Ol, we thanked God that for five long months we would leave the twentieth century with its roar and rush, and live as the Mongols live.

The first hunting camp was eighty miles south of Urga, after we had passed a succession of low hills and reached what, in prehistoric times, was probably a great lake basin. When we pitched our tents beside the well, they seemed pitifully small in the vastness of the plain. The land rolled in placid waves to the far horizon on every hand. It was like a calm sea that is disturbed only by the lazy progress of the ocean swell. Two yurts, like the sails of hull-down ships, showed black against the rim of the sky where it met the earth. The plain itself seemed at first as flat as a table, for the swells merged indistinguishably into a level whole. It was only when approaching horsemen dipped for a little out of sight and the depressions swallowed them up that we realized the unevenness of the land.

The Mongols told us that in the rolling ground to the east of camp we could surely find antelope. The first morning my wife and I went out alone. We trotted steadily for an hour, making for the summit of a rise seven or eight miles from camp. Yvette held the ponies while I sat down to sweep the country with my glasses. Directly in front of us two small valleys converged into a larger one, and almost immediately I discovered half a dozen orange-yellow forms in its very bottom about two miles away. They were antelope quietly feeding. In a few moments I made out two more close together, and then four off at the right. After my wife had found them with her glasses, we sat down to plan the stalk.

It was obvious that we should try to cross the two small depressions that issued into the main valley and approach from behind the hillcrest nearest to the gazelles. We trotted slowly across the gully while the antelope were in sight, and then swung around at full gallop under the protection of the rising ground. We came up just opposite the herd and dismounted, but we were fully six hundred yards away. Suddenly one of those impulses that the hunter never can explain sent them off like streaks of yellow light, but they turned on the opposite hillside, slowed down, and moved uncertainly up the valley.

Much to our surprise, four of the animals detached themselves from the others and crossed the depression in our direction. When we saw that they were really coming, we threw ourselves into the saddles and galloped forward to cut them off. Instantly, the antelope increased their speed and literally flew up the hill slope. I shouted to Yvette to watch the holes and shook the reins over Kublai Khan's neck. Like a bullet, he was off. I could feel his great muscles flowing between my knees, but otherwise there seemed hardly a motion of his body in the long, smooth run. Standing straight up in the stirrups, I glanced back at my wife who was sitting on her chestnut stallion as lightly as a butterfly. Her hat was gone and her hair was streaming, and the thrill of it all showed in every line of her body. She was running a close second, almost at my side. I saw a marmot hole flash by. A second death trap showed ahead, and I swung Kublai Khan to the right. Another and another followed, but the pony leaped them like a cat. The beat of the fresh, clean air; the rush of the splendid horse; the sight of the yellow forms fleeing like windblown ribbons across our path—all this set me mad with a wild exhilaration. Suddenly I realized that I was yelling like an Indian. Yvette, too, was screaming in sheer delight.

The antelope were two hundred yards away when I tightened on the reins. Kublai Khan stiffened and stopped in twenty yards. The first shot was low and to the left, but it gave the range. At the second, the rearmost animal stumbled over itself and ran wildly about in a circle. I missed it twice, and it disappeared over a little hill. Leaping into the saddle, we tore after the wounded animal. As we thundered over the rise, I heard my wife screaming frantically and saw her pointing to the right where the antelope was lying down. There was just one more shell in the gun, and my pockets were empty. I fired again at fifty yards, and the gazelle rolled over, dead.

Leading our horses, Yvette and I walked up to the beautiful orange-yellow form lying in the fresh, green grass. We both saw its horns in the same instant and hugged each other in sheer delight. At this time of year the bucks are seldom with the does and then only in the largest herds. This one was in full pelage, spotless and with the hair unworn. Moreover, it had finer horns than any other we killed during the entire trip.

Kublai Khan looked at the dead animal and arched his neck, as much as to say, "Yes, I ran him down. He had to quit when I really got started." My wife held the pony's head while I hoisted the antelope to his back and strapped it behind the saddle. He watched the proceedings interestedly but without a tremor, and even when I mounted he paid not the slightest attention to the head dangling on his flanks. Thereby he showed that he was a very exceptional pony. In the weeks that followed he proved it a hundred times, and I came to love him as I have never loved another animal.

Yvette and I trotted slowly back to camp, thrilled with the excitement of the wild ride. We began to realize that we were lucky to have escaped without broken necks. The race taught us never again to attempt to guide our ponies away from the marmot holes that spotted the plains, for the horses could see them better than we could and all their lives had known that they meant death.

That morning was our initiation into what is the finest sport we have ever known. Hunting from a motorcar is undeniably exciting at first, but a real sportsman can never care for it very long. The antelope does not have a chance against gas and steel and a long-range rifle. On horseback the conditions are reversed. An antelope can run twice as fast as the best horse living. It can see as far as a man with prism binoculars. All the odds are in the animal's favor except two—its fatal desire to run in a circle about the pursuer, and the use of a high-power rifle. But even then an antelope three hundred yards away, going at a speed of fifty miles an hour, is not an easy target.

Of course, the majority of sportsmen will say that it cannot be done with any certainty—until they go to Mongolia and do it themselves! But conditions on the plains are so unusual that shooting in other parts of the world is no criterion. After one gets the range of an animal that, like the antelope, has a smooth, even run, it is not so difficult to hit as one might imagine. Practice is the great essential. At the beginning I averaged one antelope to every eight cartridges, but later my score was one to three.

We spent the afternoon at the new camp, setting traps and preparing for the days to come—days in which we knew, from long experience, we would have every waking moment full of work. The nights were shortening rapidly, and the sun did not dip below the rim of our vast, flat world until half past seven. Then there was an hour of delightful, lingering twilight, when the stars began to show in tiny points of light; by nine o'clock the brooding silence of the Mongolian night had settled over all the plain.

Daylight came at four o'clock, and before the sun rose we had finished breakfast. Our traps held five marmots and a beautiful golden-yellow polecat *(Mustela eversmannii).* I have never seen such an incarnation of fury as this animal presented. It might have been the original of the Chinese dragon, except for its small size. Its long, slender body twisted and turned with incredible swiftness, every hair was bristling, and its snarling little face emitted horrible squeaks and spitting squeals. It seemed to be cursing us in every language of the polecat tribe.

The fierce little beast was evidently bent upon a night raid on a marmot family. We could imagine easily into what terror the tiny demon would throw a nest of marmots comfortably snuggled together in the bottom of their burrow. Probably it would be most interested in the babies, and undoubtedly would destroy every one within a few moments. All the weasel family, to which the polecat belongs, kill for the pure joy of killing, and in China one such animal will entirely depopulate a hen roost in a single night.

At six o'clock Yvette and I left camp with the lama and rode northeast. The plain swept away in long, grassy billows, and at every rise I stopped for a moment to scan the horizon with my glasses. Within half an hour we discovered a herd of antelope six or seven hundred yards away. They saw us instantly and trotted nervously about, staring in our direction.

Dropping behind the crest of the rise, I directed the lama to ride toward them from behind while we swung about to cut them off. He was hardly out of sight when we heard a snort and a rush of pounding hoofs. With a shout to Yvette I loosened the reins over Kublai Khan's neck, and he shot forward like a yellow arrow. Yvette was close beside me, leaning far over her pony's neck. We headed diagonally toward the herd, and they gradually swung toward us as though drawn by a powerful magnet. On we went, down into a hollow and up again on its slope. We could not spare the horses, for the antelope were already over the crest and lost to view, but our horses took the hill at full speed, and from the summit we could see the herd fairly on our course, three hundred yards away.

Kublai Khan braced himself like a polo pony when he felt the pressure of my knees, and I opened fire almost under his nose. At the crack of the rifle, there was a spurt of brown dust near the leading animal. "High and to the left," shouted Yvette, and I held a little lower for the second trial. The antelope dropped like a piece of white paper, shot through the neck. I paced the distance and found it to be 367 yards. It seemed a very long shot then, but later I found that almost none of my antelope were killed at less than three hundred yards.

As I came up to Kublai Khan with the dead animal, I accidentally struck him on the flank with my rifle in such a way that he was badly frightened. He galloped off, and Yvette had a hard chase before he finally allowed her to catch him. Had I been alone I should probably have had a long walk to camp.

It taught us never to hunt without a companion if we could possibly avoid it. If your horse runs away, you may be left many miles from water, with rather serious consequences. I think there is nothing that makes me feel more helpless than to be alone on the plains without a horse. For miles and miles there is only the rolling grassland or the wide sweep of desert, with never a house or tree to break the low horizon. It seems so futile to walk; your own legs carry you so slowly and such a pitifully short distance in these vast spaces.

To be left alone in a small boat on the open sea is exactly the same. You feel so very, very small, and you realize then what an insignificant part of nature you really are. I have felt it, too, amid vast mountains when I have been toiling up a peak that stretched thousands of feet above me with others rearing their majestic forms on every side. Then, nature seems almost alive and full of menace, and it is something to be fought and conquered by brain and will.

Early in our work upon the plains we learned how easy it is to lose one's way. The vast sea of land seems absolutely flat, but in reality it is a gently rolling surface full of slopes and hollows, every one of which looks exactly like the others. But after a time we developed a land sense. The Mongols all have it to an extraordinary degree. We could drop an antelope on the plain and leave it for an hour or more. With a quick glance about, our lama would fix the place in his mind, and dash off on a chase that might carry us back and forth toward every point of the compass. When it was time to return, he would head his pony unerringly for that single spot on the plain and take us back as straight as the flight of an arrow.

At first it gave him unceasing enjoyment when we became completely lost, but in a very short time we learned to note the position of the sun, the character of the ground, and the direction of the wind. Then we began to have more confidence in ourselves. But only by years of training can one hope even to approximate the Mongols. They have been born and reared upon the plains, and have the inheritance of unknown generations whose very life depended upon their ability to come and go at will. To them, the hills, the sun, the grass, the sand—all have become the street signs of the desert.

In the afternoon of our second day I remained at the tents to measure specimens, while Yvette and the lama rode out toward the scene of our morning hunt to locate an antelope that one of our Mongol neighbors had reported dead not far away. At six o'clock they came galloping back with the news that there were two gazelles within three miles of camp. I saddled Kublai Khan and left with them at once. Twenty minutes of steady trotting brought us to the summit of a slope, where we could see the animals quietly feeding not five hundred yards away.

It was just possible to stalk them for a long-range shot, and, slipping off my pony, I flattened out upon the ground. On hands and knees, and sometimes at full length, I wormed my way through the grass for one hundred yards. The cover ended there, and I must shoot or come into full view of the gazelles. They were so far away that the front sight entirely covered the animals, and, to increase the difficulty, both were walking slowly. The first bullet struck low and to the right, but the antelope only jumped and stared fixedly in my direction; at the second shot, one went down. The other animal dashed away like a flash of lightning, and although I sent a bullet after its white rump-patch, the shot was hopeless.

The antelope I had knocked over got to its feet and tried desperately to get away, but the lama leaped on his pony and caught it by one hind leg. My automatic pistol was not in working order, and it was necessary to knife the poor beast—a job that I hate like poison. The lama walked away a dozen yards and covered his face with the sleeve of his gown. It is against the laws of the Buddhist religion to take the life of any animal or ever to see it done, although there are no restrictions as to eating flesh.

With a blanket, the Mongol made a seat for himself on his pony's haunches. He then threw the antelope across his saddle, and we trotted back to camp into the painted western sky, with the cool night air bringing to us the scent of newborn grass. We would not have exchanged our lot that night with anyone on earth.

After ten days we left the "Antelope Camp" to visit the Turin plain, where we had seen much game on the way to Urga. One by one our Mongol neighbors rode up to say farewell, each to present us with a silk scarf as a token of friendship and goodwill. Yvette photographed the entire family, including half a dozen dogs, a calf, and two babies, much to their enjoyment.

A day and a half of traveling was uneventful, for herds of sheep and horse indicated the presence of yurts among the hills. Game will seldom remain where there are Mongols. Although it was the first of July, we found a heavy coating of ice on the lower sides of a deep well. The water was about fifteen feet below the level of the plain, and the ice would probably remain all summer. Moreover, it is said that the wells never freeze, even during the coldest winter.

The changes of temperature were more rapid than in any other country in which I have ever hunted. It was hot during the day—about 85 degrees Fahrenheit—but the instant the sun disappeared we needed coats, and our fur sleeping bags were always acceptable at night.

We were 150 miles from Urga and were still going slowly south when we had our next real hunting camp. Great bands of antelope were working northward from the Gobi Desert to the better grazing on the grass-covered Turin plain. We encountered the main herd one evening about six o'clock, and it was a sight that made us gasp for breath. We were shifting camp, and my wife and I were trotting along parallel to the carts that moved slowly over the trail a mile away. We had had a delightful, as well as a profitable, day. Yvette had been busy with her camera, while I picked up an antelope, a bustard, three hares, and half a dozen marmots. We were loafing in our saddles when suddenly we caught sight of the cook standing on his cart, frantically signaling us to come.

In ten seconds our ponies were flying toward the caravan, while we mentally reviewed every accident that possibly could have happened to the boys. Lü met us twenty yards from the trail, trembling with excitement and totally incoherent. He could only point to the south and stammer, "Too many antelope. Over there. Too many, too many."

I slipped off Kublai Khan's back and put up the glasses. Certainly there were animals, but I thought they must be sheep or ponies. Hundreds were in sight, feeding in one vast herd and in many smaller groups. Then I remembered that the nearest well was twenty miles away; therefore, they could not be horses. I looked again and knew they must be antelope—not in hundreds, but in thousands.

Before us, as far as the eye could reach, was a yellow mass of moving forms. In a moment Yvette and I had left the carts. There was no possibility of concealment, and our only chance was to run the herd. When we were perhaps half a mile away, the nearest animals threw up their heads and began to stamp and run about, only to stop again and stare at us. We kept on very slowly, edging nearer every moment. Suddenly they decided that we were really dangerous, and the herd strung out like a regiment of yellow-coated soldiers.

Kublai Khan had seen the antelope almost as soon as we left the carts and, although he had already traveled forty miles that day, was nervously champing the bit with head up and ears erect. When at last I gave him the word, he gathered himself for one terrific spring; down went his head, and he dashed forward with every ounce of strength behind his flying legs. His run was the long, smooth stride of a thoroughbred, and it sent the blood surging through my veins in a wild thrill of exhilaration. Once only I glanced back at Yvette. She was almost at my side. Her hair had loosened and was flying back like a veil behind her head. Tense with excitement, eyes shining, she was heedless of everything save those skimming yellow forms before us. It was useless to look for holes; ere I had seen one we were over or around it. With head low down and muzzle out, my pony needed not the slightest touch to guide him. He knew where we were going and the part he had to play.

More than a thousand antelope were running diagonally across our course. It was a sight to stir the gods—a thing to give one's life to see. But when we were almost near enough to shoot, the herd suddenly swerved, heading directly away from us. In an instant we were enveloped in a whirling cloud of dust through which the flying animals were dimly visible like phantom figures. Kublai Khan was choked, and his hot breath rasped sharply through his nostrils, but he plunged on and on into that yellow cloud. Standing in my stirrups, I fired six times at the wraithlike forms ahead as fast as I could work the lever of my rifle. Of course, it was useless, but just the same I had to shoot.

Roy Chapman Andrews, regarded as one of the world's foremost explorers, poses here with his beloved Mannlicher rifle and a goral.

In about a mile the great herd slowed down and stopped. We could see hundreds of animals on every side, in groups of fifty or one hundred. Probably two thousand antelope were in sight at once, and many more were beyond the sky rim to the west. We gave the ponies ten minutes' rest, and had another run as unsuccessful as the first, then a third and a fourth. The antelope, for some strange reason, would not cross our path but always turned straight away before we were near enough to shoot.

After an hour we returned to the carts—for Yvette was exhausted from excitement—and the lama took her place. We left the great herd and turned southward, parallel to the road. A mile away we found more antelope; at least a thousand were scattered about, feeding quietly like those we had driven north. It seemed as though all the gazelles in Mongolia had concentrated on those few miles of plain.

The ponies were so exhausted that we decided to try a drive and leave the main herd in peace. When we were concealed from view in the bottom of a land swell, I slipped off and hobbled Kublai Khan. The poor fellow was so tired he could only stand with dropping head, even though there was a rich grass beneath his feet. I sent the lama in a long circle to get behind the herd, while I crawled a few hundred yards away and snuggled out of sight into an old wolf den.

I watched the antelope for fifteen minutes through my binoculars. They were feeding in a vast semicircle, entirely unconscious of my presence. Suddenly every head went up; they stared fixedly toward the west for a moment and were off like the wind. About five hundred drew together in a compact mass, but a dozen smaller herds scattered wildly, running in every direction except toward me. They had seen the lama before he had succeeded in completely encircling them, and the drive was ruined.

The Mongols kill great numbers of antelope in just this way. When a herd has been located, a line of men will conceal themselves at distances of two or three hundred yards, while as many more get behind the animals and drive them toward the waiting hunters. Sometimes the gazelles almost step on the natives and become so frightened that they run the gauntlet of the entire firing line.

I did not have the heart to race again with our exhausted ponies, and we turned back toward the carts, which were out of sight. Scores of antelope, singly or in pairs, were visible on the sky line, and as we rode to the summit of a little rise a herd of fifty appeared almost below us. We paid no attention to them, but suddenly my pony stopped with ears erect. He looked back at me, as much as to say, "Don't you see those antelope?" and began gently pulling at the reins. I could feel him tremble with eagerness and excitement. "Well, old chap," I said, "if you are as keen as all that, let's give them a run."

With a magnificent burst of speed Kublai Khan launched himself toward the fleeing animals. They circled beautifully, straight into the eye of the sun, which lay like a great red ball upon the surface of the plain. We were still three hundred yards away and gaining rapidly, but I had to shoot; in a moment I would be blinded by the sun. As the flame leaped from my rifle, we heard the dull thud of a bullet on flesh; at the second shot, another; and then a third. *"Sanga,"* (three) yelled the lama, and dashed forward, wild with excitement.

The three gazelle lay almost the same distance apart, each one shot through the body. It was interesting evidence that the actions of working the lever on my rifle and aiming, and the speed of the antelope, varied only by a fraction of a second. In this case, brain and eye and hand had functioned perfectly. Needless to say, I do not always shoot like that.

Two of the antelope were yearling bucks, and one was a large doe. The lama took the female on his pony, and I strapped the other two on Kublai Khan. When I mounted, he was carrying a weight of 285 pounds, yet he kept his steady "homeward trot" without a break until we reached the carts six miles away.

Yvette had been afraid that we would miss the well in the gathering darkness and had made a "dry camp" beside the road. We had only a little water for ourselves, but my pony's nose was full of dust, and I knew how parched his throat must be, so I divided my supply with him. The poor animal was so frightened by the dish that he would only snort and back away; even when I wet his nose with some of the precious fluid, he would not drink.

The morning after encountering the great herd, we camped at a well thirty miles north of the Turin monastery. Three or four yurts were scattered about, and a caravan of 250 camels was resting in a little hollow. From the door of our tent we could see the blue summit of the Turin "mountain," and we had in the foreground a perpetual moving picture of camels, horses, sheep, goats, and cattle seeking water. All day long, hundreds of animals crowded about the well, while one or two Mongols filled the troughs by means of wooden buckets.

At this camp, and during the journey back to Urga, we had many glorious hunts. Each one held its own individual fascination, for no two were just alike, and every day we learned something new about the life history of the Mongolian antelope. We needed specimens for a group in the new Hall of Asiatic Life in the American Museum of Natural History, as well as a series representing all ages of both males and females for scientific study. When we returned to Urga we had them all.

The hunting of large game was only one aspect of our work. We usually returned to camp about two o'clock in the afternoon. As soon as tiffin had been eaten my wife worked at her photography, while I busied myself over the almost innumerable details of the preparation and cataloging of our specimens. About six o'clock, accompanied by two Chinese taxidermists carrying bags of traps, we would leave the tents. Sometimes we would walk several miles, carefully scrutinizing the ground for holes or traces of mammal workings, and set eighty or one hundred traps. We might find a colony of meadow voles *(Microtus)* where dozens of "runways" betrayed their presence, or discover the burrows of the desert hamster *(Cricetulus).* These little fellows, not larger than a house mouse, have their tiny feet enveloped in soft fur, like the slippers of an Eskimo baby.

After two months we regretfully turned back toward Urga. Our summer was to be divided between the plains in the south and the forests north of the sacred city, and the first half of the work had been completed. The results had been very satisfactory, and our boxes contained five hundred specimens, but our hearts were sad. The wide sweep of the limitless, grassy sea, the glorious morning rides, and the magic of the starlit nights had filled our blood. Even the lure of the unknown forests could not make us glad to go, for the plains had claimed us as their own.

CHAPTER SIXTEEN

H. FRANK WALLACE

Harold Frank Wallace represented the epitome of the British sportsman. A gifted barrister and a talented artist, he combined his writing and artistic talents with his love of hunting to become one of the more prolific sporting writers of his era.

Born in 1881, he was educated at Eton and Christ Church, Oxford. While at Eton, he practiced continually with both rifle and shotgun, eventually joining the school's rifle team. After being called to the bar, Wallace embarked on a two-year hunting trip that would take him to Asia, Africa, Canada, the United States, Australia, and New Zealand—experiences he captured in his first book, Stalks Abroad *(1908).*

In 1911 Wallace, accompanied by Captain George Fenwick-Owen, traveled from Shanghai to Omsk through a region into which few European sportsmen had ever ventured. The pair collected several species of game, including Kansu roe deer and Przewalski gazelle. It was the bagging of the rare takin, however, that garnered them the most attention.

After Wallace's return to England in 1912, he spent time studying the trophy heads of red deer in the islands. His subsequent book, British Deer Heads *(1913), was a sumptuous production he illustrated with photographs and drawings. Over the course of the next three decades, he wrote* A Highland Gathering *(1932), which recalled his deer-stalking days in Scotland;* Big Game: Wanderings in Many Lands *(1934), a recollection of his many hunting trips worldwide; and* Hunting Winds *(1949), another compendium of sporting memories. He also wrote the loosely autobiographical works* Happier Years *(1944) and* Please Ring the Bell *(1952).*

Perhaps Wallace's most famous work recounted his earlier trip with Fenwick-Owen through China. The Big Game of Central and Western China *(1913) captured all the mystery and romance of the distant land. Readers took a great interest in his chapters on hunting the takin, an animal only a few sportsmen had ever seen or bagged.*

A TALE OF THE CHINESE TAKIN

It was on 6 August that our hopes were at last realized. The night, cold and bracing, had shone with a beautiful clear moon in a cloudless sky, and we woke to a lovely sunrise and every promise of a glorious day. By five o'clock we were climbing the hillside to the top of the ridge. The road lay for the first mile or so through meadows thick with stunted larches, whose grotesquely twisted branches blended with the gray rocks that showed amid the long wet grass. One moment I was reminded strongly of pictures of caribou country in Newfoundland, at others of nothing so much as those rhododendron thickets that one sees so often on the grounds of an old Scottish home.

Presently we struck a narrow, knife-edged ridge, which on the east descended abruptly in a series of spire-shaped pinnacles to deep gorges with bare and naked sides. Swiftly running mountain streams gleamed like silver threads below. To the west lay the large basin, a portion of which we could see from the cave. At the far end it swelled gradually to tolling tops—typical sheep country, though there were no sheep—which again descended to similar country on the far side. From the narrow ridge where we stood we had a magnificent view. Range after range stretched away to the west, a few fleecy clouds resting on the highest peaks, and a wide valley extended far below us to the north, and all, save where the rocks and slides made pronounced gray-and-white splashes, was of a vivid green. We halted to glass, the hunters squatting native fashion, while George and I pulled out our glasses and settled ourselves among the rocks. For a few moments no one spoke, and then George quietly remarked, "I've got them!" We made them out, two great yellow forms moving amid the rocks on the far side of the basin. They were our first takin, and never shall I forget that moment. Their color, I fancy, is what struck us, more than anything in their appearance. It was the reincarnation of the Golden Fleece.

The takin in sunlight are a conspicuous golden yellow, though the females are considerably lighter and more silvery in tone, like the yellow in the coat of a polar bear. The bulls are much larger and have a decidedly reddish tinge about the neck, not unlike the color of a lion. The back view of both sexes, owing to the length of hair, the formation of the hindquarters, and comparative concealment of the short, broad tail, is absurdly like that of a teddy bear. Much larger in size, they reminded me strongly of the Rocky Mountain goat (*Oreamnus montanus*), both in their heavy build and apparently clumsy lumbering gait. At times they can cover the rough ground on which they dwell with the agility of a rhinoceros. They normally carry the head low, with the point of the muzzle considerably below the line of the vertebrae. The eye sockets are prominent and close up to the horn, the curve of the nose decidedly Semitic, and the nostrils large and well formed.

The horns of the old bulls do not harden into a solid central mass but separate, and, though tapering at the tips, become worn and flattened in front. Those of the younger bulls are jammed up against each other and are soft at their bases. When the horn growth is complete, these harden and become more widely separated. Size of body is simply an indication of the excellence of the head. In other words, a big bull will almost certainly carry a big head, and a very big head is, in the case of the takin, only a matter of a few inches. The horns of the cows are considerably smaller than those of the bulls.

When suspicious, takin give each other warning by a kind of hoarse cough, and during the rut they utter a low bellow. The natives credit them with great ferocity. In the winter they are to be found among the dwarf bamboo that covers the hills at an altitude of seven or eight thousand feet. In summer they retreat farther into the recesses of the mountains and spend their time on the rock-scattered slopes and battlemented crags that tower above the rhododendron groves and thickets of the Tsinling range. When they are alarmed, unless they are badly frightened they do not go very far but stop at a little distance and start feeding again. The old bulls are very cunning and always the hardest to approach when alone. They will lie with outstretched necks in the densest thickets and refuse to move until the hunter is almost on them.

We watched the takin moving in a rather clumsy, lumbering way about the hillside and then set about getting closer. The wind was from the east, and a detour around the top of the basin was our only means of approach. The actual distance was not long, but it took us an hour to reach the spot from which we had to make our descent. Here a higher and even rockier top than those we had already traversed confronted us. From its side sprang an enormous jagged spur, which stretched into the depths of a deep gully on our left. Stopping again for a spy, the doctor almost immediately detected a herd of takin. They were lying about in the sun, directly above an almost perpendicular stone chute, or narrow gully, which seamed one side of the spur and descended in an unbroken drop for over a thousand feet. We made out eight animals altogether—three bulls, three cows, and two calves. Two of the bulls were sparring, while the calves played about among the rocks. They were in a much better position for a stalk than those we had previously seen. We accordingly decided to go after them.

An hour and a half later, we reached the summit of the mountain, attaining an altitude of between eleven thousand and twelve thousand feet, I suppose. The ascent was similar to the country over which we had already come, complete with saddles or open grassy patches. On the stunted larches that bordered the edge of these little glades rested long roof poles and coffin boards, for the country swarmed with woodcutters. There was no tree of any size, for in a country where fuel is precious every large tree is chopped down and cast into the fire with a happy disregard for the future. Other trees are sliced into coffin boards and carried down the hillside on men's backs, and on to Sianfu. Replanting is unheard of.

Both native hunters were very excited; Lou-lou was laughing and gesticulating, urging us forward, and rushing about in his rope sandals in a manner highly aggravating to anyone in heavy shooting boots.

We were now in a position to spy the takin. They had moved from their original position and were lying among the rocks, scattered over the hillside. One bull was considerably larger in the body than the other two and seemed an older animal, though both were full grown; its horns, too, looked bigger. It was lying somewhat apart from the others, overlooking the stone shoot, in an ideal position for a stalk.

We continued our advance until we had gained a position with the game some four or five hundred feet below. The ground was rocky and extraordinarily steep. Here we put on some spare hemp sandals, which, though very small and uncomfortable, were a necessity, as it would have been impossible to get within shot in our own footgear. Even so, while descending I was within an ace of dislodging a large boulder; fortunately, I managed to replace it in time. We drew for shot, the lot falling to George. He decided to go for the big bull. On hearing his shot I was to fire at one of the smaller bulls that were lying fifteen yards to the right of his prospective victim.

A steep crag of rock, sloping into lesser pinnacles, rose immediately above the bank of dwarf rhododendrons sprinkled with wildflowers on which the takin lay. George, the doctor, and Lou-lou went to the left; Yong and I to the right. Though only twenty yards apart, the rocks hid us from their sight. In Shaanxi—at any rate, when the animals are in the open—hunters take nearly all shots at *pan-yang*, or "precipice oxen," as the natives call them, at close quarters. I was, however, rather startled, on looking over my peak, to see a bull and two cows lying within twenty yards of me in blissful unconsciousness of danger. The big bull was hidden, the third tucked away beneath an overhanging rock lower down the slope.

I cautiously thrust my rifle over the rock, took a fine sight at the bull's neck, and waited. It seemed an age before George's shot rang out, but at last it did, and before my bull could spring to its feet it was dead. I heard a crash from below; the two cows dashed past me, and as they did so I had a second shot. A calf suddenly appeared, and with it the doctor's final injunctions about meat. The calf disappeared behind a rock and a second later fell fifty feet below me, though I did not know this until later. As another full-grown animal galloped across our front, Yong seized my arm and waved wildly. Thinking I had fired my second shot at a cow, I fired again, and apparently missed, for the beast carried on. I tried again as it blundered over some rocks stern on, and had the satisfaction of seeing it fall.

George appeared below, and I joined him. He had killed his bull with a shot in the brain. It had pitched straight over the ledge on which it lay and lodged in the center of the stone shoot two or three

Chinese guide Yong and the bull takin bagged by H. Frank Wallace.

hundred feet below. While he told me this, a cow—I do not to this day know where it came from—suddenly shot into the air within a few yards of us, as though propelled through a stage trapdoor. I gasped, the doctor yelled, and George in his rope sandals dashed around the corner in pursuit. Very soon I heard two shots; my companion came clambering back, and we compared notes. He had the big bull, a cow he had just shot, and a youngster at which I had made some very bad shooting earlier. The cow had pitched a good fifteen hundred feet over rocks, trees, and shoots, and the indefatigable doctor subsequently discovered her, smashed to a pulp. I had the bull I had killed with my first shot, a calf, and the animal that I thought I had wounded with my second shot and afterward, on reviving, had killed. Yong, however, who had been indulging in some mysterious maneuvers on his own account, came up and said he had found this animal, a cow, lying beside the big bull in the shoot. The other beast I had killed turned out to be the second bull, with a slightly better head than the first.

Though the bull George had killed carried a better head than either of mine, and was a much larger animal in every way, a comparison of their measurements showed that I had had all the luck. None of my three heads were damaged at all, while one of his bull's horns was broken and the cow's absolutely ruined.

Thus ended a somewhat exciting five minutes in which we secured specimens of a very rare animal. We had, in all, three bulls, two cows, and two calves. No particle of the meat was wasted, for the natives, woodcutters, and such, hearing of our success, collected and carried it off in basket loads. Takin meat, though good, is decidedly tough, and we retained the meat of the calves for our own use.

Almost immediately after we had ascertained the death roll, heavy folds of mist, which had been gradually collecting, enveloped us completely, and we spent the rest of the day in their damp embrace, reaching the cave about six. The following morning I returned to the dead animals to make some sketches, while George went after a big bull we had spied on the far side of the basin. The animal was very restless, and the men"jumped" him in dense rhododendrons. He then went off like a streak of greased lightning, stopped once, and then started on again.

George had another day after takin in dense bamboo cover. He found a herd which, though aware of his presence, did not seem much alarmed. The animals puttered on in front, stopping to graze after a bit and then going on again. George killed a cow and wounded a bull, which, unfortunately, he was unable to follow up because he had an attack of cramps. It was impossible to force a way through the bamboo because small firs, birches, and the like grew thickly in-between. It was hard luck not to kill a male, since he was out for fourteen hours and had a terribly hard day. Old Yong enjoyed it, for he found some roots that were supposed to be good for his tummy, his liver, or some other portion of his anatomy. He was always digging about and was as keen as a pig after truffles. In the middle of a stalk he would suddenly dive into a hole or some patch of undergrowth, grub for an indefinite period, and emerge, no dirtier than before (for that was impossible) but heated and triumphant, with some beastly little root, which he secreted in his rags.

I have endeavored to give the reader some idea of the takin and of the country it inhabits. It is not a graceful animal but is intensely interesting. There is still much to learn about its habits and distribution. The country is unspoiled, and there are plenty of takin for future hunters. Apart from cold, it would be much easier to pursue them in the winter than in the summer, though it is no use traveling to Shaanxi at any season of the year unless one is prepared for a long, tedious journey and some really hard climbing.

CHAPTER SEVENTEEN

THE EARL OF RONALDSHAY

Many British soldiers and civil servants stationed in India and other far eastern regions of the British Empire utilized their leaves for stalking game in the mountains, deserts, and forests of southern and eastern Asia. Among the most distinguished of these civil servants and sportsmen was the earl of Ronaldshay.

Born Lawrence John Lumley Dundas in 1876, he became the second marquis of Zetland in 1929. An extraordinary traveler with an eye for detail, Dundas first arrived in eastern Asia in 1898. In 1900 he was appointed an assistant to the earl of Curzon, viceroy of India, and he served in that capacity for over a decade. In 1916 he was appointed governor of Bengal, a position he held for six years. He became the secretary of state for India in 1935.

Effective as both diplomat and administrator, Ronaldshay was also a prolific writer. His first two books, Sport and Politics Under an Eastern Sky *(1902) and* On the Outskirts of Empire in Asia *(1904), combined descriptions of his travels and his love of big-game hunting. Subsequent works were valuable for their portraits of the peoples and landscapes of the region, including* A Wandering Student in the Far East *(1908),* An Eastern Miscellany *(1911), and* Lands of the Thunderbolt *(1923).*

By the 1920s, however, Ronaldshay's professional duties had lured him away from the pleasures of sport and simple travel. India seethed with ambitions of independence in the decades following World War I. From 1924 to 1935 Ronaldshay, an astute observer of changing times, wrote a number of books that studied the psychology of Indian unrest and addressed the steps necessary for India to achieve home rule. His magnum opus was his three-volume biography of Lord Curzon, published in 1928.

After a long and storied career, Ronaldshay retired from his position as British India's secretary of state in 1940, even as another world war was erupting. He died in 1961.

In his early years, Ronaldshay loved to stalk wild game, particularly in the rugged vastness of the Himalayas and Mongolia. This passage, taken from On the Outskirts of Empire in Asia, *recounts his hunts in the Sino-Mongolian borderlands. The quarry: trophy* Ovis ammon.

WILD SHEEP IN THE MONGOLIAN ALTAI

With my move into Mongolia my bad luck soon came to an end. I sent a man off with my Chinese passport—a gorgeous foot or more of decorated parchment—to the nearest frontier guard, a movable institution that lived in a yurt. Having obtained permission to wander where I would, with the services of a Mongol fighting man to witness that I was under official protection, I marched along the foothills on the Mongolian side of the range, halting for two or three days at distances of ten or twelve miles, and shooting over the mountains in the vicinity of my camp.

Here and there on the lower ground I came across large herds of gazelle. I shot a fine buck one day, and on another occasion I had a desperate hunt after a huge wolf, without, however, succeeding in bringing him to bag. Still, big rams seemed difficult to find and, when found, still more difficult to approach, and I began to wonder if the fears that so often assailed me were destined to come true. But a great day was coming, one of those red-letter days that stand out so clearly in the life of a sportsman.

It was 13 August, and the sun was just rising in a cloudless sky as we left our quarters on the banks of a tiny stream. But there was that hard, cold look in the heavens, which tells that you need expect no warmth from the dazzling sun, no matter how brightly it shines. Before long, a wind swept over the bare, bleak hillsides, which made progress against it a severe effort and chilled the blood in our veins till feet and hands became numb and the teeth chattered with the cold. We toiled long and hard and saw nothing, and at one o'clock, as I sat shivering under the lee of a rock, making the most of the slices of cold gazelle that made my lunch, Pombo crept up to me and, after shaking his head, pointed repeatedly in the direction of camp. The temptation was great to hurry back to the shelter of our tent, but I had been looking around and through my glasses had just caught sight of a herd of rams. I pointed in their direction.

Pombo gazed blankly, and then said, "Stones."

"*Koshkor,*" (rams) I answered.

Pombo shook his head, took my glasses, and stared into vacancy.

"Koshkor," I said again.

He looked at me, wavered, and then said, *"Malinka."* (small)

We had limited means of carrying on a conversation intelligible to both parties—a few words of Russian, English, and Kalmuk and a large assortment of gesticulations.

"Bolshoi," (big) I maintained.

Pombo refused to give way, so I took matters into my own hands. I tethered the ponies in a hollow—the other Kalmuk was not with us—and signed to Pombo to follow me.

It was a long, weary way before we could approach the rams, for the wind drove me to the top of a range of shaley hills, along the summit for about a mile, and then down again, above the spot where I had last seen them lying. To make a long story short, I found myself, at the end of about two hours, in a fairly favorable position. After taking a thorough survey through the glasses, I began crawling carefully, thinking to make my final approach. But the end of my stalk was not at hand. Five minutes later, the sheep suddenly got up, stretched themselves after their siesta, and rushed helter-skelter down the mountainside and across the valley bottom to some low foothills on the far side, where they proceeded to graze on the scanty herbage between the stones.

I heard a hoarse, demoniacal chuckle behind me and turned around to see the Kalmuk's ugly saturnine countenance in a wide grin. That decided me. I became desperate, and I determined at all costs to get even with him. Putting a ridge between myself and the rams on the far side of the valley, I ran down to the bottom, where I confronted a flat open space, half a mile across. My situation certainly appeared hopeless, but a little lower down I noticed a shallow gorge in the valley bottom, where a stream flowed down the mountainside into the main stream in the middle. I decided to follow that, hoping it would afford sufficient shelter.

Shall I ever forget the crawl along that stony channel of water? It was so shallow that I had to wriggle like a serpent, moving a yard or so at a time. Keeping my glasses fixed on the heads of the rams as they fed, I lay like a log whenever one of them lifted itself from the ground in suspicion. Though I did not notice it at the time, there were a dozen bleeding cuts on my hands and knees. Somehow I reached the main stream, where a fairly high bank allowed a few minutes' rest in an upright position. Then, peering anxiously over the top, I saw the five big rams still grazing quietly about a quarter of a mile from me.

It was even more satisfactory that they were grazing slowly away from me, and that immediately in front of them rose a low ridge. Provided they continued in their present direction, they would soon pass out of sight, giving me a chance to cover the few hundreds of yards of open ground that still lay in front of me. Pombo, who had been left some way behind, now came up and, seeing how near I was to getting a shot, forgot his "I-told-you-so" attitude. He got a bonus for every big head I secured, and he became as keenly interested in the proceedings as I was. How slowly the beasts moved! And evening was fast settling down. Sometimes a blade of grass would catch the eye of one of them, and the bull would turn back to crop it, causing a delay of several precious minutes. At last, however, they reached the summit of the ridge and began moving out of sight on the far side. For some minutes the last of them stood gazing around on the crest, but, once satisfied, it too went on, and the way was clear.

Now was my chance! I pulled myself together, climbed out of the riverbed, and ran—ran as though my life depended on it, across those few hundred yards of flat, stony, coverless ground, till I was on the very ridge the rams had just crossed. I took a moment to catch my breath, and then—all thought of the next step was instantly banished. A puff of wind or the sound of a falling stone reached the invisible rams, and the next moment they were streaming back across the valley.

My first shot brought one down. *"Malinka,"* hissed Pombo, and I aimed again. But now they were traveling fast, and, try as I might, I could not cover one. The hoarse bark of a wolf came from behind me. The rams hesitated, pulled up for a second, and looked around. I had the three-hundred-yard sight up and fired at the leader, a gray-haired beast with a massive head. It went on for a few yards and then sank, while the rest disappeared up the mountainside. Pombo shrieked a triumphant war whoop and nearly spoiled everything by dancing a wild fandango across the valley bottom and halfway up the hillside opposite, for, as I soon discovered, the beast was very far from being dead. After capturing the Kalmuk and subduing him with threats of summary justice with the butt of my rifle, I proceeded to make a careful stalk after the wounded beast and was lucky enough to steal up unobserved and give it a death shot at six o'clock.

It was a magnificent beast, with a perfect horn 57 inches along the curve and 20 inches in circumference at the base. But there was no time to waste, for night was upon us, and camp was a long way off. I sent off Pombo to fetch the ponies from the hollow where we had tethered them and occupied the interim in skinning and cutting up the beast. By the time we had loaded up the horns and turned our heads toward camp, it was dark, and for the next two hours we picked our way at a funereal pace over ground I didn't much care to ride over in broad daylight. But what did that matter when I had a 57-inch *ammon* head tied on at the back of my saddle! What did it matter if I did not reach camp until ten o'clock, after fifteen and a half hours of toil over mountains of shale. The joy it is given to the hunter to know is deep, and I was tasting it to the full. I even abstained from railing at Pombo for trying to persuade me to turn back early in the day.

It would be easy to dwell at length upon every stalk I enjoyed during my sojourn in Mongolia, for the details of every one are all burned deep into my memory, but it would be tedious for my readers. The *ammon* are plentiful, and big heads are far from being scarce, though the bareness of the ground makes them difficult to approach. The extraordinary weight of an old ram's horns seems to be a handicap in its race for life, a fact that is doubtless appreciated by the packs of wolves that frequent the country. I came across a regular Golgotha one day, with many horns in an excellent state of preservation, and carried off a horn measuring 58 inches from among them. Looking around through my field glasses, I lit upon a pack of wolves on a hillside not far off and counted no less than eleven in one place. It is in large part because of the presence of these beasts and their carnivorous tendencies that the rams are always on the alert and so sensitive to the presence of danger.

Camp life is pleasant enough, if you are not averse to a little cold. Except for occasional snowstorms—which are indescribable while they last—I found the climate fine and dry. The cold in the winter must be intense, for on 17, 18, 19, and 20 August the thermometer registered 22, 19, 7, and 15 degrees of frost, respectively. I observed on the first of these days that it was a freezing 15 degrees while I was partaking of breakfast. On that day I was fortunate enough to secure another ram, with a very fine head measuring 55 inches and 20 inches in circumference. I came across it quite by accident when starting to stalk a herd I had spied some distance away.

An even more exciting day was 20 August, when I was lucky enough to secure a right-and-left, both rams carrying horns over fifty inches in length—not, however, before I had passed through some

anxious moments. The first ram fell dead to the shot, struck at the base of the neck, but the second went gaily away with a broken hind leg.

Having watched it till it lay down, I pointed it out to Pombo, gave him the glass, and impressed upon him by signs and forcible expressions that I desired him to remain where he was to keep an eye on the wounded ram while I proceeded to stalk it. I started off, but I hadn't reckoned on Kalmuk number two, who, before I had gone very far, seized the opportunity to lead a white pony along the skyline behind us. Of course, the ram was up and away like a flash. Soon it lay down again, this time mercifully out of sight of both Kalmuks, who evidently imagined that it had gone off for good. They then began to skin and cut up the dead beast.

I marked down the spot where it was lying and went off as hard as I could to get around it. I had to cross a valley and climb far up a steep, shaley mountainside, and it was not till an hour later that I found myself crawling down toward the spot I had so carefully marked. I was soon able to make out a horn straight below me, and I knew that it was still there. A few more yards and I would have been in a position to shoot, but the next moment, to my consternation, I saw the ram spring up and bolt. Looking for some cause, I descried the evil features of Pombo appearing over a ridge straight in front of me. Evidently he was blissfully ignorant of the presence either of myself or of the wounded ram, but there was no time to be lost, and, running on to a slight eminence, I apprised him of the position by emptying the contents of the magazine after the flying beast. By a stroke of good luck, I brought it down and the next minute was standing exultant beside it. It carried a fine horn of 51 inches, and, since the first also had a horn of just over 50 inches, I congratulated myself on bringing my trip after wild sheep to a highly satisfactory conclusion.

The following day, 21 August, I stayed in camp, packing the horns and head-skins and making various preparations for leaving the country on the morrow. I had been out shooting exactly fourteen days, and during that time I had shot ten rams and a gazelle, an excellent bag, considering the bare nature of the country and the wildness of the game. I need hardly add that we had worked hard to secure this result. I had not taken a rest once during the fortnight, and the day's work averaged at least fourteen hours during all that time, since my habit was to leave camp at 5 or 6 A.M. and return by dark or as soon after dark as possible.

The trophies I had secured were all fine heads, with the exception of a small one that I discarded. They included four heads of over 50 inches, as follows: 50¾, 51, 59, 56½, and 55 inches. The measurements of the six best heads in the latest edition of Mr. Rowland Ward's *Horn Measurements* were 62, 60, 59½, 59, 56½, and 55 inches.

On 22 August I bade farewell to my Mongol soldier, who, by the way, had just concluded an agreement with my Kalmuks to meet them at a spot in the mountains of the frontier with thirty bricks of tea, for which he was to be paid twenty-five rubles. By evading in this way the vigilance of the Russian customs officials at Kosh Agach, they no doubt expected to do a good stroke of business: The price of this particular brand of tea in Russia was 1 ruble, 40 kopecks per brick.

Two days later I reached Kosh Agach, and a march of eight days brought me to the Russian village of Onguidai. Here I was able to get post-horses again, and I reached Biisk on wheels five days later. I took the steamer from there down the river Ob to the Siberian railway.

CHAPTER EIGHTEEN

J. WONG-QUINCEY

Wên-hsien Wang (J. Wong-Quincey) was that rare breed of native Chinese not only well educated but inculcated with a passion for sport in the European style. He inherited his sporting bent from his father, a high-ranking police official in Hong Kong, who had worked with the British Army in England and had developed a love of shooting and collecting fine firearms.

Born in 1886, and supposedly named by none other than the historical personage General Charles "Chinese" Gordon, young Wong-Quincey spent time in schools in Hong Kong, Tientsin, and Shanghai, eventually earning his undergraduate degree. When not in school, he armed himself with his father's Greener shotgun or Winchester .44 repeater and prowled neighboring marshlands, canals, and even cemeteries for wild game.

In 1908 he left China for England to attend graduate school, and in 1913 he graduated from the University of London with a degree in Shakespeare and seventeenth-century English drama. He returned to China and served briefly in the diplomatic corps, then took a position as a professor at Tsing Hua College in Peking (Beijing), a post he would hold until driven out by invading Japanese troops in 1937. During his professorship, he made two trips to the United States. On one of them he purchased a Savage bolt-action rifle in .250-3000. That rifle would be his constant companion during his numerous big-game hunting trips.

Wong-Quincey began his big-game hunting in 1916, journeying to the rugged hill country of Shanxi Province in northern China. He bagged wild boar and goral and also hunted pheasant and other game birds. By the mid-1930s, he had ventured into Inner Mongolia, following the Peking-Suiyuan railway before embarking by foot and horseback into the interior. At nearly fifty years of age, wearing spectacles to compensate for near-blindness in his left eye, he stalked Ovis ammon darwini *(Gobi argali) among the rugged hills.*

After the Japanese invasion, Wong-Quincey fled Peking for Tientsin with his family. There he managed to write his memoirs of his hunting experiences. Doggedly banging out his manuscript on a typewriter, he also admitted to writing part of his work on a table made of suitcases stacked in a bathroom. A mere acquaintance, Sydney Cooper, carried the finished product to London.

This passage from a chapter in Wong-Quincey's only book, Chinese Hunter *(1939), describes the hunting grounds of Inner Mongolia and the author's pursuit of* Ovis ammon darwini. *He was accompanied not only by native guides but by several Chinese sportsmen he dubs Fatty, Jack, and Beau.*

BIG HORNS OF INNER MONGOLIA

Our permanent camp was not a hamlet but a single farmhouse. It was situated on a gentle incline and surrounded by walls of adobe. The enclosure might have been a hundred feet square. The farm buildings were neatly arranged within this large sloping courtyard. Rising over the back wall was a tiny structure housing the family shrine. About fifteen feet from this same wall, a long row of living rooms, facing south, ran along the whole width of the courtyard. It was divided into half a dozen chambers, all used for human habitation. At a right angle to the living quarters were smaller buildings, facing east and west, which were used as stables or for storage. The walls and roofs of all the structures were built of adobe, supported by frameworks of wood. Adobe is not a very permanent building material, but the men repair the walls annually in the springtime. The doors and window lattices were of unpainted timber. All the roofs were flat. They were used as drying stages and were easily accessible from the ground. It was amusing to see the family watchdogs sunning and playing on the housetops. Outside on a lower level were the threshing floor, the family well, and some outbuildings.

Our farmhouse was about two miles from the southern foothills. There were farmhouses in every valley where arable land was available; the whole district was dotted with them. To correct any impression of crowding, I should point out that each farm was about a mile from its nearest neighbor. Apparently the main valleys also served as thoroughfares for whatever traffic went through these hills. Occasionally one could see travelers going from south to north. Beyond this district to the northeast lay Pailingmiao (the Temple of the Larks), the famous spiritual and political capital of the Inner Mongolians. But the main route to Pailingmiao was from Suiyuan and Kweihuacheng, much farther to the east.

We were in an area sparsely and perhaps fairly recently settled by farmers. But there was evidence that this territory was the scene of much earlier colonization or military occupation. Not more than a thousand yards to the north of our farmhouse we discovered the foundations of a stone wall running continuously for miles from east to west. It was not very solidly built, consisting of flat stones placed one on top of the other without much binding material, but in its original condition it must have formed a rampart of considerable strategic importance. Now the Mongolians are tent-dwelling nomads who build nothing except lamaseries. The Chinese must have constructed this wall for defensive purposes. The Great Wall of China is far to the south, so this rampart must represent some supplementary outer defense, marking the limit of a former Chinese advance. It was a pity that our party did not include a historian who could have enlightened us on this subject.

Our first supper on the farm was especially prepared by "Jack." I had had no previous experience of his culinary ability, and his cooking turned out to be pretty rotten. But for a keen appetite, no one would have eaten the messes he dished up. We strongly advised Jack to allow the regular cook to attend to his duties, but this man also proved to be very disappointing. That first night we were all in bed by eight thirty. I had overexerted myself that day and was too tired to fall asleep. I lay awake till ten, when I sat up and took my last tablet of Adalin. I woke at three, dozed till half-past five, and then got up. Jack objected to my early rising and especially to my lighting the camp lantern at an unearthly hour, and I believed the others silently supported him. They received with reservation my dictum that in big-game hunting the early riser gets the game. They were either unwilling or unable to follow my advice and example. I was always the first to leave for the hunting ground and the first to return home.

On the second day of our hunting it was my turn to go out with Jen, the elderly guide. Our assigned direction was east. Fatty had somehow arranged with Jack and Beau to keep Sung, but he took care not to mention the fact to me. Fatty went to the west, while Jack and Beau, accompanied by Li, hunted toward the north. I liked old Jen. He was really only forty-eight, about my age. I liked him because he went uphill slowly, avoided any unnecessary climbing by making detours, stuck to the top of ridges as much as possible, and seconded my desire for a short rest every two or three miles. Both he and I had passed the exuberance of youth, and now I preferred to do my hunting with the most economical expenditure of physical energy and the greatest use of intelligence.

Jen was tall and gaunt. His cheeks were hollow, his cheekbones were prominent, and he had a dried-up, wrinkled, and hungry appearance. He was slow, silent, lugubrious. A rich, drooping, black mustache added to his air of sad dignity and made him look older than he really was. He was not decrepit: He held himself straight and could walk as far and last as long as the best among us. He never spoke of his own accord, but, if encouraged, he would talk very interestingly in his quiet way. Li told me Jen had been a mighty hunter in his youth and had killed over a hundred bighorn sheep, but in recent years he had lost two grownup sons, one after the other, and since then he had been incurably sad. That shocking bereavement certainly had something to do with his doleful outlook. In China grownup sons are of great economic and spiritual value: They work to keep the parents at ease until they die, and then the sons worship their spirit. On the other hand, I thought Jen's temperament was naturally reserved and lacking in aggressiveness. Misfortune had only accentuated these characteristics. He was a slow and intelligent guide, and I liked him in spite of his shortcomings.

Jen and I left the farm and proceeded northeast. We had to climb up and go down several times before we reached the higher ground. From northeast we turned directly south, intending to follow a triangular route that would ultimately bring us home. We saw a few crows but not a single animal, except many flocks of domesticated sheep in charge of shepherds. When we passed by a farm in crossing a wide valley, I said there was no use looking for bighorn near farm dwellings. Jen quietly contradicted me and pointed out that wild sheep often went down to the vicinity of a farm to find any civilized food they could pick up. They were not afraid of the farmers, who were unarmed, and would not leave even if the farmers shooed them away. But if they saw a man carrying a gun, they would become immediately suspicious. Li had told me the same thing the day before. I recalled their prediction that we would see bighorn from the farmhouse, and all this information set me thinking.

We were still going south and had covered about seven miles since leaving home when I suddenly discovered that I had forgotten to bring the bag containing my lunch. Looking for game on an empty stomach was totally against my principles. I told Jen to lead the way straight back to our farmhouse. That meant a shortcut directly west by crossing a very steep range of hills. The climb was rather exhausting. I had been wet and dry all morning and was now again soaking wet with perspiration. The weather was still mild, but every day a strong wing blew from the south, and this wind could be quite chilly. The wind made steady shooting very difficult, but it helped to cool the damp body. One does not catch cold easily in the open air, provided one does not rest too long in clammy underwear. We reached home after a five-mile walk across difficult country. We had done twelve miles between breakfast and lunch.

I prepared lunch by myself to make sure of a tasty and square meal. I consumed a deliciously tender omelet made of six eggs and half a pound of chopped sausage, drank an unlimited supply of hot tea seasoned with milk and sugar, and finished up with a dish of prunes. After smoking a cigar in calm repose, I was ready for fresh adventures. Jen and I went southeast to the foothills on the edge of the plain to look for bharal. When we reached the scene where Fatty had slaughtered five blue sheep the evening before, shepherd boys who had been eyewitnesses told us eloquently about the fireworks. Fatty had fired fifteen shots to kill his five animals, and this fusillade had caused a panic among the remainder, who were now scarce and wild.

We were climbing among the welter of boulders when a bharal ram popped up only fifty yards away, exposing its whole body except its legs for a standing shot. I was just kneeling down to make sure of a steady aim when in a flash the beast was gone. We rushed up to the top of the ridge, but the animal had completely vanished among the confusion of rocks. Jen told me that bharal are temperamental creatures, and one must shoot quickly. After climbing around for another five minutes, we caught a distant glimpse of another bharal, flashing uphill in and out of the boulders. I could not have hit that one with a shotgun. I refrained from wasting a rifle cartridge.

We scrambled to the top of a pile of huge boulders and sat down for a rest. We examined the opposite hillside with minute care. The background was such excellent camouflage that it was almost impossible to pick out an animal if it kept still, but after waiting ten minutes a bharal ram, which had been there all the time, lost its nerve and quietly walked into the shadow between two huge rocks for greater safety. The animal thought it was well hidden, but I could just make out the white patch on its rump. The range was about 150 yards. The wind was now blowing powerfully right across my front. I had plenty of time but found it impossible to hold the barrel steady. I leaned my back hard against the rocks and took careful aim, sighting very low this time, since I had consistently overshot the day before. At the report of the rifle the animal fled and disappeared in a moment. Jen told me my shot was two or three inches too low.

We continued to climb for half an hour but saw nothing more that day. We returned by way of a winding valley, which involved an easy walk of about four miles. That afternoon we did eight miles, making a total of twenty miles for the whole day. I was not exhausted but felt tired enough. I was now wearing a pair of top boots studded with big nails. They were too heavy for these hills, in the absence of snow, but they were well worn and comfortable.

On the walk home I was filled with bitter reflections. Why did civilized people spend hundreds of hard-earned dollars, go through infinite trouble, and suffer unspeakable discomforts and physical exhaustion just for the sake of killing a few harmless wild creatures? There is a world of interest in the reply. Moreover, I felt I was getting too old for big-game hunting. I was only one year short of fifty. I could still do my twenty miles a day uphill and down, but I became too exhausted after a climb and had not the reserve strength to hold the rifle to a fine aim. My eyesight was also deteriorating. Why continue at my age to undergo this savage pilgrimage? The day before, I had disgraced myself with Li. Today

I had missed a standing shot with Jen as witness. Did I have to repeat this ignominious performance before Sung? Bitter thoughts accompanied me all the way home.

When we got back to the farmhouse, I brightened up at once on hearing that the other hunters had been cursed with bad luck and rotten shooting. Fatty had seen two bighorn sheep at long range and had fired thirty shots at them for nothing. After all, I had only shot once and missed. This young, energetic, keen-eyed hunter had missed thirty times in one day. Jack and Beau had also come across bighorn and had fired repeatedly without result. Intrinsically, my performance had not been so bad; comparatively, it was much better. Human beings derive much comfort from the misfortunes of their fellow men, and why should they not, so long as it does not hurt the other fellow?

The odds are all in favor of God's wild creatures, so free, so lithe, so graceful, so swift and surefooted, and so physically efficient. Think of a bighorn sheep carrying a head that weighs seventy pounds and going uphill like the wind where there is neither road nor path. Naturalists who have actually timed their speed declare that a bighorn is capable of galloping at the rate of twenty-five miles an hour for short spurts. That is very slow compared with the amazing speed of the deer and especially of the antelope, but quite fast enough to make the running bighorn an elusive target.

I might make mention of the weapons used by various members of our party. Jack and Beau each had a Springfield sporter fitted with peep sights. Fatty used a similar rifle with a very handy telescope sight. My weapon was the same .250-3000 bolt-action Savage. Fatty, the youngest member of the party with the best eyesight, had the advantage with the telescope. I was the oldest of the group, had the poorest eyesight, and was the only member wearing spectacles. However, it is possible to exaggerate the importance of rifle sights. Intrinsically, the telescope is the best sporting sight, but habit and familiarity count for a great deal.

Before I fell asleep that night, I did some hard thinking. I was no match for the younger hunters and guides in the matter of hard hunting. I was even less of a match for the wild beasts in physical prowess. If I were to get a worthwhile trophy soon, I would have to depend more on cunning and intelligence. On and off all day I had been cogitating on the information that bighorn come down to the farms to look for civilized food. We had not met with any animal so far, but I came to the conclusion that bighorn frequent the neighborhood of the farms only in the very early morning when no human beings are about. I determined to get up very early next morning to try out this theory. I fell asleep for the first time without the help of drugs and slept soundly till midnight. I dozed off again until the flashlight revealed the fact that it was nearly 4 A.M.

I got up quietly and made my preparations in great stealth in order not to disturb the others who were still sleeping soundly. I had much difficulty in arousing Li. He was a young man who liked to sleep and hated to get up when it was still pitch-dark, but once awakened he cheerfully entered into the spirit of my idea. After a hurried breakfast we crept off the farm, just as it was beginning to get light. It was our turn to go north, and we started in that direction. I felt absolutely fit because of a good night's natural sleep.

We were going up the main valley. The farm was only a few minutes away. Li and I were talking quietly and walking side by side through a ploughed field only a few feet from the lower edge of a slope. On glancing up we suddenly saw a pair of bighorn sheep on the skyline about five hundred yards above us. We ducked immediately behind a bank. My mind became frigidly clear and concentrated. I instinctively realized that the chance of a lifetime was now within my grasp. The pair of bighorns consisted of a ram and a ewe. One glance had shown me that the ram was a magnificent creature with horns that had described more than a circle. I had no doubt the animals had seen and heard us, but they showed not the least sign of disturbance and must have taken us for peasants.

In tense whispers I impressed upon Li the necessity of approaching the quarry with deliberate slowness. On no account were we to press them. They might now be a little suspicious, but they were not excited. I saw them standing at ease or moving only at a walking pace. We had to keep them in that mood at all costs. Another reason for climbing slowly was to prevent me from getting winded. My heart had to be quiet and my breathing normal when the moment arrived for the decisive shot. I emphasized these points with dramatic gestures, whispering as little as possible for fear of being overheard. Li contributed to the plan of campaign by suggesting that we approach the animals along the right flank instead of frontally. This was less likely to disturb the sheep and would place the sun behind my back. I heartily approved of his strategy.

We began the easy ascent by circling to the right. Every step was took with deliberate caution. There was absolutely no cover on these hills. The surface was bare and smooth. There were small rocks here and there, but they were too low to afford protection. The dried grass was exceedingly sparse and only a few inches high. The only method of hiding was to take advantage of the contour of the hills. After much careful and quiet maneuvering, we approached the point on which the bighorns had stood when we first saw them from the valley floor. We crept up by inches to the skyline, and peeping cautiously around protecting small rocks, we had the intense satisfaction of seeing the two animals standing on the next skyline about three hundred yards distant and a hundred feet or so above us. The situation was completely satisfactory. We had gained two hundred yards on the quarry without frightening them in the least. They were leisurely on the move and entirely unconcerned.

We allowed them to disappear and then began another encircling movement. This time we proceeded even more gingerly, because we felt that the quarry was now within easy hearing distance, although unseen. At last we reached a little hollow the animals had recently vacated, within thirty feet of the skyline. I instinctively realized that the great moment of decisive action had at last arrived. I eased a cartridge into the chamber and slipped off the safety catch. I took off my hat and laid it carefully on the ground. Then Li and I wormed ourselves up those remaining thirty feet. I was a little in advance; Li was crawling up on my left. At last I got my head behind a rock on the skyline only a few inches high. As I peeped cautiously over the stone, the sight that greeted me was fit for the gods. If I live several hundred years I shall never forget those next few moments or the next five minutes.

The pair of bighorns stood on the next skyline absolutely motionless, like beautiful living statues. I estimated the range to be no more than one hundred and fifty yards. The conditions were perfect either for shooting or for taking photographs. The ground rose slightly in front until it reached the next skyline about twenty feet above me. It continued to rise gently to a small mound at right angles to my position, and then it descended in a ridge parallel with me and hidden from my view. The pair of wild sheep stood in the center of a small amphitheater. The early morning sun was behind my back, illuminating every detail of the beautiful quarry and yet making it difficult for them to see us because the sun was shining right into their eyes. There was only a gentle cross-breeze. It was quite fresh. The two animals stood broadside on, the ram on the left and the ewe about a yard to the right, head to head, as if they were holding a consultation. The sheer beauty of the ram in that statuesque pose, with its magnificent horns, its deep chest, and lean hindquarters, took my breath away.

I was conscious of intense concentration. I was far too excited to show any outward signs of excitement. I was like a boiler subject to intense pressure but with the steam under good control. The sight of that pair of wild sheep standing in such calm unconcern gave me confidence. I knew they would not move if we did not disturb them. I wriggled several times until I settled into a comfortable shooting position flat on my stomach. Slowly I pushed the rifle barrel forward, poking the muzzle between two or three blades of dried grass and resting the barrel finally on the small sharp rock in front of me. I had time to notice that the grass stalks ended in pods full of seeds. So vividly did the mind take in every detail in that tense concentrated moment!

As I looked through the sights, the front bead wobbled slightly. I was not actually winded, but the climb had somewhat increased the rate of my breathing. I rested for a few moments—it appeared to me like minutes—but the sheep obliged by continuing to stand still. I aimed for the exact center of the ram, which was a point just six inches behind the shoulder. Li lay beside me in miserable agony. He did not know what was going through my mind and could not understand my inexcusable delay. When the front sight wobbled to the exact center of the animal, I gave the last squeeze to the trigger.

At the sharp report of the rifle, both sheep started to gallop madly away, the ram showing no sign of being hurt or even of being inconvenienced. Li and I rose to our knees in speechless consternation with our mouths wide open, paralyzed. In a single moment I passed through all the depths of hell and vaguely cursed myself for scoring a clean miss when missing was quite impossible. If I had only hit a leg, I would not have felt so completely blank. The bighorns were galloping side by side and crossing our front toward the right, where they would go over the ridge and disappear downhill. Of course, I should have reloaded and fired again while they were in full sight, but I was completely paralyzed, and so was Li. After running thirty or forty yards, I noticed that the ram was leaning against the ewe while going at full speed. Li said he saw their horns interlocked. This sign of the ram's distress completely broke the spell that had held us motionless.

Li jumped up with a whoop and shouted for me to give him the rifle, since he could shoot at the wounded ram much more quickly than I. I refused to give up the weapon, determined to win or lose by my own efforts. Together we raced like mad around the top of the amphitheater, intending to follow up the sheep that had just disappeared over the ridge. That 250 -yard dash seemed to have been done in record time, but actually it must have taken nearly a minute. In my heavy nail-studded top boots it was a mercy I did not slip and break my neck, but I kept up with the younger and more lightly shod Li. I felt sure when we got to the ridge the wounded ram would offer me a few more shots downhill. I was grimly determined to follow that wounded prize all the way to Outer Mongolia or to Siberia if necessary, until one of us dropped dead. As soon as we had crossed the edge of the ridge, we unexpectedly found the ram lying on its right side in a small depression, apparently stone dead. The ewe had vanished.

The sudden discovery of the dead ram, when the utmost we could have hoped was to see a wounded beast romping away beyond our range, brought on an overpowering revulsion. Out of the deepest hell I was abruptly transported to the seventh heaven. Li was young and volatile. I had always prided myself on my reserve and self-control, but both Li and I abandoned ourselves completely to our feelings. We danced up and down like wild Indians. We shouted at each other incoherently. When, in our mad gyrations, we came within reach, we thumped each other hard on the back. When we had worked ourselves into a state of utter breathlessness, we plumped down beside the beautiful trophy.

While we were regaining our breath and composure, the fallen beast made a slight movement. I was driven into a momentary panic. What if the animal should struggle to its feet and run away. My rifle was lying on the ground somewhere behind me. I made a sudden move in the direction of my weapon while plucky little Li got ready to pounce upon the huge beast. The bighorn ram made one slow convulsive movement and lay still for good.

While we were standing around the fallen monarch, we caught sight of another bighorn ram on the skyline about three hundred yards to the east of us. I examined it casually through my monocular. It was somewhat smaller than the one I had just shot but large enough to make a very desirable trophy. This ram had heard the report of my rifle and had come up to the skyline to investigate. I could not work up any excitement; in fact, I was hardly interested in this new opportunity. I could have taken a shot, but the distance was long and the sun was shining right into my eyes. Li thought my chance of hitting it was not very good.

The animal stood gazing at us steadily, shifted its position calmly once or twice, and then, evidently not liking our looks, slowly disappeared northward. We could easily have followed it, but I was not interested. After all, I was not a bloodthirsty man. The wonderful trophy I had just obtained should have satisfied any hunter for a lifetime. My fear of losing the prize that lay on the hillside had something to do with my restraint. Li had told me of a fallen and unguarded bighorn that was mysteriously stolen. I did not feel safe until the precious cargo was under lock and key in the farmhouse.

The sight of the priceless trophy filled me with inordinate pride and admiration. I behaved like a baby, I must confess. I caressed the amazing horns with the palm of my hand and stroked the velvety fur. The animal had looked large enough at 150 yards, but at close quarters it appeared immense. It was as big as a large donkey. The farmhands who carried it home assured me that the animal weighed between three and four hundred pounds. By looking at the teeth, Li guessed the beast was about eight years old. Of course, the horns were the most astonishing feature. No buffalo weighing over a thousand pounds could boast of such massive horns, curving in majestic grace. These horns were of a dark slate color. The surface was covered with a close succession of lateral folds or rings. I measured one horn with the span of my hand along the curve and guessed the length to be over forty inches. The fur was velvety but not thick. It was medium gray in color, but the underpart of the body and portions of the legs were almost white.

Li lost no time gutting the beast with my sharp hunting knife. I watched with interest the great care he took in reeling off the long intestine. He showed no concern for the other parts of the viscera. He told me he could sell the long intestine for a dollar. Later on I learned that China did a brisk export trade in casings. These are sent to foreign countries, and especially to America, where they are used for sausage coverings or are made into gut for tennis rackets. The wild sheep has a longer and commercially more valuable intestine than the domesticated variety. It is a strange world when people from different hemispheres can be so strangely connected.

Li went back to the farm to fetch help, for it would require four men to carry that beast without damage to horns and skin. I was left alone with my prize and contemplated it with endless wonder. The noble animal was now fallen and gutted but remained every inch a monarch. I had to wait almost an hour, but I was not in the least bored. I was supremely happy; I was fresh and not even damp; the morning was delightful, the sun was shining, and there was hardly any wind; I found plenty to occupy my mind and to consume my energy. I walked to the top of the mound and behaved and felt like the stag who was the lord of all he surveyed. When I became tired of attitudinizing, I turned my attention to more practical occupations.

I walked to the scene where I had fired that triumphant shot and measured the distances with great care. I paced the ground and found that I had shot the bighorn at a range of 160 yards. I had taken a fine sight, and for once I had made no mistake. I also paced the distance the stricken ram had run and discovered that the beast had galloped 100 yards before it collapsed. Li and I, therefore, had covered 260 yards in our mad dash after the wounded animal. I like to be exact, even if it is only to please myself.

Li duly returned with four farmhands carrying two stout poles and a large coil of rope. They also brought the watchdog from the farm to eat the offal, saving certain delicacies for themselves. The bighorn sheep proved a heavy load even for four men. The carriers perspired liberally and rested frequently. The hill was no more than five hundred feet high and easy to descend, and the farm was only half a mile away. We reached home in triumph at 10 A.M. I was sorry none of the other hunters were there to envy me. Human beings require the misery of other people to complete their own happiness.

I ordered the bighorn sheep to be placed over a pole to be photographed, with Li and I posing beside the animal and grinning idiotically. The cook took the snapshots and proved to be a better photographer than a culinary artist. When we got back to the farm, we learned that the inmates had received a message announcing the fact that Jack had shot a bighorn ram some time after I had shot mine. Toward noon his animal was carried back to the farm and proved to be a much smaller beast than mine. It was about four years old, weighed under two hundred pounds, and carried horns that had not yet described a full circle.

All morning I was filled with an unaccustomed elation. I had good reason to have a swelled head. After all, I was not too old for big-game hunting, when the conditions were right. I had the honor of being the first of our party, and probably the first Chinese sportsman, to kill a bighorn ram, and my trophy had a pair of horns that sportsmen would be willing to travel halfway around the world to obtain. I liked to think that I had been rewarded because I had been modest in my expectations and had been humble about my misses during the first two days. In three days I had only fired five shots. Considering everything, mine was not such a bad record for a man of fifty.

CHAPTER NINETEEN

PERCY W. CHURCH

Born in 1867, Percy William Palmer Church entered a period in history when the British Empire was approaching its zenith. Like many other young men of his era, he enjoyed sporting activities throughout the British Isles, Continental Europe, and especially the rugged haunts of Central Asia.

In the summer of 1899, Church and his hunting companion, J. V. Phelps, trekked from Srinagar to Leh and Yarkand. They continued into the shooting grounds of the Tian Shan range and Chinese Turkistan in pursuit of wapiti, ibex, and roe deer. After a successful hunting trip, they proceeded to Kuldja, where temperatures plummeted to 40 degrees below zero, before returning to India.

A fellow of the Royal Geographical Society and the Zoological Society in London, Church contributed several scientific papers describing his journey in western China. His only book, Chinese Turkistan with Caravan and Rifle *(1901), swept readers to a virtually unknown area of the globe. In this passage from his book, Church describes hunting the massive Altai wapiti, also known as the maral.*

WAPITI IN CHINESE TURKISTAN

On the last day of October I started, taking only a small tent and traveling as light as possible, since the Koksu roads were said to be very bad.

An easy day's ride took us to the entrance of Koksu, a deep and imposing gorge. We descended into it next morning, fording the Koksu River and then turning up the valley on a pretty rough path, a portent of worse to follow. Before midday I was met by the head Kalmuk of Koksu, a very nice old fellow, who had an *aül* already pitched for me. He advised me to stay there for the night, saying that the road ahead was very bad for a long way and that there was not enough time to reach a good camping ground.

The next day the chief Kalmuk accompanied me part of the way to see me safely over the worst part of the road. Certainly, he had not exaggerated the badness of the road; it ran high up along the hillside and was narrow and precipitous. In two or three places there was not room for a loaded pony to pass, so we had to remove everything from it, but the good old chief had sent a lot of men to assist, so this did not take long. After crossing a spur we scrambled and slid down a steep and stony zigzag track into a side valley, after which things were a bit better. Up this valley we turned, threading our way through a large pine forest, and, after a march of nine hours, we camped just above the last pine trees, three or four miles from the top. It was a cold spot; some milk we had brought froze solid during dinner. I saw some old, shed horns here, and Durji told me that once it had been a great place for stags but that none came there now.

The next day we turned out of this side valley into another, traveling over a pass of about eleven thousand feet. The north side of the pass was already covered with snow. From there we descended again by a very steep path to Big Koksu, another nine hours' march for the ponies. On the way down we saw a large herd of ibex, but they were in a hopeless place, so, after watching them for a time, we went on. One of the bucks was very big, certainly well over fifty inches, and had a most remarkable spread of horn. As Durji remarked, the horns grew out from its head, more like those of a sheep, and it was with some regret that I abandoned the attempt to obtain them.

Farther on we saw another big buck, a single one this time, and we went a long way down and around to try for it, but it was traveling too fast, and we could not catch up with it. I reached camp sometime after dark, having had a long and rough walk for nothing. Camp was by the bank of the Koksu River, near a large pool of clear, blue water that should have held fish, though I saw none. Below this the river runs through a cliff-bound gorge, which is passable only when the ice bears.

In the morning we crossed the river by a deep and bad ford. The bottom was all boulders, and the ponies stumbled, so it was rather a wet job, and a cold one too. Just after crossing, one of the ponies fell off the path and very nearly went into the river, and we spent some time getting its load off and hauling it up again. We then went up a big side valley, where it was necessary to climb up and along the hillside—in fact, we all got off our ponies and walked bits of the way. The path is indeed a rough one when a native of the Tekkes prefers his own two legs to his pony's four!

After some eight or ten miles of this, we got down to the stream again and pitched camp on a small flat by the side of it. Here we were at the wapiti ground, and my hopes had already been raised by seeing the track of a good stag on the hill just above.

In the afternoon Durji proposed going out to have a look, so away we went, floundering in and out of the stream for a mile and then scrambling up the hill, the first part of which was barely usable for the wonderfully surefooted ponies. After tying up the ponies in a convenient hollow, Durji and I went up a ridge and settled down to watch the surrounding country and enjoy the last of the afternoon sun.

The valley we had left was deep and narrow, so the bottom of it only got the sun for an hour or two in the middle of the day, but we were now well up the hill. From our post we could see a large area of ground. Opposite, looking south, was the valley where camp was—first, pine forests and grassy glades, then cliffs, and above all the snow; on either side of our ridge were side valleys that were said to be good places. Presently the sun went behind a hill, and immediately it turned very cold, while a nasty, penetrating little wind began to blow. I had foolishly left my sheepskin coat with the ponies and now simply shivered when I sat, or rather crouched, against a rock. It was getting dark, and I was nearly frozen when two white objects appeared among the bushes on the far side of the upper little valley. Joy! Two stags, no doubt. We hastily produced the big telescope, and the remains of the rapidly fading light just served to show that one of them was a really big stag, the other a small fellow.

Stag wapiti are very light-colored in the late autumn and winter; in fact, from above they look almost white. The hinds are much darker, and, for almost as far as the beasts are visible, one can see the difference at once with the naked eye.

Of course, it was far too late to do anything. We waited until it grew quite dark, for fear of being seen as we retired, and returned to camp in cheerful mood—Durji full of confidence, saying I should shoot the big stag next day for sure; I myself less certain of it, but hopeful.

The next day, accompanied by two other Kalmuks, we started before four o'clock in black darkness. When we had reached our observation post of the day before, we sat down to wait for dawn. It was bitterly cold, and I was nearly frozen in spite of a heavy fur coat, but when it began to get light, after what seemed hours, there was the big stag feeding alone on a grass patch among some bushes, close to where we had seen it the evening before. Its smaller companion had apparently gone elsewhere during the night, as we saw no more of it.

The hillside on which the stag was feeding was mostly covered with bushes about six feet high, but the leaf was now gone, and the only thick places were the northern sides of some little rocky ridges, where there were a few scattered pine trees. The heavy forest did not begin until farther down.

There was nothing we could do until the stag settled down for the day, so we lay in a small hollow behind a sheltering rock and admired it through the telescope. It was worth looking at, too—twelve points and a great spread of horn—and even the Kalmuks agreed that it was very big. One might well imagine how eagerly I longed for a shot, and how I hoped I would make a good one when the critical moment came.

Meanwhile, it was interesting to watch the precautions this noble beast took for its safety. Having finished its morning feed, it went into the bushes and stood there listening for a time, after which it lay down, but this was only a ruse, for from time to time its head went up, and not until it had shifted its position three times did it finally decide that all was well. Then it went off to a small clump of pine trees to lie down for the day. By this time it was ten o'clock.

Now was the sportsman's opportunity. After giving the stag half an hour or so to go to sleep, we left one Kalmuk on the watch and, having safely crawled over a short space of ground that was in view, we started off. I was glad to stretch my cramped limbs again and get my feet warm, for up till now they had been almost devoid of sensation.

We had to take a long, steep detour that went up and down, and not till nearly three o'clock did we get near the end. At last, only one ridge separated us from the stag's resting place. With the glass I could see the watching Kalmuk lying by his rock; he made no sign, so we knew that the stag was still there and waited some time in the hope that it would get up to feed before dusk. It grew late, and the wind, never very steady, began to get shiftier, but still the stag did not move. Finally we decided that I should creep up to the last ridge while Durji went above and tried to shift it out toward me.

This all worked out beautifully. After a due interval, I heard Durji give a warning shout—a most unnecessary proceeding, since I was all eyes and ears—and the stag appeared about four hundred yards off, heading through the bushes toward me. At first it was traveling fast, but it soon settled down to a walk, seeming inclined to go farther up the hill, which would not have mattered much, because I surely would have had a shot, though possibly rather a long one. My great fear was that the stag would turn down and be lost to view, since the ground that way was a hollow into which I could not see. When the stag was a bit over one hundred yards off, it stood still, undecided which way to turn, facing almost directly the place where I lay concealed. Afraid to wait longer, I covered the point of its shoulder and, chancing a few intervening branches, let drive. A heavy stumble in answer to the shot showed a hit and gave me time to loose off the second barrel. The stag turned down the hill and was at once out of sight. I dashed down the ridge, reloading as I ran, and, getting a glimpse of its back, fired another shot, which, as I afterward found, hit it in the ribs too far back. The first shot had broken its shoulder, and the second, hurried and high, had gone through its ear.

The ridge ended abruptly in a small cliff, and when I arrived there the stag was already a long way below. It was going slowly, obviously hard hit. I was so far above it that the bushes did not greatly hinder my view, and I could see the whole length of its back, so I sat down to try and stop its career. Resting the rifle on my knees, I missed the first shot, but the second broke its hip, and down it went. It must have been nearly four hundred yards away, and this shows the advantage of the .303 rifle. But the first shot of all hit it fair on the point of the shoulder, and if the bullet had come from a .450 it would probably have finished the business at once.

I got down as quickly as possible, and a shot behind the shoulder finished the stag. I had time to admire its horns and congratulate myself on my good luck, though I felt somewhat ashamed of such an

inartistic performance. Not until later did I realize what a prize I had got—twelve points and a little snag that might almost be reckoned a thirteenth; massive and wide, with a great development of the fourth tine; and a slight palmation of the tops. This head is, taken all round, the finest specimen of an Asiatic wapiti I have seen, and, since the horns are an article of trade, I saw lots of them afterward in Kulkja.

Durji and the other Kalmuk soon arrived, and we congratulated one another. Durji at first tried to conceal his delight under a "There, I told you so" sort of air, which he could not keep up, while the other Kalmuk, a cheerful soul and a great friend of mine, kept pointing out the ridge to him and wondering at the distance.

It was nearly dark by the time we had got off the head and skin, but I cared little now for rough paths or cold. The Kalmuk we had left behind managed to get the ponies up within half a mile of us, so presently we started for camp. We arrived there late and tired, and wet-footed from the deep fords on the way downstream, but overall a very cheerful party.

Having got what I wanted, I would now have been quite willing to leave Kooks and go to Jigalong for roe deer, but the energetic Durji, who did not mind the cold at all, was bent on my getting another stag and some ibex as well. He said that the ibex here were even bigger than the Akjas ones and that it was pity to come so far and not shoot a few of them. It was true that there were lots of ibex, and big ones too, but it was now altogether too late in the year to face the high and steep ground of the valley I was in, and, as will be seen, I did no good with them.

The next morning, 6 November, I did not go out. Our men were busy mending their footgear with the stag's skin, so I amused myself writing in my diary. First I had to thaw the ink over a fire, though it was twelve o'clock and the sun was out and, besides, I had wrapped up the ink bottle most carefully.

In the afternoon we went out and saw some ibex and an enormous brown bear, but they were all on the other side of a deep valley and far out of reach. The wind began to blow hard, and it was so cold on the ridge that we gave it up and returned.

I do not think that the bear here are the same as the red bear of the Himalayas. This one looked to me much bigger, and, since it was only about half a mile beyond the ibex, I had something with which to compare its size. The natives say these bear are very savage; the Himalayan red bear certainly is not, and it rarely, if ever, assumes the offensive, even when wounded.

The following day we moved camp a bit farther up the valley but saw nothing worth going after. It blew so hard at night that we dared not have a big campfire for fear of setting the whole place alight with flying sparks, so I turned in early, bed being the only place where there was a chance of keeping warm. The wind lasted all night, bringing snow up with it toward morning, and all the next day it was too bad to go out, so it was an off-day for all hands.

On the morning after the blizzard there was still a little snow falling, but the day turned out fair, so we moved camp a little farther up and in the afternoon went out to look for ibex. We saw several herds and started to try and stalk one lot, but it was rather late in the day and intensely cold. So when my boots were frozen hard and my feet quite numb, I gave it up, afraid of frostbite.

Up in the valleys the cold was by now pretty severe. One's hands, if wet, froze instantly to any piece of metal touched, and one's moustache became attached to the edge of the glass in the act of drinking.

On 10 November we saw lots of ibex but only one within reach. The days were now too short for this sport; the ground was very steep and cut up by deep valleys, which made it difficult to get around quickly enough. The snow was just beginning to melt in a few exposed places, but clear nights and cloudy days delayed its disappearance.

We did manage to bring off a stalk the next day, but it was not a very successful one. The ibex saw us just too soon and, of course, began to move. I lay down to shoot, but the hillside was steep, and I kept slipping down it in the fresh snow. At last Durji, seeing my predicament, held my feet, and I hit one buck but did not get it. The herd went up the hill and scattered in every direction, though they did not all go at once, for, as Durji said, they seldom heard a shot or saw a man up there and hardly knew what to make of it. With the glasses I saw a big buck and three females lie down again farther up, so we went on. After another two hours' climb, we got there, and I shot a buck all right—with 47-inch horns.

The snow had made the going dangerous in places, and we nearly came to grief once or twice. One scree with a cliff below was particularly nasty to cross. Even Durji reluctantly confessed that the season for ibex shooting was now about over. On our way down we saw ten or twelve hinds and a small stag, the only deer we had seen since 5 November. There were a few tracks in places but not nearly as many as there should have been, and Durji was disgusted and puzzled at their absence. We had found an old campfire and a horse's tack in one place, however, so we thought that some other shikar must have been there. On our way back we met him—a Kazak—going up for the skins of two stags he had shot during the calling season. He had hidden them under the rocks.

Next day we had another try after ibex, but just when we were getting on terms with them they moved and took up a position where the wind barred all approaches. The Kalmuks proposed trying to drive them, but this, as I expected, turned out a failure.

I had now had enough of it. I wanted to get back to a less rigorous climate and again be able to take some of my clothes off at night instead of having to put more on. So next day we returned down the valley to the camp from which I had shot the stag, and another short march took us down to Big Koksu. The drift ice coming down had jammed in places and then frozen solid, so we crossed the river on an ice bridge, which would have borne a siege train, though the river was not yet frozen where the current was swift. The rapid stream in the side valley we had left was frozen along the sides but not in the middle. It was girth deep, and we had to ford it about once every hundred yards, which was most unpleasant. When the ponies reached the edge of the ice without falling through, they nearly always stumbled in getting off the ice into the water, so one's feet were always wet, and a nailed shooting boot is not the warmest of footgear, even without a thin coating of ice.

Both days I tried to stalk ibex but without success. Either it is their custom at this season to be always on the move, or the broken weather had unsettled them, for they never stopped long enough in one place to give one a chance to get up to them, and it is poor fun climbing up a hill for hours, only to find that your game has moved on.

The descent to the big river had seemed pretty steep, and the ascent from it only strengthened that impression. A whole day's toil still left us some distance from the top of the pass. We crossed it on 16 November, going down to the bottom of the side valley and camping just before we reached the bad bit of road. The whole place was white with snow, and camp was comfortless enough. On the pass we met some of Durji's sheep in his son's charge on their way to winter quarters up the valley.

The good old chief Kalmuk had again sent men to help us over the bad places, and he met us just on the other side and came down with us to the entrance of the Koksu Valley, offering to have an *aül* pitched for me.

Here I heard from the other two Kalmuks of their change of plans. I decided to follow them along the foothills, looking for roe deer on the way.

The weather was cold, and my small tent was a cramped dwelling place, so I arranged with the chief to have a small *aül* made and sent after me as soon as possible. It eventually reached me on 28 November—pretty quick work, as by then I had traveled some way. The chief said he could supply me with one ready-made, but when I found that this meant turning out a family until a new one could be made for them, I said no.

CHAPTER TWENTY

HARRY CALDWELL

Though Harry Caldwell was well known in China as a tiger hunter, he was equally famous for his stalks of a wide variety of Chinese big game. His book Blue Tiger *also recounted his hunts after argali, goral, wild boar, and wapiti. In this passage from* Blue Tiger *(1924), Roy Chapman Andrews joins Caldwell on a hunt after wapiti in Shanxi Province.*

ON THE TRAIL OF SHANXI WAPITI

To speak of wapiti among American sportsmen is to talk about something not immediately recognized by many hunters, but to mention elk is to talk in terms understood by all. The facts are, however, that the wonderful animal *Cervus canidensis* of our wooded Northwest is not the true elk at all but is the wapiti, and in all probability is an offshoot from the big stag of Central Asia.

If the theory now advanced by many scientists is true, the wapiti of Central Asia led the nomads of Mongolia across the narrows now known as the Bering Straits, the animal to become the American elk and the man to become the American Indian. Whether or not this hypothesis is true, it would seem to be a fact that the so-called elk of the American Northwest is close kin to the giant stag of Asia. The true elk is a large deer with palmated horns, common to Scandinavia.

There has been considerable discussion in recent years as to the number of distinct species of wapiti to be found in Asia, and even today scientists have not definitely decided just where to draw the line between the seemingly different species of stag found in Manchuria, Mongolia, and northern China. They have practically agreed, however, that there are no less than ten species to be found in this area, and within the past year I have definitely located what seems to be an entirely different species in the mountains of Fukien Province in southern China.

The wapiti found in northern Shanxi Province is a wonderful animal, closely allied to both the Manchurian and Kansu species but sufficiently different that it may prove to be another species of this handsome deer found in Central Asia.

The wapiti by nature is an animal of the heavily wooded wilds. When in 1919 Mongol guides proposed to me, after winding up a most successful expedition after bighorn sheep *(Ovis camosa)* in Shanxi, that we move along three days' journey on horseback to the east in order to hunt the great stag, I took it as a joke, knowing the mountains in that region would be equally denuded of all tree life as those where we had hunted bighorn. But after the Mongol guides assured us repeatedly that we would find herds of wapiti feeding like cattle on the barren mountains, it was not difficult to persuade ourselves to remain another week or ten days in the far north during the bitter cold in order to secure a series of this rapidly disappearing deer.

To find the bighorn sheep among the barren mountains was no strange thing. That animal has every advantage of the enemies of earlier days, since it is very much at home on the rugged cliffs and crags where it has been able to care for itself. The advent of the high-powered rifle in China, however, supplemented by the building of railroad from Peking northward to within a few miles of the sheep country, seals the doom of both sheep and wapiti. Three years ago it cost us nineteen days' travel on horseback in order to get specimens of bighorn and wapiti, but today sportsmen can visit the same places with very little effort. The finding of these wonderful animals in northern China will soon be a thing of the past.

Leaving the sheep country, our route led along the foothills skirting the fertile Kweihuacheng plain. This city is destined to become the gateway to both the Gobi and Ordos desert regions, both of which will someday blossom and produce as a garden spot under the skilled hand of the Chinese farmer.

The Mongol is a nomad by nature, spending his time in the saddle hunting and rounding up herds. These vast arid regions will always remain desert unless cultivated by the Chinese, who are gradually filtering into the country, converting the barren grasslands into wonderfully productive fields and gardens.

By making forced marches we could have reached the wapiti country in two days, but an accident landed our cart, containing specimens and supplies, upside down across a chasm and delayed us a full half-day. It was fortunate that our entire outfit was not dashed to pieces at the bottom of this pit across which the cart rested like a well-placed bridge. The ropes that had been securely laced around the loads held things in place to such an extent that we really lost nothing more than our patience and the few things we carried in open carriers.

This experience is but one of the vicissitudes of travel in such a country. Let it be understood that one pays dearly for every trophy he takes out of this mountainous region, where patience and endurance are assets indispensable to the sportsman.

As we approached the region where the hunters assured us there were both wapiti and roebuck in abundance, Mr. Andrews laughingly said, "Caldwell, I would as soon expect to find a snowman standing on Fifth Avenue in July as to find either wapiti or roebuck in such open country as is ahead of us."

After establishing ourselves in a small village jammed in a nook under the overhanging cliffs, we prepared for our first wapiti hunt. Leaving camp at an early hour in the morning, we followed the frozen streambed through a most wonderful gorge until we emerged into more open uplands. There were still no trees or cover in sight, and we wondered all the more where the big deer would conceal themselves.

Far up at the head of the ravine we had traveled for four hours was a vast grassy plateau, cut deep here and there by ravines into which the sun never shines. Our guides now began to talk in whispers, scanning the snow-covered slopes with care. We began to see many signs of wapiti, and all was tense as we approached the mouth of a ravine sparsely wooded with low blasted birch.

My companion turned up the wooded ravine while the guides led me on toward the uplands. Soon there were roebuck scampering around in large numbers from the sparse cover through which the others were working their way. The guides also put up three wapiti out of this cover, which gave me my first glimpse of one of these huge wild deer. The Mongols did not seem the least perturbed at seeing these animals disappear over the skyline. There were two cows and a bull carrying a wide spread of horns. Mr. Andrews saw the big bull behind a gnarled birch at close range, but he could not maneuver for a shot on account of the lay of the land.

After climbing out of the head of the ravine that I had followed for more than four hours, I crossed a mile of rolling uplands with patches of drifted snow that showed signs of deer everywhere. When I came within six hundred yards of a sparsely wooded slope across a shallow ravine, I saw a dark object that looked much like an upturned stump standing out against the snow.

Raising my glasses, I saw a wonderful sight. There stood an immense stag, knee-deep in drifted snow, as if guarding eight cows resting in the snow at points but a few yards distant. The bull had a wonderful spread of horns, so I paid no attention to any of the other animals.

Approaching another sixty yards to a point where the slope broke off into the ravine, I decided to risk a shot. The bull now gave a sneezing snort and dashed up the hill, followed by a mad rush of cows. I fired point-blank at the animal as it topped the skyline, striking it in the shoulder. It went down in a mass with a thud but was soon struggling to get over the divide, across which the cows had already disappeared. I fired a second shot through the fleshy part of the neck, which did no damage.

The big bull got to its feet and shambled down the slope a way, where it stood for a time while being bombarded by Mr. Andrews from a long distance. It finally went down in its tracks, after being hit several times through the body. My first shot had completely shattered the left shoulder, part of the ball ripping great holes through the lungs. The metal jacket passed through the right shoulder blade and was found just under the skin on the off side. It was a demonstration of the terrific shocking power of the .250-3000 cartridge.

It is quite a task to skin out an animal of this size on the bleak barrens of the far north with the strong wind from the deserts sweeping across the uplands. After the job was finished, we sent one of the hunters to camp with the skin and head while we continued our hunt.

A few days later, my companion routed a large cow and yearling from some cover where we had put up and fired at a roebuck. I crouched low, letting the animals pass me at less than thirty yards' distance. I was soon rewarded, for I could see, far up the glade, the horns of a big bull glistening in the sunlight as it raced down toward me. It doubtless had caught some sign indicating danger from the cow as it passed me, for, instead of following the cow, the bull swung far to the right, coming into sight far up the creek bed I had been following. At the crack of the gun the animal collapsed in the stream. I saw that it was unable to proceed farther, so I watched it slowly get on its feet and walk away from me with an unsteady gait.

I knew the animal was shot through the lungs and waited to see how long it could remain on its feet. After slowly walking up the stream bed thirty yards, it stood for a few seconds and then toppled over at the foot of an abandoned terrace. This too was a very fine specimen, though not as large as the first.

There is a combination of forces militating decidedly against the wapiti in the open country of northern China. In the first place, there is absolutely no cover in the region, other than dwarfed wild pear and blasted birch. Fuel gatherers are fast destroying this scant cover, making daily excursions for wood with donkey trains and marketing it at fabulous prices in the settlements of the plain. Thus the big deer is constantly exposed to danger, either while at rest in such cover as it can find or while feeding on the grassy slopes.

The second factor auguring evil for this splendid animal is the fact that the horns while in the felt are very valuable for medicinal purposes, bringing as much as three hundred dollars a pair in the city markets. For this reason wapiti are rounded up and persecuted annually.

I very much wanted to get another goral, so we decided to take a day off from hunting wapiti and go up among the cliffs after these fine little goats. It is easy to locate them but exceedingly difficult to get a shot except at long range.

My guide frantically beckoned me to come to him. He was looking off toward a point of the cliff fully a half-mile away and far above us. I could see nothing with the naked eye and could see only two faint spots, which I could not discern as living objects, with the use of my field glasses. The guide declared that these were goral, but, if so, it seemed to me impossible to get a shot. After some consultation, he intimated to me that we would work our way up to the base of the cliff while the other man made a wide detour in order to get on top of the range. It seemed a big program, involving hours of time with little hope of getting a shot, but these men know pretty well what they are doing.

My climb across the ravine and up the slope to the position the hunter had indicated stands out as the most strenuous work I did on the whole expedition. Soon after we had reached our positions, I saw the head of the other hunter appear far up on the top of the precipice. My man signaled him to make the drive.

To me it seemed that there was absolutely no chance for any animal to get down the face of the cliff to where we were. As we waited, my guide said, "Be ready when the goat comes, for it will come very quickly."

I sat with rifle in a position for a quick shot. Suddenly a gray object shot forth, zigzagging from point to point on the face of the cliff, followed by a second. I would not have believed it possible for any animal to come down that precipice as did those two gorals, had I not seen it. They both disappeared from view for an instant, to appear again barely one hundred feet from us, and then only as they lunged from one high point to another point fifty feet below.

I raised my rifle and fired when the first animal was midway between the two points. It turned over just enough to land upon its back on the point with force, which wedged it in-between two rocks. The second animal landed squarely upon the first. There was no other place to land, and one was following the other so closely that there was not time to change its course. The second animal made another flying leap into what looked like open space and disappeared.

I found that I had struck the first animal, at which I had fired in midair, behind the shoulder, totally obliterating the heart. It was by far the most wonderful, though likely accidental, shot I ever made with a rifle. It is the kind of a chance that the sportsman often has to take, however, when out after these wonderful little cliff goats.

Our last day after wapiti added another fine bull to our series. We had routed a herd from a draw that was being driven from above when my companion fired at a roebuck that ran temptingly close. The big deer broke back up the hill, almost running over the eight beaters. We spent the rest of the day wandering from one patch of possible cover to another, trying to locate the herd. The deer had scattered; we found only two of them at widely different places. I had a wonderful opportunity to watch one fine bull making its getaway from the beaters. It was a most satisfactory study. The animal was just a little too far for a shot, and, since it was so nearly a duplicate of the second one I had shot, I really cared little about securing it.

On the trip I had been using peep sights kindly loaned to me by my friend Castle, with whom I had hunted serow in Chekiang Province. But that morning I had replaced them with my own open sights, hoping to find an opportunity to try them out at long range in the wonderfully clear atmosphere of the far north. We had long since headed home, and Andrews had his rifle thrown across his shoulder with a sling. We were traveling down a deep ravine single file when I heard a rustling in the brush far up to our left. Looking up, I saw a big wapiti bull just breaking cover. I took quick aim and fired, splintering a sapling just over the back of the deer, bringing it to a sudden halt. My second shot, which I fired before my companion could get his gun in shape for action, grazed the back of the animal.

It was impossible for me to line my sights in the darkness of the deep ravine, so I was shooting with a very coarse bead and consequently shooting high. Mr. Andrews by this time was ready for a shot, and, falling upon one knee, he took careful aim through his peep sights and brought the giant stag rolling down the slope. It was a beautiful specimen, but smaller than either of the other specimens we had taken. With a series showing a varied spread of horns, we were satisfied with our hunt and agreed not to take the life of another one of these wonderful animals.

These were wonderful specimens, representing the most magnificent species of living deer, yet I saw fossil heads taken from the Fen Ho Valley that showed a much larger horn than any of the deer we had taken. The same was true of the fossil bighorn sheep that had been taken in the same region. These and other fossils recently collected serve to show that wonderful fauna once inhabited that area, at the time when it was most probably heavily forested. The living specimens of today, though magnificent, do not compare in size with the fossils representing the fauna of a few thousand years ago.

CHAPTER TWENTY-ONE

FREDERICK (GILLETT) LORT-PHILLIPS

Sporting literature of the late nineteenth and early twentieth centuries abounds with the recollections and journals of hunters who traveled six of the seven continents in search of big game. Often wealthy and well established, they contributed to sporting journals or privately published their memoirs. In some instances, these sportsmen collected their notebooks, edited them, and had them printed by major publishing firms. Such is the case with Frederick Gillett.

Born in 1872, Gillett had his first sporting experiences at sixteen, when he joined a hunting trip to Norway in search of reindeer. After stalking big game in the Rocky Mountains in 1892, he turned his attention to Africa. As a member of A. Donaldson Smith's expedition into the Arusa Galla country of Somaliland, he hunted game and gained valuable experience in assembling caravans for his own future forays. By 1896, while traveling in Persia to hunt tiger near the Caspian Sea, Gillett became an on-the-spot correspondent for London newspapers, reporting on the upheaval in the region after the assassination of Shah Nasr-ud-Din. Before the turn of the century, he had taken additional hunts in Somaliland, Norway, and Canada.

Gillett, who changed his name in 1926 to Frederick Lort-Phillips in honor of his mother's oldest brother, gained social recognition as well. An officer with the Geographical Club, he was also elected vice president of the London Zoological Society in 1906. With mounting business concerns and a family to care for, he decided a hunting trip after ibex and wild sheep in the Tian Shan Range would be his last.

Arriving in Russia in May 1908, Gillett traveled by rail, then caravan, to the Tian Shan Range in western China. He used native Khirgiz and Kalmuk tribesmen to guide his party through the treacherous passes of the range. In this passage taken from his book The Wander Years, Hunting and Travel in Four Continents *(1931), Gillett, accompanied by a German interpreter named Höger and his Khirgiz shikaris, has crossed the Chinese frontier in search of ibex* (Capra sibirica).

HUNTING IBEX WITH KHIRGIZ AND KALMUK

On Friday, 29 May, four weeks since I had left London, we crossed the Chinese frontier, where our affairs were dealt with expeditiously and courteously, and we sped on our way down an avenue of trees in which the magpies built, past a toylike mud fort with buttressed walls and pagoda-roofed towers. Clustered around the fort was a Chinese village. The people looked rather attractive, with roses stuck under the rims of their hats and hanging over their left ears. Chinese nobles attended by their suites passed us on the road, and it was evident that we had passed not only a frontier but from one culture to another, though we were soon again in the open country, and one Khirgiz is much like another, whomever his overlord may be.

At Kuldga, where we exchanged our wheel traveling for the horse caravan that would take us to the mountains, the Russian consul entertained us. He did all he could to help us, lending us his Cossack servant to do our buying for us and secure us a cook. A Russian officer named Vodopianof, to whom I had brought introductions, was also very civil and obliging, and Father Raemdorck of the Belgian mission gave us much good advice. Having exchanged somewhat tedious courtesies with the mayor of Kuldga; having engaged a cook-servant with a gift of tongues who spoke Russian and the languages of the peoples of the Tian Shan; and having hired our horses and made such additions to our outfit and supplies as were necessary, including several Chinese visiting cards for use when communicating with the Kalmuk Ottomans, we at last set out for the mountains.

On Thursday, 4 June, we started. Ours was quite an imposing cavalcade: Höger, who had never ridden before, was on the smallest of the horses; twelve packhorses; I with my .410 shotgun over my back and my .375 rifle on my saddle; and Jarmee, our cook-interpreter, carrying my .256 rifle. We got along at a fair pace, but it was six hours before we reached the Illi River, over which a ferryboat took men and baggage; the horses swam, held up on either side. Thanks to the energetic and kindly Khirgiz who volunteered his help, we made an expeditious crossing of this swift and dirty river and, loading up again, made our way to the house of a Taranchi, where we stayed the night.

Starting next morning, the idea occurred to me to take a photograph of our caravan as it moved off. I did so, but on remounting, with one foot in the stirrup, my horse gave a bound and started off after the others, dragging me with it. I failed to get my foot free, and the horse, lifting its hind legs, kicked me in the stomach and sent me flying, luckily releasing my foot. Though stunned for a moment, with my head and left leg feeling pretty bad, I found that no real damage had been done, except that the fall had snapped off the stock of my .410. Naturally, now that the shotgun was damaged, we immediately began to see sand grouse.

The passage through the foothills was dreary going, but as we approached the mountains, riding beside a mountain torrent that we had to cross from time to time, the vegetation increased, and presently we were in a region of such beauty that I used the word "divine." The trees and bushes were all in bloom, and the flowers were superb; it was as if we had come upon the nursery of all English flower gardens. Orange Iceland poppy was growing in great profusion, so, too, was a dark, almost black-red aquilegia. There were masses of phlox, not yet in flower, and, perhaps best of all, the many buttercup-yellow flowers: a wild rose and clumps of a plant with a flower nearly as large as a wild rose, all of the same brilliant yellow. There were lots of buttercups; a white rose; a creeper with a pale yellow bloom the size of a passion flower, which simply covered many of the bushes; and dozens of others whose names I do not know and whose like I had not seen before. To see such a wealth of beauty would alone have been worth a journey from England.

On reaching the pine tree elevation, we camped, though it was not the best camping ground, being on the side of the hill. I had brought with me several pen sketches of animals to show the natives, and when I talked to them they were of great assistance. After supper, Jarmee, who proved an excellent servant, ran to tell me there was a tiger on the hill. I went out at once but saw no trace of it. On returning, I saw a good many red peonies that I had not noticed before. The next morning I discovered some yellow violets, and it struck me how many of the flowers I had seen ran to yellow. At 9:20 we reached our highest point, and from the top we looked across the Tekkes to the Tian Shan. The country on the other side of the pass was great rolling hills of grass with clumps of fir.

From this point, our journey across the Tekkes to the hunting grounds was, on the whole, wearisome and monotonous, a test of the temper that Höger seemed to find particularly trying. There are, of course, interludes of interest and excitement. We sighted roebuck and wapiti; saw some interesting geese, red with yellow heads; and from time to time, as the nature of the land or the elevation changed, we passed through vast pastures deep in verdure and flowers. The chief interest, however, was human.

After crossing the Tekkes we were made welcome at Khirgiz Yurt. Yurts—great felt tents—are extremely comfortable, though inclined to be hot. They are circular and high, and packed around the inside are bedding and saddles in beautiful order. There are rugs on the ground, and in the center is a fire. We had one side at our disposal, opposite the door. Two young girls of about fifteen, with their black hair hanging around their faces in small plaits and with fur-bordered hats on their heads and long boots, attended to the fire. On the other side reclined three Khirgiz and our men.

We handed around a box of biscuits, and everybody took one. They gave us some boiled cream for our tea, which was a pleasant change; up to then we had been drinking it without sugar or milk, as there is so much camp work to teach the men. We stayed an hour, and then, giving the lady of the yurt fifty kopeks, or one shilling—which pleased her so much she wanted to kill a sheep for us—we shook hands and went outside. The principal Khirgiz held my stirrup for me while I mounted; another came to put us on the right road. The Khirgiz people throughout our journey proved almost invariably courteous and hospitable.

At one yurt I saw a fine eagle kept for hawking; Khirgiz are very fond of this sport. From another yurt they brought me a great bowl of koumiss, which I passed on to the men, and I secured an excellent photograph of them all drinking it, including a woman with her white headdress and bunch of keys. I entrusted this woman with a letter to my wife, which I hoped but did not really expect would reach its destination, but it did. In these great open spaces of the world, where communications are difficult and peoples are scattered, messages, whether native and verbal or European and written, seem to have something sacred about them that impels their bearers to deliver them at all cost.

Their chief, I found, was eager to help. His yurt was by far the best I had seen. We exchanged compliments, and a huge bowl of koumiss was placed before us. Now, if I hate anything, it is koumiss; however, it was not only necessary to taste but to drink deeply or offend the man who could help me to my sport. So three bowls of the stuff passed from the big bowl to my inside, every drop of which I loathed. Then I told the Ottoman that I wanted two hunters as guides—the best in the country—and two good mountain horses. He replied that he had heard from the Chanjung that I was coming and that he had to go to Kuldga for a big conference to settle tribal disputes, but that he had put off his journey for me, and while I was in his country everything I wanted was mine.

He then mounted his horse and led the way to show us where to camp. He chose a lovely spot in the valley of the downs, ablaze with yellow flowers, with a perfect view through a *V* of pine trees of mountain ranges in the distance and snowcapped peaks at the other end. Through this miniature valley ran a stream, and on the hill behind were the holes of ground marmot. He placed some felt on the ground, and he and his following watched with interest while we put up our tents. Before we fed them a meal, they examined everything. Our spread consisted of pieces of bread, a pot of jam, a tin of potted meat, and tea and sugar, and they put away five great slabs of bread among them, which I then thought a feat but do not now.

After this meal, we turned to business and discussed the question of men and horses. He appointed, as my guide, a man whom he said knew all the country and was a good hunter, and he promised another man for the next day. I was to pay them thirty-five rubles each a month. I tried for thirty, but he said I ought not to kick at the extra five rubles, because I would have first-class sport, so I agreed. He also said he would give me two A-1 mountain horses for fifteen rubles a month each; he would take all risks, and the loss would be his if a horse died or broke a leg. To this I also agreed. Then came the question of sheep, and I agreed to purchase half a dozen extra-large ones from him for thirty-six rubles.

Of course, this was not as simple as I write it; everyone had much to say, and it was a long time before we settled everything. I then took a picture of the group and paid the Ottoman for the sheep. He asked for the money for the horses for a month, and I replied that I would pay on my return; he said, however, that he must have the money now. He told me that, years before, an Englishman, a dark fellow, had been there and that he had returned the horses but did not pay. I told him there must have been some mistake, that I would pay him the money now and that in doing so I was trusting him, though he would not trust me. He said I should have two of his best horses and the men would show me all the game I wanted.

When all this was settled, they fingered everything about the camp. I wanted to write to my wife and my mother and send the letters by the Ottoman to Kuldga, so I dismissed them, promising to come to supper with the Ottoman later. I had very little time and scribbled for all I was worth, and then the Ottoman came back to call us to supper. The yurt was not far away, so we walked. Masses of wild onions were everywhere as we threaded our way over the hill.

The Ottoman's two sons, thirteen and fourteen, came to meet us and escorted us to the yurt, but not to the one we had been in that morning. Inside was a huge cauldron in which was boiling a whole sheep. We sat on a rug, and three women prepared the meal, while the Ottoman and his sons and two brothers sat around with a couple of other men. Two children hung around the women; one, three years old, butted his mother in the breast like any lamb, and she at once opened her dress to him.

When the sheep was boiled, pieces of it were ladled into large bowls. Water was poured over our hands and dishes were set before us, full of great hunks of boiled sheep, very fat indeed. Everyone who owned a knife (and there were few) used it, taking the meat in the hands and cutting off hunks of fat and what little lean there was; the rest used their fingers and teeth, gnawing at the bones and sucking out the marrow. The head fell to one man's lot, and he cleaned it even to the eyes. I managed to find some lean bits, but Höger could eat nothing, and the Ottoman rather felt it that we did so badly. As

each one cleaned a bone, he or she threw it into the middle of the yurt, as clean as though scraped. They swallowed astounding hunks of fat. In a very short time nothing but the clean bones were left of the sheep; they stuck the skull up in the yurt, and they then drank the soup. We washed our hands, at least the principals among us did; the rest rubbed theirs on their boots to grease them. After this we had a small bowl of tea each, and the Khirgiz, having stroked their beards or chins and muttered "Allah Akbar," rose and left the yurt, and we said good night. The eldest boy's manners, considering he lived such a life, were an endless wonder to me. He held up the flap of the yurt for us to pass out, and we made our way back to camp.

We were up at 6 A.M. and got everything packed and the tents down to show that we meant to start that day. On a carpet we ate our breakfast, and then the two wives of the Ottoman's brother arrived with a present of cream, so I gave them ten kopecks apiece and took their photographs. Soon after they had gone, the Ottoman himself appeared, and then his brothers and satellites. He brought along the two horses I was hiring from him, and my two guides, Joanai Baiseet and Souno, appeared. The only thing remaining, therefore, was the six sheep. Jarmee came along, almost crying, to say that they had given us six of the very worst, so I pretended to be in an awful rage and told the Ottoman that his name would stink in the nostrils of the whole world for trying to treat his guest in such a manner. I got six good sheep, and we packed up and started, my guides carrying my rifles.

Just before leaving, the Ottoman asked for a souvenir; he had taken a great fancy to Höger's knife and wanted that.

Höger said, "I have only one; you have three wives, would you give me one of them?"

"Certainly," the Ottoman replied. "Take your choice and hand over the knife," and he was quite cross that it was no bargain.

On reaching the Kunsoo Valley, Joanai said there were lots of ibex about, so I determined to stay a few days. On Friday, 12 June, my guides called me at 4 A.M., and at 4:30 we were off, the beginning of my hunting. We rode our horses up the hill, and jolly steep it was, but the grass was not as bad as I had been led to believe; of course, the horses felt the climb, and although it saved one's legs it is no small exertion lifting a horse up a hill at these altitudes. I was very glad of a cardigan jacket, sweater, and fur gloves, and I may here say that a walking stick and a pair of kid gloves are invaluable. The former helps tremendously, and the latter saves one's hands from getting full of the spines of a plant that grows more freely than necessary.

First of all, we saw a fox. It was a small beggar, and, though it was anxious to get away from us, the hill was so steep that it had difficulty getting up at all. Then, by not taking sufficient care, the men scared a couple of ewes. Afterward, with my glass, I spotted four ibex, two females, and two males with small horns that at once commenced fighting. The wind was changing into every direction, but I attempted a stalk, which proved a failure. Then we started a band of female ibex. With my telescope I counted twenty-five of them and fourteen kids—some had one kid and some had two—and I daresay several were young males, but there was not a male horn worth having among them. The climbing was stiff work on account of the elevation, and I found it necessary to sit down often, but it was not at all difficult or dangerous. There were a lot of snowcock, but they were very wild and flew from one hillside to another far out of reach. I spent the afternoon in camp, and the following day we moved down the valley and ascended the next ridge.

It was a fruitless climb, during which all we saw was what I assumed to be a band of female ibex, though the men said they were rams with short horns and many twists. Shooting one for the pot demonstrated that my assumption was right. Later we came to a place that looked likely and dismounted, and I began to spy and before long made out a band of rams. I pointed them out to the men, and then, leaving Souno with the horses, started with Joanai. Through my glasses I had seen there were eleven rams and that one of them carried a grand head, so I decided to make the stalk myself, and Joanai followed me. When I got to where they ought to be, there was no sign of the band, so I tried one direction without result. Joanai said they had seen or smelled me, which I knew they had not done, so I told him to look for tracks. These he found, and we followed. Just in time I spotted the ibex and dropped to the ground, and Joanai followed suit; as a gunbearer he is quite good.

What a sight it was, this band of great rams! A sight that repaid one for the long and wearisome journey. I took the rifle from Joanai and tried to get to close quarters, but they had got themselves in too good a position, and the best I could do was about two hundred and fifty yards; with the naked eye I could not see their horns. With my glasses I saw the band was restless, facing my way, and that the master ram was lying down, so all I could do was to wait for him to get up. There were some good rams in the bunch, but the master ram was by far the best of the lot. At last it got up, and I fired. I was quite steady, and, as far as I could say, I made a good shot, but it dashed away, and I thought I had missed it. The band ran downhill at its very best pace, but stopped a second, and I fired again at another, but they all went on. The distance was so great that I knew it was only a chance to hit.

They were now too far to shoot any more. I took up my glasses and then saw the master ram was hit: Blood was running down its legs. I pointed it out to Joanai, and he said, "Yes," which was the only word of English he knew. We ran like hares to the horses and then tried to find the band again. When we did, they were going up the steep side of the opposite valley. I counted them, and there were only ten. I thought the big ram was mine, but when I got out my telescope I saw, alas! It was with them, but sick, very sick, and its foreleg was quite red with the blood pouring down it from the top to the bottom, but I could not actually see the wound.

The other ram I had fired at was lying somewhere, but I was too keen on the big fellow to think about it then, and we watched the wounded one for an hour. I thought it could not possibly follow the others, but it managed to do so and, with three others, reached the summit and disappeared. The other six went in another direction, but I did not trouble about them.

It was now late, so I returned to camp. I got there at 6 P.M., having been out thirteen hours, five of which were taken up with the two stalks. In the evening I had my two hunters up to find out what they thought of the day's proceedings. They agreed that the big ram must die and had great hopes of dining on it the next day. Joanai also said that he had never seen such horns in his forty-one years and that no

European had ever killed one like it. He also said that the other ram must be dead somewhere and that we would probably find it.

Unfortunately, the prediction was not correct. Although we spotted and stalked the smaller of the rams, it passed over the ridge and, when at last we got around, was nowhere to be seen. During the morning there were a lot of foxes about, the size of the Arctic fox but gray and brown. I saw eight altogether, and they were all getting their breakfast by pouncing like cats on the mice in the grass.

The following morning we again took to the mountains. The first place we reached was an ideal spot for game, but my two men began talking at the top of their voices and startled a maral hind and calf. The next valley—or, rather, succession of valleys, for we could look over several ridges—contained a band of forty-seven female ibex with their kids and three male ibex, who were easily distinguished by their heavier build. With my telescope I could just make out their horns. I decided to go after them, and it took one hour and fifty minutes with the horses and forty minutes on foot to get to the place we had last seen them. But there everything ended; we could not see them anywhere among the rough country into which they had gone, although we hunted for them a long time. It was now very hot, and there was nothing more to be done, so we made tracks for camp, getting there at 2:30. I found by my aneroid that one rides up to about 11,700 feet and hunts the rest on foot.

At about ten thousand feet the flowers were usually at their best. There were great quantities of a large yellow flower like a marsh marigold, and also of a white flower like a multiflora narcissus. There were many other flowers and something like a wild cabbage; real wild rhubarb; and two kinds of wild onion, one with a blue and the other with a red flower. While we were looking for the ibex, I saw a most beautiful snowcock, or rather snow hen. Its body was speckly brown, its head was yellow with two broad bands of dark chestnut along each side of the face. With it was a brood of chicks. (On my return home I looked through the snowcocks at the South Kensington Museum but could not find anything like it among them.)

On the way back, within an hour of camp, we came upon the winter quarters of the Kalmuks, and I took a photograph of their primitive dwelling. Farther on I came on two Kalmuk hunters crouched on a ledge of rock that they had selected for their camping ground. I took a photograph of them also and stayed while Joanai and Souno talked with them, and then we galloped for camp. Between camp and our hunting ground of that day ran the Kunsoo River, and when we crossed it that morning it was comparatively shallow—that is to say, I got across only wetting my boots and puttees. But when we returned in the afternoon it was a different story; the sun had been burning down on the snow for hours, and a thousand rivulets and streams had been adding their volume to the river's own water. Although the river was narrow, a raging torrent divided us from camp.

Joanai took away my whip and told me to wind the horse's mane around my hands; then he took my bridle, and Souno on the other side also held onto the mane, and thus we entered the water. In a second the horses were washed off their feet; the men yelled; the horses strained every nerve to reach the other side as the water washed over the saddles and wetted us to the middle. For a few seconds I thought we would be carried away into the river. Then the horses found their feet and carried us safely to land. Last year, they told me, fifteen Khirgiz drowned in this way. It was not an experience I wanted to go through again.

CHAPTER TWENTY-TWO

H. FRANK WALLACE

H. Frank Wallace had already been recognized as a stalker extraordinaire after years of hunting red deer in Scotland. While on his hunting expedition through China's Kansu Province with George Fenwick-Owen in 1911, he utilized his stalking skills in pursuit of bharal, the famous blue sheep of northern China.

Wallace said the sheep's horns were "smooth, growing more or less at right angles to the skull, and curve upwards and backwards at the tips." With respect to color, he noted the sheep were usually "gray-brown, though in certain aspects there is a decidedly blue tinge, hence the name 'blue sheep.'"

In this chapter from his book The Big Game of Central and Western China *(1913), Wallace describes his pursuit of blue sheep.*

BLUE SHEEP OF KANSU

It was on 25 September that our luck turned. The morning dawned clear and bright, and we were off at sunrise. For the first mile or so we went along the banks of the little mountain river on whose northern bank we were camped. We had decided the night before that George was to hunt on the "Matterhorn," as we had christened the snow-covered triangular mass of rock that rose at the far end of the valley. I branched off to the north with Lao-Wei, as I had seen a number of ewes with a ram on this ground a few days before and had not been able to get near them.

We went for half a mile through thick bush, past a woodcutter's camp, and presently emerged on a small flat from which a steep ridge gradually rose to the higher tops. We had hardly pulled out our glasses when my hunter exclaimed, *"Ngaiyang!"* Far, far above me, where the first rays of the morning sun were just striking, I saw four ewes. They were leisurely walking over the skyline, stopping to nibble every now and again and gazing down into the shadows of the valley. We hurried on through the belt of trees that grew along the lower slopes of the valley, and at our next spy we saw the whole herd of a dozen animals lying amidst the rocks, surrounding a ram whose head was silhouetted in magnificence against a backdrop of deep blue.

It was an easy stalk; the wind was strong from the east, and the ground was favorable. Though not overly prone to count my heads before they have fallen, I confess that I felt very sanguine about getting a shot at the ram within the next two hours. I accordingly set out on the climb that lay before me. When we were about halfway up, Lao-Wei suddenly remembered he had left my camera behind. I sent him back for it, climbed on, and spied again. The herd was still lying peacefully on the crest of the ridge where we had just seen them—a good view of the corrie before them, the wind on their flank, and the pinnacle of rock rising one hundred and twenty yards behind them, from which I expected to obtain my shot.

I turned to look for the hunter and saw him wildly gesticulating and waving on the slope below. At a loss to understand his frantic signals, I followed their direction and was horrified to find no less than three Tibetans, bent double under their loads, wending their deliberate and preordained course immediately through the center of the corrie. The sheep were bound to see them, and my hopes sank to zero.

I am loath to confess it, but I have in the past entertained feelings of aversion to several individuals. I hated a Scotch shepherd who appeared on the skyline within fifty yards of a very fine stag I was stalking; I hated a Mormon baby in whose company I once traveled to Salt Lake City; I hated a man who got too windward of me on a rough day crossing the Channel; but never did I hate anyone as I did those three wretched Tibetans! I rushed up the hill ("rush" is a purely metaphorical word), and Lao-Wei rushed after me. The three miscreants, seeing a foreign devil armed with a rifle, his empurpled and streaming visage lifted toward them, and understanding—as I did not—the guttural anathemas of his follower, rushed precipitately over the crest of the hill, and the sheep, alas, catching momentary glimpses of these events, leisurely disappeared over the ridge.

It took us a good half-hour to reach the spot. Cautiously we peered over each crest; stealthily we crept along a knife-edge of rock overhanging a big basin and spied; Lao-Wei even threw rocks down in disgust; but not a thing stirred. A great eagle swept around us in ever-widening circles, silently contemplating the scene.

On our way up the hill we had seen a couple of ewes with their lambs. They had whistled derisively at us, but, in spite of my companion's earnest solicitations, I had refused to shoot. The sheep we were after seemed to have vanished. We could see them nowhere in front, so, as a forlorn hope, we retraced our steps to the ewes. They placidly fed where we had left them, and no ram gladdened our eyes. Had the herd passed them, they would certainly have moved, so it seemed that the ram must be somewhere in front of us. We clambered back up the hill—after I had made a sketch or two of the ewes, much to Lao-Wei's disgust, for his bloodthirsty mood had not evaporated—reached the top, and sat down to eat our sandwiches. It was then that, very faint and far away, I heard two shots. George, at any rate, had had some luck.

We now faced the opposite side of the corrie down which we had stealthily crept an hour or so earlier. The eastern side was overgrown with rhododendron bushes; the western side presented a chaos of rocks, slides, small patches of grass, and an ineffectual covering of bushes and stunted firs. In desperation, I pulled out my glass for one last spy—and found it focused on five sheep. There was no ram among them, but the rest of the herd could not be far off. I pointed them out to my companion and held up five fingers. He took the glass and held up nine. It was ten minutes before I made out the rest, and then discovered twelve in all, including the ram. They moved slowly and with agility across the face of the cliffs, reached the slope of the face, and turned helter-skelter back for no apparent reason. In a few minutes they settled to feed up a narrow crevice in the rocks, and we, crawling out of sight, pounded up the slope.

They were in full view when we reached the summit, feeding away among the rhododendrons three hundred yards below us. It seemed certain they would cross into the corrie from which the three men had dislodged them in the morning, so we continued on our way and presently lay safely sheltered among the rocks. Every second, I expected the leading ewe's head to appear, but half an hour passed in silence, and the suspense became too great. We crawled down the hill to a spot that commanded a view of the basin and looked over. There we saw them, well out of shot, their old course abandoned, working steadily away from us. We went back and around the shoulder of the hill, then down the ridge they had to cross to leave the basin.

As I peered through the grasses, I fully anticipated seeing them within shot, but there was not a sign of a sheep anywhere. Lao-Wei declared that they had already crossed and that we were too late. It seemed scarcely possible that they had had time to do so, but he seemed certain of it, so I sent him back to a spot from which he could spy, to see if they were still below us. He disappeared over the rocks, and presently I saw him, a diminutive figure, far back on the ridge. He moved stealthily from rock to rock, peering into the mass of boulders beneath him, then straightened himself. He was right and I was wrong! Up the hill I went again, and he joined me.

Hope still flickered within me, but it was faint. The evening was drawing in, and as I looked over into the corrie where the sheep had fed in the morning I felt anything but sanguine. There lay the big ram, and there too, within shot of me, as I realized with a gasp of surprise, were the sheep, placidly feeding, after all the fluctuating fortunes of the day. It seemed as if they had never moved from the spot where I had first seen them. These are the moments that come back to one, and that is the moment I remember as I conjure up again the grassy corries and rocky tops of the Kansu sheep ground. Those last few yards—how exciting they are, when the stalker's skill and experience, pitted against the marvelously acute senses of a really wild animal, seem at last as if they are about to triumph. The big ram and a smaller one, the ten ewes, and the two mothers with their lambs were there.

I doubled back around the hill, Lao-Wei after me. Three minutes later, we lay in a convenient hollow, sheltered by a rock within a hundred yards of the beast. It was partially hidden by a dip in the ground; another three yards would have brought it broadside on in full view, but the aggravating animal lay down. I could just see the tip of one of its horns. There we lay for half an hour, suspiciously watched by a malignant and youthful ram. During the wait, Lao-Wei carried on a violent altercation with me, employing signs and grimaces, and he ended in sulky subsidence. His object was to induce me to fire at the small beast, whose attention he had gratuitously attracted by his gesticulations, and to take my chance at the big one afterward. I was equally determined to wait until a good chance at the latter presented itself.

The light was fast waning, and at length, somewhat reluctantly, I made my follower pitch a few small stones onto a rock slide that ran down the hill on our right. The first had "absolutely no effec' wha'ever," as my wine merchant at Oxford used to say of his favorite claret. At the third, the small ram leapt from its rock as if shot from a catapult; the alarm spread, and the whole herd made off. The big ram, mercifully alone, stood for a second—and I ignominiously missed it! As it galloped after the ewes, I again pulled the trigger. Result—a misfire. Just on the edge of the corrie—the ewes were already streaming over—it paused for a last look. As I fired, a couple of stragglers came up, and they dashed out of sight in a bunch. We tore to the crest of the ridge. A second later, the sheep appeared.

In vain I scanned each head. The ram was missing. Who has ever adequately depicted the mingled waves of hope and fear that fill the stalker's heart at such a moment! And yet my hopes were strong, for, unwounded, the ram would have been well to the fore. For a moment or so we stood there waiting, while Lao-Wei openly expressed his grief at my miss. Then, from behind a tuft of grass emerged a horn. It swayed, drooped, and was followed by a head. It was the ram. It walked a few paces very slowly, wavered, and hesitated. Then its legs collapsed, and with gathering speed it rolled five hundred feet to the foot of the gully.

CHAPTER TWENTY-THREE

ST. GEORGE LITTLEDALE

St. George Littledale, one of the Victorian era's most renowned sheep hunters, left no books to recount his adventures in the Altai of Mongolia, the Caucasus, the Pamirs, or Kamchatka. His written works, for the most part, appeared in journals and consisted of detailed descriptions of his travels in remote regions of Central Asia. One such article, "A Journey across Tibet from North to South and West to Ladakh," appeared in an issue of the Geographical Journal *in 1896 and is indicative of his keen eye for terrain, climate, and the customs of indigenous peoples.*

Though an ardent explorer and geographer, Littledale's passion was hunting bighorn sheep. His wife often joined him on his expeditions, and he, in turn, accompanied the famous Russian sportsman Elim Demidoff on various shooting excursions. A subspecies of sheep he collected, Ovis ammon littledalei, *would be named after him.*

Littledale contributed several articles on Asian sporting experiences to the Big-Game Shooting *volumes of* The Badminton Library of Sports and Pastimes *collection, which exalted all kinds of British sport, from dancing and boxing to the shooting sports. This excerpt appeared in that collection.*

THE *OVIS POLI* OF THE PAMIR

The Great Pamir, or "roof of the world," forms the nucleus of the whole Central Asiatic highland system. It consists of a vast plateau formation of some thirteen thousand square miles, with a mean elevation of at least fifteen thousand feet.

This, briefly, is what modern geographers have to say of the home of *Ovis poli* (Asiatic wild sheep):

> The plain is called Pamir, and you ride across it for twelve days together—finding nothing but a desert without habitations or any green thing, so that travelers are obliged to carry with them whatever they have need of; northeast, you travel forty days over mountains and wilderness, and you find no green thing. There are

> numbers of wild beasts—among others, wild sheep of great size, whose horns are a good six palms in length. From these horns shepherds make great bowls to eat from, and they use the horns also to make folds for their cattle at night.

Marco Polo wrote in a similar way of the Pamir six hundred years ago, and, six centuries earlier still, some Chinese pilgrims described it as "midway between heaven and earth. The snowdrifts never cease, winter or summer: The whole tract is but a dreary waste without a trace of human kind."

These descriptions are nearly as true today as they were when they were first written, and this Pamir is the home of the grandest of all the sheep tribes, *Ovis poli*.

Until recently, the Pamir was considered one of the most inaccessible places in Asia. The Trans-Caspian Railway, which opened in May 1888 from the Caspian to Samarkand, has completely altered this state of affairs, though the Russian government looks with disfavor on English travelers wishing to use the line it so cheaply and expeditiously constructed for purely military and strategical purposes.

Had it not been for the several months of untiring effort of Sir Robert Morier, our Ambassador at St. Petersburg, I should never have allayed the natural suspicions of the Russian officials in the Asiatic and War Department and obtained the necessary permission to travel by that route. I entirely owe the success of our expedition to his efforts, and I can never sufficiently thank him for the trouble he took.

But had I known as much about Russian Central Asia as I do now, I would not have waited for the railway. I would have crossed the steppes to Khokand and from there traveled south to the Pamir, years ago. There are three routes by which it is possible to reach the Pamir. The first is from Ladakh over the Karakoram to Shah Dula, and then west, either from Yarkand or from a point before you reach the city. For this route it would be necessary to have a passport from the Chinese government, which, though much easier to obtain now than it was formerly, is still by no means easy to get, and, having obtained it, there is no certainty that the government would not throw obstacles in the path of anyone wishing to visit the Pamir from the

Chinese side. The second route is via Gilgit, Yassim, Chitral, and Badakshan, but the political difficulties at present render this out of the question. The third is by the Trans-Caspian Railway.

I have made two visits to the Pamir, the first in 1888 and the second in 1890, and Mrs. Littledale accompanied me on both occasions. In 1888 I did not know anything about the country or the chances of sport, beyond the mere fact that the Pamir was the habitat of the *poli* sheep, but as to which particular district I ought to visit, or what special outfit I ought to take with me, I could obtain no information, either in England or in Russia. However, I had the good fortune to meet the Rev. Dr. H. Lansdell, who gave me valuable advice as to the route to Khokand.

From the Russian officials we received the greatest civility on all sides. Whatever antagonism there may be between the two countries politically, it begins and ends with politics, for socially at the present day there is no nation more popular in Russia than the English, nor do I know any country wherein a man bearing proper letters of introduction will be made to feel more at home than in Russia.

Saturday, 5 August 1888, found Mrs. Littledale and myself camped in a valley, flat as a billiard table and about two miles wide. It was one vast riverbed of soft shingle, cut up into countless channels that varied day by day, almost minute by minute. One or two hours of sunshine brought down a flood like a mill race, which cut new channels and left old ones dry, making a channel that was difficult to ford in the morning almost dry by night, and moving the main stream maybe half a mile away.

The place was an idyll of desolation; there was not a shrub, a bird, or a living soul in sight. The few blades of grass that appeared here and there among the debris fallen from the cliffs above, had a halfhearted air, as if they knew that they were out of place. The mountains on either side were forbidding. Down their rugged sides dashed torrents from the glaciers above. The head of the valley was blocked by grand peaks that reared their proud summits to a height of twenty thousand feet or more. There they stood (and stand), unnamed, unmeasured, and unknown, waiting for someone to conquer their virgin snows.

It had been no easy task to persuade our Kara-Kirghiz hunters to come to this place at all. They asked why I wanted to go. They said there was no grass there, that the horses would die of starvation, and did I think that the *gulja* (the Kirghiz name for *poli* rams) would stay in a place where there was nothing to eat? For generations their fathers had been hunters, and did I, a stranger, know better than they?

I pointed out to them that we had everywhere found skulls of fine old rams from ten to fifteen years old, and yet we had hitherto seen no ram over five years old in the flesh. How did they account for that? They replied that no Kirghiz had ever seen one of the big ones alive. "Then," said I, "come with me, and I will try to show them to you," for I felt perfectly certain that the *poli* were no different in their habits from the *Ammon* and the bighorn, and that it was only a question of time before we found the old rams in some secluded spot, away from the females. The event would show that I was right.

We left camp one morning around 4:30 A.M. and rode up the main valley for an hour or so. This brought us to the mouth of a side valley, and we turned up it, keeping to the east side so as to be in shadow. The elder Kirghiz, named Dewanna, soon detected something about two miles away, on high, undulating ground across the valley. He was using binoculars, and though I tried to use my telescope my fingers were so numb with cold that it was quite impossible to hold it steady. After some little scrutiny, we all decided that the beasts were *arkar*, or female *poli,* and continued on our course about another mile, when we came to some extremely likely-looking ground, which made us pause again to take a good look ahead. By this time a little warmth had come back into my fingers, and I was able to use my Ross's telescope again. After carefully spying over the ground and finding nothing, I turned the glass to our old friends, the *arkar*. The moment the glass was still, one look was sufficient. Down went the telescope, and I crept forward, dragging my pony out of sight, while the Kirghiz, divining that I had seen something, promptly followed my example.

What a sight that glass revealed! Twenty-six old *poli* rams in a band, and the smallest of them larger than anything I had yet seen. Luckily for us, we had kept under the shadow of the rocks, but for that, we would have been in full view of the rams for a quarter of an hour. They were still quietly feeding, unconscious of the deadly peril to which they were exposed.

Men who are not sportsmen can hardly realize what my feelings were when I discovered that at last I had in front of me so many splendid specimens of an animal that for years had been the dream of every British sportsman in the East. Years before, when in Kashmir, my wife and I had discussed every possible means of getting at the noble beast, but the more we talked with those most likely to know, the more we were convinced that any attempt during those times would be hopeless, and we had to content ourselves with the thought that, when in the Gilgit country, we had been within sixty or seventy miles as the crow flies from the inaccessible Pamir.

I may remark here, in passing, that the honor of having brought to Europe the first entire specimens of *poli* is due to the Russians Karelin and Severtzoff. I believe the members of the Yarkand Expedition can claim "first blood" among Englishmen.

As I looked at those old rams, some browsing, some lying down, my thoughts wandered back a dozen years to when, on the slopes of that stupendous Nanga Parbat in Astor on a misty morning in May, three ibex (the smallest thirty-eight inches) bit the dust. Again my imagination jumped forward to an autumn in the frosty Caucasus, when three royal red deer stags fell in almost as many seconds. On occasions like these, one's thoughts are always rose-colored. It is only the red-letter days that come forward. Pushed into the background are the long, trying stalks, when perhaps for an hour you have stood up to your knees in an icy stream, not daring to move, for movement meant instant detection. Forgotten, too, is that last critical moment when, as your head rose higher and higher above the rock that had been your objective point for hours, your hopes sank lower and lower until the hideous truth became plain to you—that the head you had almost counted as your own had gone, never to gladden your eyes again. Or it may be that there was even worse luck to forget: when, on account of wind or light or a tired man's labored breathing, a .500 Express bullet was driven by six drams of powder *just over* a big beast's back!

The rams we had sighted were on the other side of the valley, the bottom of which was about a mile and a half wide, quite flat and without any cover. To get at them we either had to retrace our steps for about two miles, when we could cross unseen, or go forward about a mile. The Kirghiz were both in favor of going forward, but I wished to go back, and it was very much against my will that I let them have their own way. The rams were on the lee side of the hill and near the top, which is always a most difficult position; in fact, if the game is within one hundred or one hundred and fifty yards of the top, and the hill is pyramidal in shape (which this hill was not), I think "it passes the wit of man" to approach them, for, from whichever side you try, you will find them either with the true wind or with the shifting eddy leeward of you. It is a position of nearly absolute safety for the rams.

We kept behind the moraine of an old glacier, and a shoulder of the hill finally shut our quarry out of view so that we were able to cross the valley. In the middle of the valley there was a rapid stream, and the younger Kirghiz, having stripped, carried Dewanna and came back afterward for me. Unfortunately, when we were nearly across, my carrier slipped and almost came down, wetting me to the knees in ice water as cold as only fresh water from a glacier can be. After a stiff climb of about an hour, we reached the top of a small ridge from which we expected to view the rams, but, though we glassed every yard carefully, we could see nothing of them. All the while I knew that we were standing on wrong principles, and when at last, after a most careful climb, we found we had run into an eddy of wind and the sheep had vanished, it caused me no surprise.

For several hours after this, we walked on slowly, spying every yard as we went, for tracking on this stony ground was hopeless. On reaching a spot where the hill broke off sharply, we lay down and examined the ground, which was very much broken up into little valleys filled with great boulders. The lee side of any one of these valleys was a likely place for the rams.

When the Kirghiz hunters first joined us, I had told the interpreter to explain to them the use of field glasses. They had all laughed at the idea of finding game with such things; now they constantly wanted

to borrow them. For about half an hour we lay spying, both with binoculars and telescope, and Dewanna had just risen to his feet, saying there was nothing, when I saw by the young Kirghiz's manner that he had seen something. I was just in time to drag Dewanna down when, over a brow below us, came a fine *poli,* followed by two others, all beasts with good heads. After a few minutes, the three lay down close together near the bottom of a small ravine, and we had a good look at them through a telescope. They were magnificent fellows, possibly part of the big group we had seen in the morning.

The Kirghiz wanted to drive the rams, and I promptly vetoed the proposition. What is it, I wonder, that all over the world makes the natives so desperately keen about driving? I could easily account for it if the general knowledge of stalking were as limited as that of the Kirghiz, who spoiled several of my earlier stalks by showing themselves behind me while I was "worming" my way up to game, and who seemed quite ignorant of the fatal results of showing oneself upon a skyline. But it is not only the Kirghiz, for in the Caucasus two men whom I employed, perfect masters of the stalker's art—quite as good as the best of the Kashmir shikaris—were always tempting me to "drive." I am glad to say that the only time I was weak enough to yield to their solicitations the drive ended in a fiasco. Taking the younger Kirghiz with me to carry the rifle, and leaving Dewanna to watch and to signal to us the direction of any movement on the part of the rams, I took the precaution of picking up a good supply of small stones with which to pelt my man whenever I found him going too fast ahead of me. The fellow had most wonderfully quick sight, so I used to send him ahead of us. On previous occasions he had got so carried away with excitement that I had to be perpetually running after him to stop him. At that altitude (more than sixteen thousand feet above sea level) I found that I could not shoot unless I had been walking with the greatest circumspection, so it was necessary to recall him now and again by this simple and easy system of telegraphy.

Keeping well out of sight along the ridge, we found a little watercourse down which we could descend without being seen.

Having carefully searched every inch of ground to make sure that there was no other *poli* in our path that might spoil our stalk, we crept down to within three hundred yards of where we had last seen our three rams. Here the Kirghiz took off his sandals, while I took the Henry double express out of its cover, made sure that all was ready, and then handed it back to him, because every extra pound one carries adds to the difficulty of keeping one's breath.

I was shod in tennis shoes with red rubber soles three-quarters of an inch thick. To my mind these are the perfect footgear for stalking, because they are perfectly noiseless, will outwear two ordinary leather soles among the rocks, and are only dangerous on snow or ice.

Softly as mice we crept up the slope of a little ridge on the farther side of which we had last seen the *poli*. Our man on the hill made no sign, so all was right so far. A little short of the top, I took the rifle and crept up the last few yards alone. Peeping over the top, I could just see the tip of a horn behind a rock about one hundred yards below. I took off my cap to place my rifle upon it, for, if it were fired resting on a rock without a pad, the jar would send the bullet wide. I cocked the weapon and lay there waiting.

The wind was right, and the moment the sheep moved they would be at my mercy. While waiting, I sent the Kirghiz about ten yards to my right to see if he could make out in which position the big one was lying. From my point of view they were half hidden, and it was difficult to say for certain which was the big head.

Suddenly they jumped up and stood for one moment looking up the hill. The big one was end on, facing me, but I had had a good rest, my heart had ceased to beat wildly, and my hand was steady, so I squeezed the trigger gradually and firmly. The report was followed by the loud smack that tells an old hand all he wants to know. Not wasting a look on the big one, I shifted the sights to one of the others and fired just as it bounded off. Another smack told me that bullet, too, had found its target, but the beast made off with its companions.

Dashing frantically down the hill and up the other side of a small ravine, I saw one *poli* standing and looking about, two hundred and fifty yards off. Lying down, I tried to take careful aim, but I found the rifle was pointing ten feet over its back one second and twenty feet below it the next. This was no good, so I lay quiet in the hope that the sheep might be so unsophisticated as to stay there until my poor panting frame recovered its steadiness, but, alas, in a few seconds it was off.

I was satisfied that the beast was unhurt, and the wounded one probably lay between us and it, so at once I took up the search for the lost sheep. Dewanna, on the hill, now came in handy, directing us by a prearranged code of signals.

Presently Dewanna got very excited and kept signaling "below, below." We were then at the bottom of the valley, and were at a loss to know how to go any lower, when out from behind a large boulder came the *poli,* very sick indeed, but, to make sure, I gave it another barrel and rushed up to gloat over my latest prize, measuring 59 inches along the left horn and 58½ inches along the right.

I then started up the hill back to where the first one lay. When I got up to it, I was rather disappointed because I had thought that it was bigger than its comrade. I pulled out the tape and began to measure: "Sixty, sixty-one, two, two and a half"—thank goodness, at last I had got a trophy that would hold its own in any company, and one that will still be a comfort, a joy, and a thing of beauty when old Time has so stiffened my joints that this most glorious and exciting of all sports will be only a memory.

Having skinned our beasts and packed their heads on one pony, the younger Kirghiz, careless of the possibility of a fall and consequent impalement, somehow twisted himself in among the horns on the pony's back, and he rode while we went on foot back to camp. The waning glories of the sky—the dark shadows stealthily creeping across the snows and the little rills frozen into silence—warned us that the Night King was coming and that it was well to hurry. When we reached camp, our interpreter met us, and I think everyone echoed his *"Vraiment, c'est assez grand!"* as the men scrutinized my first big head.

In 1888 we had wandered about until we found the valley in which the above took place, and then, having discovered a good hunting ground, got to work. We bagged fifteen rams, all but four with horns over fifty inches and several with horns longer than sixty inches.

In 1890 we decided to try the southern Pamir, since all the natives agreed that the farther south one went, the bigger the heads became. But a visit to the southern Pamir meant much more elaborate preparation than before, and our modest little caravan of twelve horses in 1888 swelled to the considerable number of forty in 1890. It was necessary to take food for ourselves and our men and also for the animals, and for each horse carrying a load of baggage we had to have an extra horse carrying barley to feed it. Besides this, we took four or five horse loads of firewood, for there are long stretches of the Pamir that are absolutely devoid of vegetation of any kind—places where even the travelers' "standby" fuel, *Boortsa eurotia,* is not to be found. Without *Boortsa eurotia*, life on the high timberless plateau of Central Asia is indeed hard, for that insignificant-looking plant affords splendid fuel. Green or dry, it makes a blazing fire, and though it wants constant attention and soon burns out, where there is no dry dung it is a perfect godsend.

We had made up our minds not to return by Turkestan if we could get across the Hindu Kush and down into India, but our chance of getting through was very uncertain, so we were obliged to secure our retreat by establishing, along the return route, depots of barley, flour, firewood, and the like, all of which entailed extra transport.

Our tent was lined and had a double fly, but, during the furious gales that even in summer sweep over the Pamir, we found it so cold and troublesome to keep upright that on our second expedition we took with us a couple of Kirghiz yurts in addition. The yurts are not fastened to the ground in any way, but because of their domed shape they never showed the slightest tendency to blow over. Once inside our yurt we had no fear of a stormy evening, nor did we ever have to rush out in scanty garments on a bitter night to refasten some yielding tent peg.

On the Abchur Pamir there were immense quantities of *poli* horns, most of them of very large. One head measured about sixty-nine inches, though Sir Frederick Roberts showed me an even larger one at Simla and kindly allowed me to photograph it. The Maharajah of Kashmir had given the head to him, and, as far as I know, it is the biggest head on record: length, 75 inches; tip to tip, 54½ inches; circumference at the base, 16 inches.

Let me recall one day of my 1890 expedition as another sample of *poli* shooting I have done. At the end of June we had camped by Victoria Lake, which was still three-quarters frozen, and after a short and fruitless hunt we had recrossed to find the Alichur Pamir. The weather was changeable and the wind shifty, but our sport had been fair. One stormy evening I spied three rams a long way off. Before we reached them, a flurry of snow hid them from us, and when the snow cleared we could not see them. We decided that they must have gone over the hill for shelter, but when we looked for them they unfortunately got our wind and, bolting out from some rocks, dashed across an open piece of ground.

I put the two-hundred-yard sight up and fired at the center one, which was a monster, towering above its two companions. It was by far the biggest sheep I had ever seen—its horns, I should fancy, certainly measured something over seventy inches. I saw the dust fly just over its back and had no time for a second shot before the sheep disappeared in a dip of the ground. I felt low at missing such a grand fellow, but it was a running shot at quite two hundred yards, and a hit would have been more or less of a fluke.

The sheep were a very long time coming up the other side of the ravine, so we went to see what had kept them and found that the two smaller sheep were waiting for the big fellow, who was lagging wearily behind. As soon as they had got over the ridge, we followed them and found their track, which was very bloody. My bullet, instead of going over my beast, must have gone through it without expanding, and it was not long before we found it lying down on a snowbank streaked with its blood. Here I could have stalked and finished it, but one of the Kirghiz, in his excitement, showed himself and made the beast get up again. After this the beast kept lying down at intervals, traveling a shorter distance and resting longer each time.

The vitality of *Ovis poli* is something extraordinary. Here was a beast shot through the lungs, as was proved by the frothy blood that poured from its wounds, and yet it went eight hundred or a thousand feet up a snowy slope. Having allowed it to get out of sight, we followed it, but just as we reached the top of the slope a heavy storm obliterated everything in six inches of fresh snow. As soon as the storm was over, numbed and cold though I was, I tried to follow by kicking the new snow away with my feet till I found blood, but eventually I lost the ram and had to leave it. It was a terrible disappointment, for I fear I shall never look upon its like again.

I now had to turn my attention to my Kirghiz companion, who had become violently ill and lay there unable to move. I had no brandy to give him and not even a coat to wrap him up in, for we had left our sheepskins at the bottom of the hill. However, I rubbed his hands vigorously, and after a time he recovered sufficiently to descend, leaning upon my shoulder. I believe it was nothing but the altitude that affected him. Extraordinary as it may seem, two weeks before, two other Kirghiz who regularly spent four or five months of the year on the great Altai, as their forefathers had done before them, had succumbed to the additional two or three thousand feet elevation at which they found themselves with me and had been compelled to leave the Pamir.

CHAPTER TWENTY-FOUR

CAPT. J. N. PRICE WOOD

Capt. John Nicholas Price Wood was typical of the brotherhood of British officers who traveled, explored, and hunted in the vast reaches of the British Empire. Wood, an officer in the 12th Royal Lancers, had planned for several years to take his leave time for a shooting trip to the Tian Shan Range. The frontier locale shared by Imperial Russia, China, and Great Britain, however, was a sensitive strategic region during the early twentieth century, as competing powers played the Great Game to achieve dominance and security in the remote areas of central Asia.

Eventually Captain Wood received the necessary permits to travel. He journeyed through lofty landscapes, finally reaching the shooting grounds of the Koksu region of Chinese Turkistan. There he enjoyed a wealth of big-game hunting experiences. Wood's only book, Travel and Sport in Turkistan *(1910), captured the flavor of this remote area, its tribal peoples, and the excitement of the chase.*

A MIXED BAG IN THE KOKSU

August 26—The day started badly but improved, and later on the sun came out. I saw only two lots of ewes, but we shifted camp about seven miles in the direction of Karatash, and the men behind with my baggage saw six *(Ovis ammon) karelini* that they said were shootable. I had passed them in the mist when I first left camp. I noticed a place exactly like that made in England by a man digging out a rabbit burrow. I asked what this was and was told it had been made by a hungry bear looking for a marmot. I hope the bear caught it.

August 27—A fine day. Went north and spied everywhere but could only find some ibex. I shot the best of these for meat, as I had not had a shot since leaving the Pamirs. Unable to get near, I guessed the range at two hundred yards but went low and only got my beast (41½ inches) with the third shot, as it foolishly came toward me when disabled by my second shot. I then transferred my attention to the next-biggest ibex, which I hit through the middle. This beast lay down close, too, but when I pursued, it made off and reached the opposite side of a steep gully, which I could not cross. I expended no less than thirteen cartridges on finishing it, chiefly because my man, watching through a glass, kept telling me that my bullets were going high. The fact was that, as often happens, what he took for the strike of the bullet was really a ricochet or stone, thrown up perhaps as much as five feet above where the bullet had really struck. The distance was actually about three hundred yards. Of course, one ought not to shoot at an animal so far off, but it was only a question of finishing off a beast that could not go far, and there was no danger of wounding any other, so no harm was done. Rain again commenced about 6 P.M., and continued until I went to bed at 9:15 P.M.

August 28—We started late again (about 10 A.M.) on account of the rain, and moved camp another seven miles toward Karatash. Around 2 P.M. I set out from this new camp, but I had no sooner reached the place from which I wanted to spy when down came the clouds again, and we could see nothing. We therefore returned to camp in a good wetting rain. On the way we found the skull and backbone of a *karelini* some months dead; its longest horn (the tip of the other was broken off) measured 55½ inches. I wish I could manage to find and shoot one or two of that size. Elevation of camp, 8,700 feet.

August 29—Clouds low all day and rain most of the time, so it was useless to leave camp. Snow fell last night to the 10,500-feet level. In the afternoon, too late to stalk, we saw some animals descending over the snows to the north. We hoped these were *karelini*, but Namgoon, on being sent to reconnoiter, reported they were all ibex.

August 30—It was a fine morning, and we left camp at 6 A.M. and tried the hills to the south. During the first five hours I saw only a herd of ibex, and then, at 11 A.M., we came on a herd of seven *karelini* in a nullah. They either heard Namgoon or winded us, for they moved off at once. The first was a dark-colored animal and the second very light; both of these and one other seemed to carry nice heads. When they had vanished, we followed, and I twice tried a stalk but failed each time to get within range. They were very suspicious, and the wind was

shifty and may have caused their uneasiness. During my third stalk, I was still separated from them by a deep nullah when I suddenly saw them descending the opposite side of the nullah, coming toward me but evidently bent on making off. I could not reach the side of the nullah in time to have a shot as they descended, so I ran to a rocky and very steep point that formed the "gate" by which the nullah debouched into the open. As I reached this, I saw some *karelini* at the bottom, rapidly departing. There was no time to use the glass, so I followed the rule "When in doubt shoot the leader" and, sitting down, put up my two-hundred-yard sight and let drive. Greatly to my own surprise, I made a brilliant shot and got it just below the heart.

I then turned my attention to the next, which I luckily missed. Having now fired two shots, I suddenly saw on my side of the nullah, one hundred yards below me and about to gain a corner, the three biggest beasts. I had no time to alter my sights but managed to shoot my dark friend through the backbone above the last rib (it was moving little faster than a walk). I then fired twice at the light-colored one as it made rapid tracks down the hill. Abdul said I had hit it, but it went out of sight downhill in the direction of camp. We tracked it some distance but found no blood and, after spying all the likely places on our way home, had to give up looking for it. The first one I shot was only 39 inches. I am sorry it went to its death in the confusion. The second was 50 inches—a very fair head for a *karelini*.

It was now about 2:15, and, as the ponies came up, I had lunch—a small cutlet, about three spoonfuls of cold rice pudding, two slices of indifferent cake, and cold tea. When we had cut up the slain and rested somewhat, we started for camp, and before we got in at 4:30 P.M. I was the victim of a fit of indigestion—the result, I suppose, of bad cooking and hasty meals. The attack luckily did not last long.

A *karelini* is very like a *poli*, except *karelini*'s horns are greenish, and those of *poli* are nearly white. A *karelini*'s horns are also more deeply wrinkled and thicker around the base than a *poli's*, though not so long.

Most of the time we had been stalking above the snow line, and, though there was not much sun, the skin of my face peeled off again; it has already suffered in this way five or six times during the trip.

Sunset was now about 6:30 P.M. Only one hailstorm came today, and it lasted only two minutes, thank goodness.

August 31—Another fine day. Started out southwest at 7:45. About two miles from camp we came on two "wild dogs" (*i.e.,* wolves), at which I had a couple of long shots. The only result was that I got a cut above the eye from the telescopic sight of my rifle. I believe I could have got nearer, but the shikaris said it was hopeless to try. About an hour afterward, as we were ascending the slope at the head of the valley toward the *gulja* (sheep) ground, two *illik* (Siberian roe) got up in front of us. I went to try to see where they had gone but, having failed, returned to the ponies, which were standing on top of a mound where two ridges met at right angles. I had sat down when suddenly, about six hundred yards below us, I saw the two *illik*, which in the distance rather resembled gigantic hares, galloping toward us, the buck pursuing the doe.

I ran to cut them off, and as they passed me at about one hundred yards I fired and broke the buck's hind foot to smithereens. It did not know what to make of this and stopped about 120 yards away. My second shot missed; my third smashed its knee. Abdul did not want me to fire again because we were near the *gulja* ground, but the buck was so active that it went out of sight, and we nearly lost it. Finally,

I caught sight of it, lying with its head behind a rock about one hundred yards from where I was. I thought I could not miss it, but my bullet went low, cut a furrow six inches along its belly, and smashed its other hind foot. In spite of this third wound, it made off again, but a bullet in the rump settled matters. Its horns from burr around outside curve to tip measured 13 inches and from tip to tip 12½ inches, with 6 points.

I saw no *gulja*s but on my way home had another shot at a wolf. It was a fair chance, and I ought to have got it, but I misjudged the range and only put my two-hundred-yard sight up, so the bullet went low. I think it was really three hundred yards away.

September 1—Another fine day. Started at 7:45 A.M. and went east. We had just struggled up to the top of our ground when we saw five *gulja*s on some steep ground below us. We easily gained a ridge overlooking them, and my shikaris persuaded me to shoot at the biggest as it was lying down. I put up my three-hundred-yard sight and taking, as I thought, a very steady aim, fired. All the *gulja*s at once sprang up and galloped off. When out of range they went more slowly, and we watched them all going off, apparently unhurt, till they were hidden by a ridge nearly a mile away. From behind this ridge only four emerged, and the shikaris at once said that the big one, if not hit, would not have left the others. We made a long search but saw no more of it, and I do not believe I touched it. I ought to have waited for my shot till the big ram got up.

As we were looking for *gulja*, a bear appeared. The wind was wrong, but the shikari was keen to get it, so I said I would have a try. We accordingly started a stalk, but we had only gone a quarter of a mile when I heard a shout from a man we had left behind to watch. I looked up and saw the bear going across my front from left to right. I ran forward about fifty yards and sat down on a hillock. As I did so the bear appeared and stood a moment, about 120 yards off and above me. I fired at once, and down fell the bear (hole of entrance, inside of left shoulder; exit, point of left shoulder), but it was up again in a moment and, with the ground in its favor, went off at a surprising pace. It came into view again within eighty yards, and I shot it through the heart.

CHAPTER TWENTY-FIVE

BRIGADIER GENERAL R. PIGOT

Great Britain's sprawling empire provided innumerable big-game hunting opportunities for military men and civil servants in a variety of exotic venues. If one were to choose a single book that reflected big-game hunting opportunities on several continents, one could easily argue that the best is Brigadier General Robert Pigot's Twenty-Five Years' Big-Game Hunting *(1928).*

Pigot's love of the pursuit of big game carried him to Africa, Canada, New Zealand, Sardinia, Norway, and various locales in Asia. In 1923 he traveled to the Tian Shan Mountains in Chinese Turkistan, though he admitted there were difficulties in gaining access because Russia's nascent Soviet regime controlled some transportation routes. Eventually Pigot received the requisite passes to enter Chinese territory and embarked on an expedition that would garner him prize trophies.

I have adapted this excerpt from a chapter in Pigot's book that describes his shooting trip to the Tian Shan.

WILD SHEEP OF THE TIAN SHAN

For several days we continued marching east without seeing a man of any sort, and I was beginning to doubt if we were ever going to find the Kalmuks when suddenly we came on their encampment on the eastern side of the Yuldus plain.

The Kalmuk chief, so I learned, was away, but in answer to my repeated demands to see the head man a cavalcade eventually arrived at my tent. Who was I, where had I come from, and what did I want, the spokesman of the party asked. Thinking that these Kalmuks must be under the rule of the governor of Ili, I said that I had come from there, which was true enough, since I had come through the Ili district. I said I wanted to shoot some *gulja* (wild sheep) before returning to Kashagar via Kucha.

"You are robbers," they answered, "and have come to steal our horses. We do not take orders from Ili, only from Urumchi, and we will not give you any help."

I told them that I would write to the governor of Urumchi and complain of my treatment at their hands and that he would be very angry with them. On hearing this they started to confer among themselves and then, after asking me many more questions, said that they would send a hunter with me if I would go away the next morning. But later on they returned and said that they would give me no help of any sort. The next day we moved on east, and, since no help was forthcoming from the Kalmuks, I had to make up my mind to find the sheep for myself.

During the next month I hunted every nullah for a hundred miles east of the Yuldus plain. In most of them there were a few sheep but mainly ewes and small rams. At this time of year (early and middle October) the big rams are still by themselves, and there was nothing unusual in my not being able to find them easily, but the lack of old horns and particularly of big horns lying about showed that it was no good looking for the big rams here. I had great expectations in the Narat nullah, where Major Biddulph had picked up a seventy-inch head in 1910, but there was nothing but a few small heads lying about even here. Where rams are plentiful in any bit of country, one finds their horns lying about wherever they have been killed by wolves or native hunters, and it is a waste of time to hunt ground where these horns cannot be found.

One can ride over most of the sheep ground in the Yuldus, so I was able to cover very large areas every day. On reaching a big nullah like the Narat or Adynkur, I camped for a day or two until I had thoroughly explored it in every direction. When the nullahs were small, Rahmana and I would leave the caravan to go on while we went up the nullah to spy and hunt for signs of the rams, rejoining the others in camp in the evening. All this ground looked excellent for sheep, but it was evident that the Kalmuks grazed their horses here in the summer, and this might have driven the sheep away.

After a time I reached a small Kalmuk camp where rams were reported. Here I spent a few days, covering miles of country each day with a Kalmuk hunter but with always the same result. There were ewes and small rams in quantities but never a sign of the big one I was looking for. Subhana, my old Kashmiri cook, got more and more depressed each day as I returned to camp without a head, and I was beginning to wonder if I had been wise to cover the ground so quickly. I imagined all sorts of things. Perhaps I had lost the art of spying. Perhaps there were no big rams left in these days. I had seen ewes and small rams in sufficient quantities to assume that there were big rams about, yet I had failed to find any sign of them. Something, however, seemed to tell me that I would find them farther east, though I had already passed the country where other Englishmen had killed them not more than ten years before.

We occasionally met Kalmuks as we moved on to the east. They sometimes volunteered to show me where the big rams were, but still I failed to find them. Each morning as I started out from camp I had hopes of finding them at last, but day after day I returned disappointed. And then one evening I returned to camp after a bitterly cold day on the hill to find that Subhana had waylaid two Kalmuks who said they could show me where the big rams were. These men told me that there were very few sheep in all the country I had been hunting but that there were plenty of them two marches away to the south and that the rutting season would be starting in a few days.

The next morning we marched south, accompanied by the two Kalmuks. On the second day's march I let the caravan go on ahead while I stopped to spy some ground, and when I caught up with them later I found some of the men gathered around some object on the ground. Joy, it was a pair of big horns such as I had been seeking for over a month. Again I questioned the Kalmuks and got the reply that a little farther on we would find plenty of horns as big as these and bigger. They said that up at the head of the nullah, which they pointed out in the distance, we would find the big rams themselves. This was encouraging. The sight of that pair of horns filled me with great hope, and even old Subhana became quite cheerful. All the rest of the march we kept on finding old horns, most of them big ones. We were indeed on the track of the big rams at last.

I had only spied for a few minutes the next morning before I found a herd of sheep and among them five big rams. There was no mistaking those enormous horns and the white throat ruffs. So it had not been my spying, after all, that had been at fault during the last month.

The sheep were in an impossible place for a stalk, and there was nothing for it but to send one of the Kalmuks around to try and move them. On seeing him the sheep went slowly off down the nullah in the direction I had anticipated. I ran hard to try and cut them off but failed to do so. However, here they were in the flesh at last, and, since the rutting season had evidently just commenced, I did not worry much about not getting one of these.

The next morning I was early on the same ground, but a blizzard came on, and we had to return to camp without finding the rams again. The temperature was down to –12 degrees, so I was glad enough to spend the rest of the day in my sleeping bag. The two Kalmuks said that they could not stay any longer, but they told me of another nullah close by that was a sure find for rams, if they had not already joined the ewes.

I was away early the next morning en route for the nullah the Kalmuks had told me about. It was bitterly cold but fine. Again, with my first spy I found more rams, four by themselves, and this time they were in a perfect place for a stalk. Leaving Rahmana behind with the ponies, I had a long but easy stalk and got up to within forty yards of the rams, which were lying down fast asleep. What a sight! I looked them carefully over with the glass and could see no difference in the size of their heads, but I picked out one whose head I could see without any doubt was a real big one. I killed it where it lay. The others went off, offering easy running shots, and I fired again but missed. Had I waited, they would probably have stood again at one hundred and fifty yards, but I could not resist the running shot at such close range. Rahmana and I got back to camp that night dead tired after a bitterly cold day but very happy. To me, not the least enjoyable part of that day was the grin on Subhana's face when he saw the ram's head at last.

Skinning a head by candlelight far into the night with the temperature many degrees below zero is not much fun, but one must do it if one wishes to be off hunting again first thing the following morning. I did not get to bed that night till the small hours of the morning. I spent ten days in that camp before I got the heads I wanted. On several occasions it snowed hard all day, and I had to stay in camp. All the time the cold was severe, with the exception of the last day.

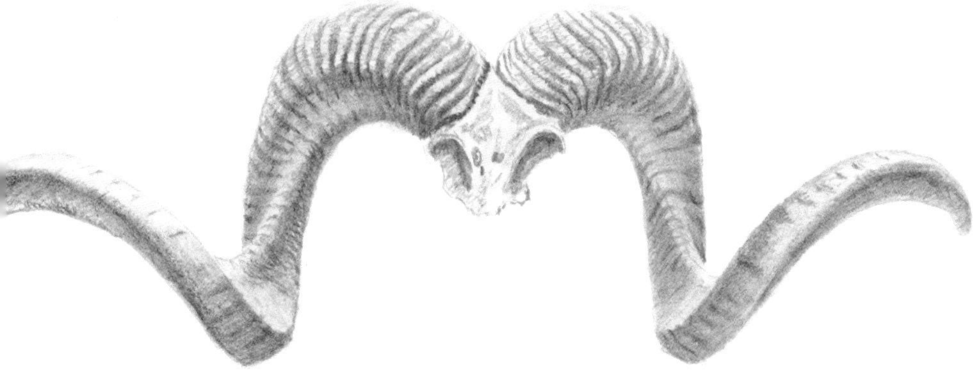

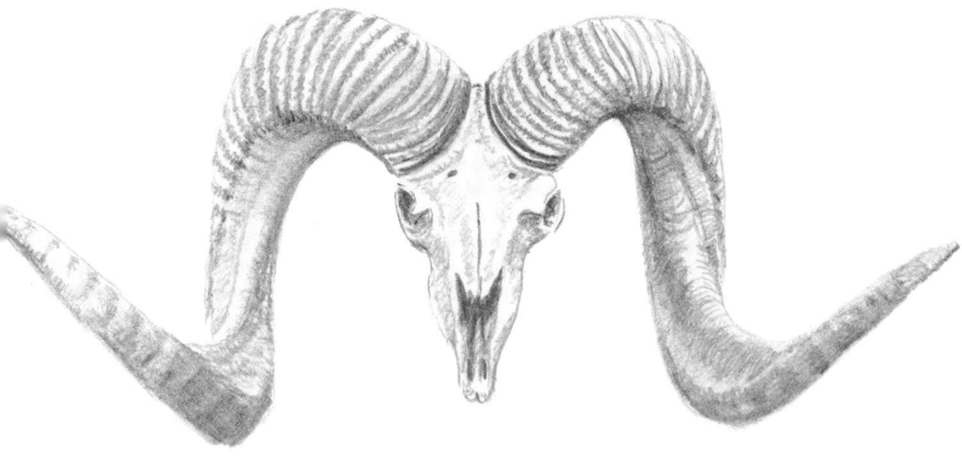

The day on which I killed my third and last ram was perfect. Not a cloud in the sky, not a breath of wind, and a bright sun. For over a month I had hunted for these rams, suffering continual disappointment, but in the end I had succeeded, and it almost seemed as if this last perfect day were an invitation to me to stay a little longer and get perhaps a record head. Having killed three, however, I could not bring myself to shoot another.

There is to my mind no finer big-game animal than the wild sheep of Central Asia. Whether they are getting scarce or not I do not know. Certainly I found no big rams in the country where other Englishmen have found them before. The Kalmuks kill a lot, without a doubt, but this country is so enormous that the sheep have ample room to change their ground, as the Kalmuks drive them on, for many years to come. It seems certain to me that during the rutting season I should have found the big rams in the Yuldus country itself, since there were quite sufficient ewes to attract them. These rams would no doubt come across from the northern side of the bit of the Tian Shan Range that bounds the Yuldus plain, returning there when the rut was over. Since there are few, if any, Kalmuks left on the Yuldus plain by the time the rutting season starts, there would be no hunters to kill the rams, and this would account for my not having found the old horns lying about.

The next day I marched south to Karashar, arriving there five days later. I left the Tian Shan mountains with many regrets, though I hope the day is not far distant when I shall visit them once again.

CHAPTER TWENTY-SIX

J. H. MILLER

When the famous British explorer Douglas Carruthers (1882–1962) mounted an expedition into the remote regions of Mongolia in the early twentieth century, he was following in the footsteps of a mere handful of Russian explorers of that region. Jack Humphrey Miller and M. P. Price accompanied Carruthers on the expedition with the backing of the Royal Geographical Society.

The group's caravan wound its way through eastern Siberia to the upper reaches of the Yenisei River and the frontiers of Mongolia. The expedition made a detailed scientific and photographic record of its journey and published its findings in the two-volume Unknown Mongolia: A Record of Travel and Exploration in North-West Mongolia and Dzungaria *(1913). For his efforts, Carruthers would receive the prestigious Gold Medal from the Royal Geographical Society.*

Jack Miller contributed three chapters on sport to Unknown Mongolia. *Little is known of his early life or of his subsequent travels, but there is little doubt that he was an accomplished shot and sportsman. I adapted this piece from his chapter on sport in Dzungaria, a remote region between the Altai Mountains and the Tian Shan.*

ON THE SHEEP GROUNDS OF DZUNGARIA

The middle of June found us once more among the mountains, reveling in the balmy breezes that ruffled the flower-studded grass of the Barlik-Maili Range. Life was again enjoyable, and we had further proof of the complex nature of Central Asia in that, in two short marches, we had risen from the enervating, furnace-like heat of the insect-infested plains to a restful, green land of bubbling brooks and matchless pasture. Wisps of smoke hanging lazily in the air and the presence of numerous flocks and herds added to the peacefulness of the surroundings and proclaimed the presence of large Kirei encampments. The Turkish words *maili* (fat) and *barlik* (everything) give the best idea of how this region appeals to the nomads, for it is indeed a "fat" land, possessing everything the heart of a herdsman could desire.

The chance of procuring specimens of that rare sheep—*Ovis ammon sairensis*—lured us to this region, but our quest was tantalizing and unsuccessful. The range of this sheep, which was first discovered by Mr. St. George Littledale in the Sair Mountains at the eastern end of Tarbagatay and southeast of Lake Zaisan, extends southward through the Urkashar and other small ranges as far as the Maili-Barlik group. This is also its eastern limit. How far its range extends westward along the Tarbagatay seems to be imperfectly known. Wild sheep exist in the low mountains to the north of Balqash, but whether they are *Ovis ammon sairensis* or *Ovis ammon nigrimontana* is a question that requires investigation.

The head of the River Kosho, which divides the Barlik from the Maili, runs through a broad, grassy upland, thickly dotted with ancient burial mounds. It is here that the chief of the western Kirei had his headquarters.

Early one afternoon, under the guidance of a herdsman, we reached his residence and lost no time in paying our respects. Instead of the usual picturesque group of yurts, we found ourselves confronted by a high enclosure built of mud with a formidable iron door. Inside the walls was a low building of the Russian type, containing the living rooms and a storeroom. Two large yurts, used for the kitchen and servants' quarters, occupied most of the remaining space.

The great man and his family received us at the entrance to his house. It was with the utmost difficulty that we maintained a dignified demeanor, for the greatness of his position had spread to his person in an alarming degree. He must have weighed a clear twenty stone, and his voluminous Kirghiz costume accentuated his corpulence. His wife was almost as large, and his sons and daughters showed great promise.

Tea and sweetmeats were placed before us in a room gaudily decorated with carpets—some of them old and good—many-hued tin boxes, and trashy goods from the Chuguchak bazaar. Somehow the whitewashed room did not suit either the occupants or their belongings. The smoky interior of a yurt would have been much more appropriate.

The old chief was decidedly suspicious of us at first and laughed at the idea that we wanted to shoot wild sheep; he undoubtedly thought we were spies. But when we had produced our Chinese passports, and had proved to him our acquaintance with the Russian consuls at Chuguchak and Kulja, he began to look at us in a friendlier light.

Like so many of these frontier nomad chiefs, though he was a Chinese subject he was thoroughly in with the Russians, so as to be on the safe side whichever way the cat jumped. Before we left, we had made friends with our host and had the satisfaction of hearing him order men and horses for our use.

Two marches along the foot of the mountains—crossing numerous boulder-strewn watercourses, and dodging protruding buttresses—brought us to the Karaul, which guards one of the few passes over the Ala-tau. In 1908 I had crossed this very pass on my way from the Altai to Kulja, via Lepsinsk. The appearance of the country had then struck me favorably, but a lengthy program and a short season had prevented me from investigating it.

With the exception of a small post of three men farther up the valley, we had now left the last habitation behind, so we decided to move along slowly, hunting as we went.

Carruthers and I agreed that he should have the monopoly of ibex, since he had not yet secured a specimen, while I had shot several good ones in the Tian Shan, and that the sheep were to be my portion, since he had shot them on the Aksia plateau.

The southern slopes of the Ala-tau drop very abruptly into the valley; they are steep shale and grassy slopes, with protruding buttresses; there are no foothills in the proper sense of the word. The spruce forest that darkens the northern declivities is entirely absent here, though the torrents that leap down from the snowy crests are fringed by thickets of willow, poplar, and much rich grass.

We called a two-day halt in one of these delightful spots while we made a thorough exploration of the surroundings. Carruthers ransacked the higher nullahs for ibex, and I scoured the lower slopes in search of rams. We shot a female ibex and a ewe for food, also five wolves. In those two days I must have seen not less than three hundred ewes and young, but not a single ram.

Carruthers saw a few female ibex and a stag with fine horns though still in velvet. Ibex ground without any tree in sight is a curious place to see a stag; it had probably fled there for protection from the native hunters, who at this season would be busy among the northern forests.

All the wolves in the neighborhood seemed to have collected in the vicinity of this abundant meat supply, for I saw no less than fourteen in the two days. On the first evening we surprised an old wolf and six well-grown cubs on the prowl; after watching them for some time sniffing at marmot holes and playing on the hillside, I shot two of the cubs, whose fur, though short, was in beautiful condition.

We decided to make a long march up the valley without stopping to hunt; by so doing we hoped to get beyond the ladies' quarters into the domains of their lords and masters, for such large numbers of ewes meant fine heads somewhere not far off. At that time frequent severe thunderstorms swept over us; though unpleasant while they lasted, the cool, clear atmosphere they produced was ample compensation.

As we moved up the ever-narrowing valley, we sighted a few gazelle, but they were in absolutely unstalkable positions. Here and there bleached sheep heads lay about; they were uniform in shape, unlike the mixed types we had found on the Yuldus, and in appearance between *ammon* and *poli*. Five days after leaving the Kalmuk camp, we pitched our tents close to the river, where the valley narrows to such an extent that the mountains rise almost directly from the riverbank. In its western portion the Ala-tau is an imposing mountain mass; some of the jagged peaks that frowned down upon us were a good fifteen thousand feet high. The view to the south was blocked by the less imposing, round-headed shale ridge that divides the Borotala from its large tributary, the Urta Saryk. From each dark crest, grassy slopes with outcrops of rock and patches of shale, deeply seamed with numerous small watercourses, dropped toward our camp.

Just as we were about to unload the horses, we sighted a bear with two cubs on a terrace across the river. They were only about four hundred yards away and in full view of the caravan. Thinking that they would sight us any moment, and forgetting what poor sight a bear possesses, we hurriedly forded the river and made toward where we thought it to be, without stopping to take our bearings. We were peering about, expecting to come face-to-face with them any minute, when suddenly a dark head and shoulders appeared for a moment above a rise a hundred yards to our left. We had hopelessly misjudged the bear's position. Even now we probably would have got it if the ground had been favorable, but a hollow hid the bears from our view until the they appeared again a good five hundred yards away.

I should be ashamed to say how many cartridges we expended in the next minute or two. Even a musketry instructor at Hythe would have marveled at the rapidity with which our bolts worked! But, though dust was spurting up all around that hurrying, shaggy figure, the distance was too great, and the bear showed no signs of being touched. The last we saw of that trio was the old bear looking defiantly back at us from a hilltop, waiting for those two precious balls of fur it had outpaced in its flight. I should feel inclined to omit this regrettable incident were it not an excellent example of what *not* to do under similar conditions. This bear was unusually dark; most of the skins we have seen in the bazaars are of a brownish-yellow color, but it was nearly black and of large size.

Large piles of *tezek* and stone kraals proved that herdsmen must have visited this region in winter. During the summer, not a single Kalmuk dares to venture into the upper Borotala or Urta Saryk because of their fear of the Russian Kazakhs from the north. These freebooters from over the border lose no opportunity of swooping down upon any outlying herds and shooting down with impunity any Kalmuk who interferes. At any rate, this was the tale we heard, and it is doubtless true, though we gathered that the Kalmuks return the compliment whenever a thoroughly safe opportunity presents itself.

In the winter, when the northern regions' passes are closed, Kalmuk herdsmen overrun the upper Borotala and Urta Saryk. In addition, considerable numbers of Chinese Kazakhs, who summer on the eastern side of Sairam Nor, move into these more sheltered regions, paying a considerable sum to the Ambans for the right to graze their domains. On this first day in the new locality, Carruthers took the ground across the river while I scoured the slopes to the north, and, as luck would have it, he came upon numbers of rams, and I found a large herd of ibex.

Leaving camp when the last of the stars were still struggling against the first streaks of dawn, my hunter and I zigzagged up to a lofty, commanding position. I dignify my companion with the title of "hunter," but he and all our other Kalmuk followers were quite useless in this respect, though they were thoroughly willing and helpful in their knowledge of the country. A herd of a dozen buck ibex were feeding on a crest some way above us, showing up well against the sky. There seemed to be one or two fair heads among them, so, after ascertaining that they were thoroughly settled in their present position, we left them undisturbed and continued our search for rams.

A short way farther on we found nine rams. Only one carried respectable horns, and I estimated them to be short of fifty inches, but I determined to try for it. Our hungry crowd had already demolished the two beasts recently killed, and the meat would be acceptable. While making this stalk, the rattle of stones drew my attention to another lot of ten rams, all strung out on a narrow sheep track, crossing a steep shale slope above us. There was no mistaking the size of one or two of those heads, but it was useless to attempt to follow them up because they were evidently thoroughly alarmed. Led by a grizzled old fellow with fine curling horns, they plunged along over the shale, stopping frequently to gaze down upon us. It was not till the afternoon that we got on terms with the original herd, and bad shooting necessitated a stern chase before we brought the best ram to bay. It proved to be only a small head of forty-seven inches, but we had bright prospects of soon getting better ones.

Carruthers failed to find any ibex but had come across three bands of rams, so the next day we exchanged ground, he going for my ibex and I for his sheep.

At the top of an outlying bluff, overlooking a likely little valley, we settled down for a thorough "spying." At our feet ran a small stream carrying the melting snow from the drifts far above down to the Borotala; from each side of this short valley rose steep slopes that broke into numerous small arms and hollows. Right at the head of the stream and just below the shale, we could see two herds of rams feeding among some ancient grass-covered moraines. There were six in one lot and eleven in the other. We were too far off to tell their size, but they were certainly worth a close inspection. Leading our horses, we screed down to the valley bottom and were then disgusted to find that the wind (what there was of it) was blowing straight up the hill.

From a campsite in Mongolia, J. H. Miller displays a collection of Tian Shan argali and ibex bagged by him and Douglas Carruthers.

However, there was no other approach. I decided to go boldly on, trusting that local eddies would favor me higher up.

After riding only a short way, while still half a mile from my objective, I left the man and horses and proceeded on foot. Provided that the sheep were on the right side of the valley, where I had last seen them, there was just a chance that, by ascending the left, I might yet approach unwinded. It was a very slow advance. The quarry had been long out of sight, and there was no way to know where it might have moved. I had to crawl up to and cautiously peer over every little vantage point. At last, all the dead ground that remained was the farther side of one small knoll. It seemed impossible that all those sheep could be concealed behind that slight cover, but nothing must be left to chance in this sort of hunting, and I continued to move slowly forward. The wind was gently fanning my right cheek, so all was safe in that direction.

Suddenly the top of a horn appeared ahead. Raising myself inch by inch, I gazed down upon the six rams, which were lying down and facing every direction but mine. Alas! Though they were only fifty yards off, not one carried a head worth shooting; they were all four- or five-year-olds. There was still just one portion of the slope hidden from view, where the other lot must be, if they had not cleared out, so, wriggling back, I approached this also from above. This time I was not so successful, or perhaps the wind was less friendly, for that well-known alarm signal—a mixture of a grunt and a sneeze—sounded before a single beast was visible. Hastily swinging around into a sitting position, I saw the twelve rams bunched together, every head turned in my direction.

Four legs kicking in the air answered the first shot. Another whack, as they bolted, proclaimed that the second bullet had found its billet; luckily, the second ram made straight downhill, enabling me to finish it off close to the horses, much to the gratification of the voracious old Kalmuk.

One of these heads measured 51¼ inches in length; the other was a massive 49 inches, but one of its horns was badly broken, so it was useless as a trophy. After assisting my companion to skin and cut up one beast, and leaving him to deal with the other, I climbed up

to a spur that overlooked a fresh stretch of country. This district was alive with game. A large herd of female ibex and their young, and some small rams, were visible to the naked eye.

As we left the scene of our success, with the heads slung over the Kalmuk's saddle, the vultures began to assemble, for no meat is ever left to rot in a country possessing such keen-eyed scavengers as these.

This proved to be one of those red-letter days when everything goes right and big-game hunting seems to be the easiest in the world. After such a day, one is apt to forget the days of fruitless search or unsuccessful endeavor, when, sometimes through faults of one's own, and sometimes owing to sheer bad luck, one returns to camp, night after night, with fatigue accentuated by failure.

It was still early in the afternoon when, while riding carelessly down a stony watercourse, with thoughts of camp and one of Pereira's savory stews foremost in my mind, a guttural *"Tocta"* from my companion banished all such thoughts from me. The old fellow had already dismounted and was pointing over the back of his horse up a side nullah we were passing at the time. *"Tash, gulja, bilmaida,"* (Rocks or rams, I don't know) was his next remark. Spotting the gray smudges that had caught his eye, I soon focussed on seventeen rams in the field of the telescope. They had evidently just risen from their siesta and were standing aimlessly about while their leader decided in which direction they should start grazing. When it had made up its mind, it led them at a trot downhill till they were lost in a fold of the ground. The commencement of the evening meal is quite one of the best times to approach sheep; they are then so engrossed in the early courses that they relax their usual precautions.

I will not weary the reader with details of this stalk, for, except to a participant, the account of one stalk is very much like another. Suffice it to say that, half an hour later, I was on my back, doing an uncomfortable caterpillar-like slither down a steep hillside toward a *V*-shaped hollow into which the sheep had disappeared.

Descending a smooth slope in this manner is an unsatisfactory way of approaching game, because the slightly convex land formation alone conceals the hunter, and, when the quarry at last comes into view, the recognition is liable to be mutual. So it was in this case.

A mass of gray backs and curling horns suddenly appeared almost directly below. At the same moment a head turned in my direction, and suddenly the opposite hillside seemed to be alive with flying sheep. There was no time to waste deciding which was the best head, though none of them was very small, so, following that sound hunter's motto, "When in doubt, shoot the leader," I had the satisfaction of seeing the leader pitch forward on its head at the shot. My next shot received a similar reply, and, as the sheep stood for a second on the crest, yet another received its death blow and came galloping straight down the hill, falling dead on the very spot they had just left. The two best of these heads measured 53 and 48½ inches, respectively—very fair heads for Karelini, which I fancy do not average as big as the Littledale of the Tian Shan, though they occasionally reach sixty inches, as proved by a head we picked up later.

While we were busy with our knives, a terrific thunderstorm that had been brewing for hours burst over us; the rain came down in torrents, and the thunder crashed right over our heads.

With two heads slung over each of our saddles and my companion holding the fifth in front of him, not to mention several dangling legs of mutton, we slowly made our way toward camp.

CHAPTER TWENTY-SEVEN

KERMIT ROOSEVELT AND THEODORE ROOSEVELT JR.

The Roosevelt name has long been linked with travel to exotic locations and big-game hunting. Though President Theodore Roosevelt received much of the focus, his son Kermit was equally at home on the African veld or in Asian forests. Born in 1889, Kermit Roosevelt attended the exclusive Groton School, then graduated from Harvard. As a young man he accompanied his father on the famous safari to East Africa in 1910. Four years later, he was again with Teddy, this time on a physically draining expedition to the wilds of Brazil.

When war broke out in Europe in 1914, Kermit couldn't wait for the United States to enter the war—he joined the British army and saw action in the Holy Land. He recounted his experiences in his first book, War in the Garden of Eden *(1919). After America entered the war, he joined the American Expeditionary Force and served in France. Upon his return home he wrote a second book,* The Happy Hunting Ground *(1920), which detailed his sporting trips, including his trip to Africa.*

But Kermit and his brother Theodore Jr. were not about to sit on their famous name or on past laurels. The brothers embarked on an expedition to the Pamirs to collect Ovis poli, *a venture sponsored by the Field Museum and funded by James Simpson. The Roosevelts coauthored a book about their joint adventure,* East of the Sun and West of the Moon *(1926). A mixture of exotic travel and equally exotic big-game hunting, the book was popular enough to be reprinted several times.*

In 1928 the brothers became part of the Kelley-Roosevelt Field Museum Expedition, which explored and collected specimens from French Indochina (Vietnam) and western Szechuan in China along the Tibetan border. It was while they were in China that Kermit and Ted collected a specimen of the rare panda bear. Kermit and Ted's Trailing the Giant Panda *(1929) also became a best seller.*

When World War II broke out, Kermit briefly served with British forces before becoming a commissioned officer in the U.S. Army. By that time hard drinking had ruined his health. Assigned to a remote post in Alaska, Roosevelt begged pilots to let him fly with them as an observer as they bombed Japanese targets in the Aleutians. He was also instrumental in creating a territorial guard of native Aleuts and Eskimos. But his health was failing, and the thought of being bedridden was anathema to him; consequently, in 1943 he committed suicide.

The following passages follow Kermit and Ted Roosevelt on the hunting trail after bear. The first piece, from East of the Sun and West of the Moon, *describes their hunt after brown bear in Chinese Turkistan. In the second passage, adapted from the book* Trailing the Giant Panda, *Kermit and Ted at last find the trail of the elusive panda.*

OF BROWN BEARS AND PANDAS

The morning after we reached our Kansu camp, Ted took the side of the valley on which our tent was pitched, and I crossed over and started up the mountains opposite, accompanied by Khalil and Nurpay. We had been climbing for about an hour and a half when we came upon a marmot burrow scored with the claws of a bear. The bear had slipped in its attempt to catch the little rodent, and it was clear that the tracks were from the night before. Until then we had seen a great deal of bear sign but nothing more recent than three or four days old. Here was a chance for the dogs, so I sent Nurpay back to camp for them while Khalil and I climbed on up the mountain, partly to look for game and partly with the idea that we would be above the dogs and would be able to watch their line and get to them more quickly in case they came to terms with the bear.

While we were watching a herd of ibex—there were no good heads among them—I thought I heard the dogs give tongue. Khalil was sure I hadn't, so we continued to rake the country with our field glasses until the time we had allotted for Nurpay's return was almost up. We hurried back to the vantage point from which the marmot hole was visible; there were Nurpay's and Fesildin's ponies, but neither rider nor hounds were to be seen. I had told Nurpay to put the dogs on the trail and loose them. We called out, but there was no answer. We felt sure the hunt had gone away without us, but we had commanded one possible direction while watching the ibex, so off we boiled in the opposite direction, heedless of falling. I threw out my bad knee but not seriously.

Every little while we stopped to listen for the hounds, and every time we topped a ridge we hoped to catch sight of the chase, but ridge succeeded ridge, and we saw nothing. Disconsolately, we returned to the ponies. We reached them exasperated and breathless at a quarter past one and found men and dogs asleep in the grass. Through a misunderstanding, the men had not loosed the dogs and had not heard our halloing.

The trail was now far too stale to follow, for there had been a scorching sun all morning, so, after a very brief tiffin, I sent Fesildin and the dogs back to camp and plodded once more up the mountain. We had moved from one ridge to another when, at four o'clock, Khalil announced that he saw a bear. Nurpay brought the telescope to focus on it and at first insisted that it was a *tungius,* a pig, but I took one good look and felt sure he was mistaken. It was a bear, right enough, walking up a grassy nullah far off on the opposite side of the mountain.

There was a long stalk before us and no time to lose. We slithered and slipped down the bed of a ravine with a floor of slide rock. It was almost as much work as climbing. We had started from Srinagar outfitted with beautiful steel-shod walking sticks, but all except one had succumbed to the vicissitudes of mountain trekking, and the one remaining was sadly cracked and weakened. We usually could count on picking up a makeshift stick, but today I had none, and badly did I miss it. There were two steep hillsides up which to pant and struggle before we reached the nullah in which we had seen the bear.

Cautiously, we pushed ourselves through the dwarf junipers. We could see nothing, and we separated to take different vantage points. I kept a sharp eye on the other two and soon saw Khalil signaling. When I reached him, he pointed out the bear, lying curled up in the undergrowth a hundred and fifty yards away, on the other slope of the nullah. As I fired, it jumped up and rolled over and over into the bed of the ravine, shouting and howling. Khalil said it was finished, but, wishing to make certain, I fired a couple of shots at the rolling bear without scoring a hit. We launched ourselves down into the nullah, though Nurpay kept exclaiming that there was no way down and that we would all fall. We landed safely, but the bear was gone.

We caught a fleeting glimpse of something running through the underbrush, and once more I opened fire. Nurpay turned cautious; he was manifestly a great respecter of bears, but he was too loyal not to follow in our wake. Two hundred yards down the ravine we stopped to reconnoiter, and it was then that Nurpay caught sight of a bear's ears, well up the side we had descended. He had difficulty in making Khalil and me see it, but at last I did. The second shot went through the heart, and down came the bear, bounding from rock to rock, to stop stone dead within thirty yards of us.

It was an old he-bear, very fat. We had no time for taking stock and congratulating ourselves, for it was after six. I hastily jotted down the measurements and tried a time exposure with my Kodak, and we settled down to the skinning with desperate earnest. Daylight was about gone when we started back up the ravine, but suddenly Nurpay stopped; his keen eyes had picked up a blood trail. *"Yekke aya,"* (two bears) he said. Khalil stoutly maintained that there had been but one; I sided with Nurpay because a number of details, hitherto unnoticed, came back to me. First there was the color; the original bear had seemed almost white, while the one we were carrying was dark brown. Then, thinking back over the last hasty skinning, I could recall only one bullet hole. Last, I was sure that the bear could not have been down in the nullah here and have climbed so far when I shot him. Still, the discussion was purely academic; it was far too late to hope to follow a trail.

We turned our attention to the serious work of getting ourselves and the bearskin back to camp. First Nurpay and I tried to carry it tandem, but one would slip and drag down the other, and we made little headway. On a perpendicular hill slope we halted, and I skinned out the head, mainly by feel. The head with the flesh on it must have weighed twenty pounds. I hung it like a pendant around my neck. With our mufflers we slung the skin around Nurpay and once more got under way. A quarter moon appeared, but in half an hour it was hidden by clouds. We struggled along with frequent halts. Part of the time we walked upright, frequently falling among the rocks; up the steeper bits we crawled on hands and knees. There was no chance to pick our path; we got over or around whatever appeared in front of us. It was after eleven before we won our way back to the ponies; fortunately, the threatening rain had held off until we were mounted.

Once again I could see the advantages of a white hunting pony. Nurpay on his white mare threaded his way down the mountainside as only a Kazak can, over country that might well give pause in daylight. The ponies seemed by instinct to avoid the marmot holes, and when they did step into one they showed the utmost calmness in extricating themselves. When we came upon small patches of upland meadow, there were always hidden springs, and the ground was boggy; by night we could only trust to Nurpay's instinct and our ponies' experience. I had a long inward debate as to whether, if I groped around for pipe, tobacco, and matches, the comfort of a smoke would compensate for the discomfort of lighting my pipe. I made the effort and was rewarded, although my pony nearly came down when I loosened the reins to strike a match.

At half past twelve we rode into camp and tumbled from our saddles to thaw ourselves around a blazing fire of spruce logs and recount our adventures to the sleepy men who had rolled out of their blankets when they heard us coming.

In the morning Khalil was feeling too exhausted to go out, so I took two Kazakhs and went off to look into the matter of the possible second bear. Nurpay had been right; there had been two, and we followed the one I had first wounded for three-quarters of a mile down the ravine below where the other had fallen. The trail was most difficult, and at length it was lost, even to Kasin's sharp eyes. We made futile casts in every direction, but at last we had to abandon the chase. I had debated taking the dogs, and I would have done well to take them, but it was doubtful we would find the second bear, and I was afraid that a badly wounded bear might cut up our dogs and render them useless.

A few days later we both took the dogs out, thinking that if the wounded bear were still alive we might pick up its fresh trail. Either it or another bear had been working about in the nullah bottom, for

Lead immediately showed interest. He and Rollie puzzled a trail for a short distance, but it was evidently too stale to follow through to a successful conclusion.

****

About sixty years ago a French missionary, Père David, while traveling in the little independent buffer state of Muping, traded from the natives the incomplete skin of a curious bearlike animal, which scientists christened *Aeluropus melanoleuscus.* Its lay name is the giant panda. A parti-colored bear about the size of a black bear, the animal is strikingly colored. Its head and forequarters are white. Its legs are black, and a black band runs around behind its shoulders; the rest of its body is white. The correct classification of the animal had long been a cause for controversy in scientific circles. From the available skins it was impossible to say whether is was a bear or a panda or whether it belonged in a class by itself.

My brother and I made the securing of a giant panda the main objective of an expedition we were planning along the Chinese-Tibetan borderland. It was impossible to secure in advance any information regarding the exact whereabouts of the giant panda or anything concerning its habits and the best method of securing one. All we could do was to rely on the information and aid we could pick up along the route.

As a result of our inquiries we determined that the animal has a fairly wide area of distribution but is to be found only in pockets, and it is never abundant. It lives in bamboo jungles at altitudes from six to fourteen thousand feet. We concluded that we could safely assume that where there was no bamboo there were no giant panda, or *beishung*, as the natives called them. We had to check local information carefully, for even after giving a detailed description of the animal and showing a plate depicting it, we could not rely upon a native's word as to its presence in a district. Sometimes natives had hazy notions of coloration or assumed that the white crescent on the chest of the black bear *(Ursus torquatus)* entitled it to be called a panda. At other times they willfully misinformed us, either from the common impulse to give pleasant news or because the native counted on earning some money as a guide before we could discover his deception.

We were unable to account satisfactorily for the scarcity of the animal. The problem of food should not have proved difficult to a giant panda, for there was always plenty of bamboo. The natives rarely molest the panda. This is particularly true among the Lolos, who regard it as semidivine. The other wild game in the same locality would not appear to prove destructive to the giant panda, for it was very doubtful that, under any circumstances, either the black or brown bear or the snow leopard would attack a giant panda.

To the best of our belief, the panda does not hibernate. We met with fresh sign in regions where brown and black bears were hibernating, and the panda we shot was found in a locality where the brown and black bears had not awakened from their winter's nap. As a result of careful study of the skeleton of this animal, scientists have agreed that it does not belong to any known species but is *sui generis*.

We first came across unmistakable sign of the panda's existence in Muping, but in spite of hunting as arduous as either of us had ever done, we were unable to discover fresh trails or any sign of it. In all our marchings, we were continually inquiring for the beast, but it was not until we approached the Lolo country that we received any encouragement. The Chinese authorities warned us that it would be most unwise to enter Lololand, for the Lolos are an independent race and do not permit the Chinese to pass through their territory. We felt, however, that if we took things quietly, we could gain their confidence and assistance.

The distance from Kooing Ma to Kooing Hai is short as the crow flies, but the trail wound around and about, and there were rivers to cross and steep ravines to negotiate, so it was not until two in the afternoon that we came to the first of the group of houses that constitute Kooing Hai. We had taken four soldiers, leaving the others with the mules. We also had Mooka and the son of a neighboring headman.

The mountainsides were glorious with rhododendrons, varying in hue from deep purple to white. Pink was the prevailing color. In places the ground was sprinkled with small blue flowers of the orchid family. Blue lilies, forget-me-nots, primroses, and a diminutive yellow blossom dotted the path side. We were climbing up a valley, and as the altitude increased the crops were noticeably less advanced.

At moments it did not seem we would meet with a friendly reception. As we reached the hamlet farthest up the valley, designated as our halting place, the inhabitants took to the mountainside, and one man was very visible, leveling a rifle at us. Our conductors succeeded in smoothing things out, but only with a good deal of difficulty, and it was not a friendly-looking delegation that dropped down to talk things over with us. I think it was the Chinese soldiers who were largely responsible for the distrust. Hsuen told us that the Lolos usually took us for what he translated as "holy fathers," as they call Catholic priests. This honor was due to our beards.

Throughout the expedition we found that it was impossible to tell what sort of gift would prove a success. The knives and axes that had been a flat failure in Muping were now of the greatest service and went a long way to clear the horizon. On the other hand, the Lolos firmly rejected the cheap field glasses of which we had expected much. The offer of a glass of Benedictine stood us in good stead. We won over the headman of the village, but his tall, handsome old father did not appear to yield quite so readily to our attempted blandishments. It was evident that except in defense of their property they did not care to attack the giant panda. We verified the story of the raid on the apiary, which stood close to the headman's hunt and was protected by a strong fence. It had taken place a month previous. They also told us that six years ago a *beishung* (panda) had been killed during a honey raid. This was the only record they could give us of a panda being killed.

All afternoon and throughout the night it rained. In the morning the skies were overcast, but no rain was falling. Ten Lolo hunters with an equal number of dogs gathered outside our tent, which we had pitched close to a hut. We set out at half-past six for the mountains. A couple of hours' climbing took us up among the bamboos, and we were soon drenched to the skin and shivering with cold. Remnants of the winter snows lay in patches. The Lolos, shrouded in the brown or black capes they weave from sheep's wool, seemed happy enough. They appeared to feel that there was a very good chance of bagging a panda, although we could not share in their optimism. As we made our way through the dense jungle along a ridge, we twice heard the dogs running something below us. In neither case did it come to anything. We called a halt and lit a fire with much difficulty. One of the Lolos took a handful of moss and placed a bit of smoldering tinder in the center of it. With incessant blowing in relays, they eventually produced a flame.

Several of the Lolos had kept to the valley on either side of our ridge, and we had not been warming ourselves for long before a series of unintelligible shouts informed our companions that the dogs were running a sounder of swine. We did not want to shoot pig, but, after a hurried debate, we decided that it would be better for our future chances if we kept our hunters keyed up and took the opportunity to shoot game for them if it did not conflict with our *beishung* hunting. Such was obviously the present situation, for with their dogs off after wild pig our Lolos could no longer hunt anything.

The scramble down into the valley was precipitous; it was bad enough in the forested spots, but when we came to bare spaces it became all but impossible. Our hopes of finding better footing along the bed of the torrent were quickly dashed. The stream thought nothing of a forty-foot drop, but to clamber down the slippery perpendicular rock slides, securing a precarious toehold in a fissure or grasping the uncertain root of some plant, proved very difficult for us. We sustained nothing more serious than abrasions, bruises, and sprains from our falls, and we thought ourselves lucky when we emerged on a native trail where the ravine debouched into the main valley. Rain and sleet were now falling, and most of the dogs had abandoned the pursuit of the pigs. After some further futile climbing, our hunters decided to call it a day, and we returned to our tent with a practical working knowledge of the country and its difficulties.

By this time, the headman had become definitely friendly, and we sat around the fire discussing the ways and means of securing game, drifting now and then into more general topics. Hsuen's choice

of words and *tournures de phrase* were a constant delight, capable of cheering the gloomiest moments. The subject had, as usual, turned to sickness and to our small stock of medicine, which we constantly had to make a calculating effort to preserve.

Hsuen translated, "Headman say he got ghost in head. Ghost make itch all time. Other people's head not itch, so headman know he got ghost."

With great ceremony, Ted presented a small box of cold cream, saying that, if well rubbed in, it would lay the ghost. We next heard about a ghost that every January caused great mortality among the children. This was undoubtedly pneumonia, a more difficult apparition to deal with.

The rain fell continuously all night, and several holes in the tent made it an uncomfortable residence, but there was no room in any nearby hut, so we had to make the best of it. Dawn broke cold and gray, with no pause in the rain. We thought it extremely unlikely that any Lolo would stir from his hut, but we were soon undeceived, for during the next hour no less than thirty-two men straggled in, each leading a dog on a string. The dogs were identical to those we had used in the Muping country. A good deal of rain had found its way into the tent during the night, so we were a bedraggled lot even before starting—not that it made any difference, for half an hour would have sufficed to saturate us thoroughly with mud and water.

Before setting off for the mountains, our hunters "made medicine." The Lolos carve no likenesses of their gods. To cure a sick man they hold services and beat drums, or burn holes in the scapular bone of a sheep, but nowhere did we see idols of any description. Two of our hunters took sticks and whittled notches, muttering all the while. As far as we could gather, the main purpose of this was to determine a propitious locality for the hunt. Hsuen looked sagely on. Turning to us, he remarked, "They pray God," then, shrugging his shoulders, he said, "Perhaps it do good, I no know."

We burrowed our way though a different bamboo jungle along a different ridge, but there was little to differentiate this day's hunting from the previous. The dogs separated and presumably hunted valleys on either side. On each day we came across *beishung* sign, but in neither case did we feel that it indicated more than one animal. From our observations we were certain that there were very few panda about, far less than in Muping. At noon we built a fire, and from the folds of their cloaks the Lolos drew forth round lumps of bread liberally studded with beans. Among the hunters, one old fellow particularly interested us. He must have been in his late sixties, and the others looked upon him as a mine of hunting lore. His counsel weighed heavily in the decisions regarding the disposition of our forces. Somewhere en route he had gathered some white fungus, which he roasted in the embers, ate, and appeared to enjoy greatly.

Once or twice the dogs picked up the trail of some animal, but they never held it for long. Aside from *beishung* signs of questionable age, all we saw were some tracks of musk deer and a number of places where wild hogs had been rooting.

After conferring that evening, we determined to make a final hunt on the following morning and, if nothing came of it, to move on to a place where we had been told we would find takin. We paid our Lolo hunters from fifteen to thirty cents a day, offering a large reward to the man who could first point out a panda, and lesser rewards to others who had a part in the successful hunt.

The villagers enriched themselves through us in other ways. We bought a sheep, eggs, some wine bowls, and many stone pipes. One of the hunters had a curious bamboo musical instrument, which he played by holding it against his teeth and blowing on it while he snapped the taut bamboo slivers with his fingers.

Our next morning's hunt was a repetition of those of the two previous days. Again we climbed a ridge. This time, instead of rain and sleet, we had snow, but the effect was much the same. We found no *beishung* sign. Ted saw a pheasant, and I caught a fleeting glimpse of a large squirrel.

We had sent Hsuen ahead with our kit to Kooing Ma, telling him to gather the mules and to go on to Litzaping, a village near the place where takin were to be found. We followed at the termination of our hunt and reached Litzaping just before dark.

Four headmen gathered to greet us. We first gave each a glass of Benedictine liqueur. We then bought some native wine, which we poured into bowls that circulated among the headmen and their dependents. They were a fine, stalwart lot, and were very friendly. We had heard that the Lolos were heavy drinkers, but we saw no indications that it was so. Their wine is usually made from corn. It varied greatly in quality, though none of it could really be called an agreeable beverage.

Our friends were unanimous that there were very few takin about. We had heard there were many near a mountain named Tsumei Kwa, but they all denied this, advising us to go on to Yehli, where they said there were many takin and an occasional giant panda. We decided we should send back the Chinese soldiers and take with us a son of each headman. The Lolos said that we might find ourselves in difficulty with the soldiers accompanying us but that without them we would be safe. Hsuen was by now thoroughly sick of the "brother-man," to whom he referred sarcastically as "our dear brother," but he was afraid the man might do us harm if we sent him back, and for several more days we gave way to Hsuen's judgment. All of us were heartily glad when, eventually, we arbitrarily forced him to turn back.

On 12 April we set out for Yehli. A persistent rain was falling, which added to the difficulties of the trail. Our pack animals consisted of our mules and two ponies. One of the ponies missed its footing and started down the mountainside. A muleteer pluckily grabbed its headstall and went rolling over the boulders until long after it had seemed impossible for him to hold on further. A most convenient dense clump of sturdy bushes prevented pony and packer from taking the final sheer plunge into the river, which definitely would have ended the careers of both. We lugged the pony back to the trail, a half-hour delay.

Twice during the march we called a halt while the muleteers turned into road builders to overcome the work of a landslide. At length the valley opened up, and we had easy going. The country became more and more lovely. Giant pine trees grew beside the path, and we finally rode out onto a great mountain meadow with a wide grassy valley, hemmed in by well-forested mountains terminating in barren, snow-clad peaks. We felt that we might almost be back in the paradise of Tian Shan.

The hamlet at which we halted formed a part of the Yehli group. The cabins were large, and cattle and sheep had trampled the ground around them. A heavy rain was falling, and a dense fog soon shrouded the valley, making the pinewood fire in the center of the cabin most welcome.

We started immediately to resolve our hunting *bundobust* (dilemma). Two self-styled experts were summoned. One was obviously a hunter, who had shot takin and produced a head in proof; the other gave rise to doubts. Both said that it was not too difficult to obtain takin and agreed that there were a few *beishung* about but that it would be almost impossible to get a shot at one. They next volunteered a unanimous opinion to the effect that it was impossible to hunt in this weather. When we asked when we might expect an improvement, both announced that the rain and sleet were typical at this time of year and that it was not possible to foretell when it would clear up.

This was indeed discouraging, but Hsuen threw himself into the breach, bringing every argument to bear. He said the absence of the headman of the valley increased the difficulty. The headman had gone away on a journey, and the date of his return was uncertain. At length Hsuen made it clear that we could not await a change in weather and that all chance of a golden egg would vanish unless they took us hunting on the morrow. Reluctantly, the Lolos yielded. We encountered a new difficulty when we tried to secure four hunters so that we could separate. The hunter with the aura of doubt said that he would substitute his son for himself. He told us the boy was eighteen, but when we had him paraded it was obvious that he was no more than twelve. After skillful sifting, we learned that his sole qualification as a takin hunter lay in his having once eaten takin meat.

A shepherd brought in a very small wild pig he had found while tending his flocks in the hills. It was striped and spotted with white and could not have been more than a few weeks old. It was dead, and it conjured up visions of roast suckling pig at Thanksgiving dinners at Sagamore. We bought it for fifteen cents, and Hsuen's culinary efforts resulted in an undeniable success.

It was late before we had at long last straightened things out and felt reasonably certain that four Lolos would be on hand in the morning. We then crawled into a hayloft, where we slept with the four heirs apparent of Litzaping who had come along with us as bodyguards.

Saturday, 13 April, dawned cold and overcast. It had snowed during the night, covering the floor of the valley and the pine trees on the mountainsides in conventional Christmas garb. We set off with four hunters, the takin-eating boy, and five slim black dogs. A thin, misty rain set in. It was a cheerless beginning for what was destined to become our red-letter day. Four porters were to follow with our bedding rolls and those of the shikaris, for the program called for a night or two *sous les belles étoiles* (under the beautiful stars) on the mountain where takin were reported.

After three or four miles we passed the clump of cabins belonging to A'Souza, the absent headman. Farther up the valley we turned off into a ravine. It was only a short way farther on that we came upon giant panda tracks in the snow. The animal had evidently passed quite a while before the snow ceased falling, but the Lolos found some sign that was recent enough to thoroughly arouse all four natives. We had taken our ponies to ride if we should enter the jungle or if the going became too difficult, and Mooka had come along to lead them back. It was now that he rose to the occasion and reached the high watermark of his value. The Lolos hesitated to follow the *beishung,* both from religious scruples and because of the very definite instructions that we wished in hunting a takin. We could gather that a conference was under way but believed that it concerned the ways and means only, and there is no telling what might have resulted had not Mooka, as we afterward learned, stepped into the breach and explained that above all we wanted a *beishung*.

This brought the conference to a close, and we started off on the trail of the panda. It was not long before the dogs definitely demonstrated their utter lack of hunting prowess. As soon as we passed some rat burrows in a small hollow, four of our dogs lost all interest in anything beyond the burrows and devoted their entire attention to the pursuit of the rats. The one that still remained with us trotted along at our heels baying until Ted caught it a shrewd clip with a stick. It retreated yowling into the forest, and that was the last we saw of it.

We now settled down to the steady business of tracking. Only three of the Lolos continued with us. The *beishung* appeared to be traveling along in a leisurely fashion, browsing on the bamboos as he went. The amount of sign that he left made us realize that we had been correct in making a conservative estimate of the number of *beishung* inhabiting the country beyond Muping, in which we hunted. Soon we came upon a boar's tracks superimposed on those of the giant panda. This continued for a mile or more. Our quarry was evidently in no hurry. For a while he followed up the rocky bed of a torrent, then he climbed a steep slope, through a jigsaw puzzle of windfalls. The fallen logs were slippery with snow and ice. Here we would crawl through and under; there we had to climb laboriously around and over. The bamboo jungle proved a particularly unpleasant obstacle course, where many of the feathery tops were weighed down by snow and frozen fast in the ground. Drenched by rain and soaked by snow, we alternately shivered and panted whenever a moment's halt was called. For a few minutes the sun came out, and we were in dread that it would melt the tracks, but after a brief interval the murky clouds hid it again.

We had been following the trail for two and half hours when we came to a more open jungle. Tall spruce trees towered in their giant bulk above the bamboo, and lichen-covered alders dotted the landscape. An occasional blue or yellow flower poked its head up where the snow lay lighter. Here the giant panda had turned its attention more seriously to provender. Under one tree the panda had made itself a nest of bamboos. Its claw marks scored the bark, and we looked eagerly among the sturdy branches to see whether we could distinguish a black and white form crouching on a limb. Its tracks led in many directions. The tough fibrous bamboos seemed to offer but an uninviting dehydrated repast at best, and to judge from the droppings they were also difficult to digest. Below us in the valley we heard the dogs yapping on the trail of some animal, probably a hog. We earnestly wished them elsewhere, for we felt sure that the *beishung* had not gone much farther before seeking some accustomed haunt to spend the sleepy daylight hours.

It was difficult to straighten out the trail. We cast first in one direction, then in another. Unexpectedly close I heard a clicking chirp. It might have been a bamboo snapping or the creaking of the interlocking branches of two trees that swayed by the wind. I remembered the eager interest of the Muping hunters at hearing just such a sound. In that case the noise had really been made by trees. One of the Lolo hunters was now close to Mokhta Lone and me. Noiselessly he darted forward. He had not got forty yards before he turned back to eagerly motion us to hurry.

As I gained his side, he pointed to a giant spruce thirty yards away. The bole was hollowed, and from it emerged the head and forequarters of a *beishung*, looking sleepily from side to side as it sauntered forth. It was not only very large but, to us, it appeared as a dreamlike apparition, for we had given up whatever small hopes we had ever had of seeing one. And now it appeared much larger than life with its white head with black spectacles, its black collar, and its white saddle.

Ted had started along in a different direction with another Lolo, so Mokhta Lone and I eagerly signaled him. Though in reality only a short time, it was nerve-wracking wait. The giant panda, dazed by sleep, was not really aroused and was walking slowly away into the bamboos. If frightened, it would vanish like smoke in the jungle. As soon as Ted came up, we fired simultaneously at the outline of the disappearing panda. Both shots took effect. Not knowing where its enemies were, the panda turned toward us, floundering through the drifted snow that lay in a hollow on our left. It was but five or six feet from Mokhta Lone when we again fired. It fell, but recovered itself and made off through the densely growing bamboos. We knew it was ours, but, although the Lolos had all along told us that the *beishung* was not an animal to be feared, we used caution in following the trail. A couple of the dogs that had been hunting in the valley below now came bounding to us, but they very evidently did not share their masters' opinions as to the innocuous character of the *beishung*.

They trailed howling behind us, and nothing could induce them to go ahead. No help, however, was needed, for the pursuit ended in seventy-five yards when we found the animal dead. It was a splendid old male, the first that the Lolos had any record of as being killed in this Yehli region.

The shikaris, the Lolos, and ourselves mutually rejoiced, each in his own tongue. Our great good fortune had been through much effort. We had hunted hard and long, usually in the face of every adverse circumstance. The previous evening conditions had seemed at their blackest, and it did not look as if we would be able to stir the Lolos from their homes. Now all was changed, and after so long holding aloof, the hunting gods had turned and fashioned the unusual chain of circumstances that alone could enable us to shoot a giant panda, trailing him without dogs and with the crowning bit of luck that permitted us to fire jointly.

When the enthusiasm had subsided sufficiently to allow us to think of anything beyond the immediate results of the chase, there were other plans to be worked out. In the face of the rain and sleet, and handicapped by a badly burst case, I had packed my camera in my bedding. My first thought was to get it, so Ted stayed behind to struggle with difficulties of transporting the panda while I hurried down the valley. As we slithered and slipped and barked our shins and knees, we kept up a running recapitulation of the details of the chase. When Mokhta Lone paused for breath, I broke in and took up the tale. I later learned that Ted and Gaffer Sheikh had been similarly employed. Mokhta Lone insisted that the panda was a sahib, for unlike the bear it had not cried out when shot.

At length we reached A'Souza's lodge, where we hoped to find Hsuen and the mules, but there was no sign of them. It was a blow, for it further dimmed any chance of successful photography. While trying to learn of Hsuen's whereabouts, we sat for a few brief minutes at the hospitable hearth of Vooka, A'Souza's wife, who acted in his stead during his absence.

She was a tall, handsome woman, wearing the conventional hooded headdress of the Lolo women. She was smoking a long-stemmed pipe with a heavy stone bowl that she later told us had belonged to her mother and grandmother before her. Filling it with tobacco, she thrust it into the fire to top the bowl with a pyramid of embers. She then handed it ceremonially to me, reminding me of a red Indian passing the peace pipe. One of her daughters brought half a dozen eggs in a bowl made of takin hide.

There was, unfortunately, no time to be lost, so we hurried back to our last night's halting place. There we found Hsuen, and we hastily started the mules forward to A'Souza's. It was not until half past four that I again found Ted and the *beishung*. My pursuit of the camera had taken me on a fourteen-mile jaunt. It was raining and sleeting, and my numbed fingers made but clumsy work with the camera. These Lolos were unaccustomed to carrying loads, and Ted had had a weary and discouraging time of it. For a while he tried to float the panda down the stream, but after struggling in the icebound water for a short time he had abandoned the attempt and gralloched the animal. He had hoped to avoid doing so until after the camera arrived. He found no sign that the panda had varied its bamboo diet.

Great were the celebrations held that night at A'Souza's. Vooka ordered a sheep to be slaughtered and resolutely refused to allow us to foot the bill. Intermingled with it all, there was a strongly pervading element of superstition. The *beishung* was at first not permitted in the compound, and we were afraid that we would have to skin it in the rain and snow and mud. Religious scruples were at length so far relaxed as to permit the shikaris to carry it into an isolated hayloft. A deeply interested group surrounded us at our work, but not one omnivorous Lolo of the lot would try a morsel of the flesh. Hsuen told us that after we left a priest was to be sent for and an all-embracing ceremony of purification would be held, to cleanse the house and its surroundings from any shadow that the death of the giant panda might have cast upon it.

The feasting lasted late. The sheep was quartered and plunged into a huge cauldron that was raised on three tall stones above the fire. A little later the parboiled meat was fished out and hacked into smaller pieces. These were thrust back into the boiling water. A silent ring of expectant Lolos lined the walls of the big raftered building. They were shrouded in their long capes, and it was as well, for there were many chinks in the roughly shingled roof, and the rain fell ever faster. When the sheep was ready, Vooka's servants ladled great chunks into wooden bowls, and adding rice from a smaller cauldron, handed them around among the guests. Soon wine was poured into a wooden beaker and circulated through the throng. It was in the main a silent gathering, lit by the flickering fagots of pine that were thrust from time to time upon the fire. With Vooka seated beside the fire, smoking her long pipe and directing her retainers, she might well have fitted in a feudal feast in Europe in the Middle Ages. Ted and I mixed a hot toddy from the last of our brandy flask and drank the health of every one, starting with General Pereira, whose attempts to shoot panda, made in the face of so many difficulties, fortune had not favored. It was late when we crawled up into the hayloft where our bedding was laid out. Never were the sleeping bags more gratefully welcome.

BIBLIOGRAPHY

Andrews, Roy Chapman. *Across Mongolian Plains.* New York: D. Appleton Co., 1921.

——. *Heart of Asia.* New York: Duell, Sloan and Pearce, 1951.

Andrews, Roy Chapman and Yvette Borup Andrews. *Camps and Trails in China.* New York: D. Appleton Co., 1918.

Baikov, Nikolai A. *Big-Game Hunting in Manchuria.* London: Hutchinson & Co., 1936.

Bell-Irving, J. *Diary of the Ewo Party: Up-Country Shooting Trips in the Yangtze Valley.* London: Army Navy Cooperative Society, 1890.

——. "Sport in China." *The Field* (February 1, 1902): 164.

Bland, J. O. P. *Houseboat Days in China.* New York: Doubleday, Page & Co., 1919.

Caldwell, Harry. *Blue Tiger.* New York: The Abingdon Press, 1924.

Caldwell, John C. *China Coast Family.* Chicago: H. Regnery & Co., 1953.

Carruthers, Douglas and J. H. Miller. *Unknown Mongolia: A Record of Travel and Exploration in North-West Mongolia and Dzungaria.* London: Hutchinson & Co., 1913.

Church, Percy W. *Chinese Turkistan with Caravan and Rifle.* London: Rivington's, 1901.

Clark, James L. *Great Arc of the Wild Sheep.* Norman: University of Oklahoma Press, 1964.

Cradock, Lt. Christopher. *Sporting Notes in the Far East.* London: Griffith, Farran, Oekeden & Welsh, 1889.

Czech, Kenneth P. *An Annotated Bibliography of Asian Big-Game Hunting Books, 1780–1980.* St. Cloud: Land's Edge Press, 2003.

Fergusson, W. N. *Adventure, Sport and Travel on the Tibetan Steppes.* London: Constable Publishing, 1911.

Gates, Elgin T. *Trophy Hunter in Asia.* New York: Winchester Press, 1971.

Grew, Joseph Clark. *Sport and Travel in the Far East.* Boston: Houghton Mifflin Co., 1910.

Groom, Francis A. *Sportsman's Diary for Shooting Trips in Northern China, or Advice to Sportsmen.* Shanghai: 1872.

Jernigan, Thomas R. *Shooting in China.* Shanghai: Methodist Publishing House, 1908.

Lanning, George. *Wild Life in China, or Chats on Chinese Birds and Beasts.* Shanghai: The National Review Office, 1911.

Leatham, A. E. *Sport in Five Continents.* Edinburgh: William Blackwood & Sons, 1912.

Lee, Robert M. *China Safari.* New York: Sporting World Library, 1988.

Lort-Phillips, Frederick. *The Wander Years, Hunting and Travel in Four Continents.* London: Nash & Grayson, 1931.

Percival, William Spencer. *The Land of the Dragon, My Boating and Shooting Excursions to the Gorges of the Upper Yangtze.* London: Hurst & Blackett, 1889.

Phillipps-Wolley, Clive, ed. *Big-Game Shooting,* vol. 2 *Badminton Library of Sports and Pastimes.* London: Longmans, Green and Co., 1903.

Pigot, Brigadier General R. *Twenty-Five Years' of Big-Game Hunting.* London: Chatto & Windus, 1928.

Prejevalsky, Col. N. M. *From Kulja Across the Tian Shan to Lob-Nor.* London: Sampson Low, Marston, Searle & Rivington, 1879.

Ready, Oliver G. *Life and Sport in China.* London: Chapman & Hall, 1904.

Ronaldshay, the Earl of. *On the Outskirts of Empire in Asia.* Edinburgh: William Blackwood & Sons, 1904.

Roosevelt, Kermit and Theodore Roosevelt Jr. *East of the Sun and West of the Moon.* New York: Charles Scribner's Sons, 1926.

——. *Trailing the Giant Panda.* New York: Charles Scribner's Sons, 1929.

Sowerby, Arthur de Carle. *Fur and Feather in Northern China.* Tientsin: The Tientsin Press, 1914.

——. *A Sportsman's Miscellany.* Tientsin: The Tientsin Press, 1917.

——. *Sport and Science on the Sino-Mongolian Frontier.* London: Andrew Melrose, 1918.

——. *The Naturalist in Manchuria.* Tientsin: The Tientsin Press, 1922.

Sportsman, The. *British Sports and Sportsmen: Big Game Hunting and Angling.* London: British Sports and Sportsmen, 1914.

Stone, Samuel J. *In and Beyond the Himalayas: A Record of Sport and Travel in the Abode of Snow.* London: Edward Arnold, 1896.

Taylor, Mary Linley. *The Tiger's Claw: The Life Story of East Asia's Mighty Hunter.* London: Burke Publishing Co., 1956.

Valdez, Raul. *The Wild Sheep of the World.* 1st ed. Mesilla: Wild Sheep & Goat International, 1982.

——. *Wild Sheep and Wild Sheep Hunters of the Old World.* Mesilla, NM: Wild Sheep & Goat International, 1983.

Wade, Henling Thomas. *With Boat and Gun in the Yangtze Valley.* 2d ed. Shanghai: Shanghai Mercury, Limited, 1910.

Wallace, Harold Frank. *The Big Game of Central and Western China.* London: John Murray, 1913.

Williams, S. Wells. *The Middle Kingdom.* New York: Charles Scribner's Sons, 1882.

Wilson, Ernest Henry. *A Naturalist in Western China, with Vasculum, Camera, and Gun.* New York: Doubleday, Page & Co., 1913.

Wong-Quincey, J. *Chinese Hunter.* New York: The John Day Company, 1939.

Wood, Capt. J. N. Price. *Travel and Sport in Turkistan.* New York: D. Appleton Co., 1910.

Younghusband, Sir Francis. *Peking to Lhasa: The Narrative of Journeys in the Chinese Empire made by the late Brigadier-General George Pareira.* London: Constable & Co., 1925.

CLIVE KAY IS THE ARTIST
RESPONSIBLE FOR ILLUSTRATING THIS BOOK.
ALL DRAWINGS ARE AVAILABLE (FRAMED) FOR PURCHASE.
SOME HAVE BEEN COLORED. FOR FURTHER INFORMATION ON THE
ARTIST EMAIL/PHONE/WRITE TO:

CLIVE KAY
34 GREENWOOD RD. RR#1
KIRKFIELD, ONTARIO, K0M 2B0 CANADA

WEBSITE: WWW.CLIVEKAY-ARTIST.COM
EMAIL: CLIVE@CLIVEKAY-ARTIST.COM